W9-BRG-852

DATE DUE

SEP 1 6 1998		
OCT 2 6 1999		
OCT 1 6 2001		
JUN 1 0 2002		
JUN - 5 2003		
DEC 1 3 2003		
DEC 1 8 2003		
GAYLORD		PRINTED IN U.S.A.

LEGAL, ETHICAL, AND POLITICAL ISSUES IN NURSING

LEGAL, ETHICAL, AND POLITICAL ISSUES IN NURSING

TONIA DANDRY AIKEN RN, BSN, JD
President and CEO, Aiken Development Group
President, The American Association of Nurse Attorneys (TAANA), 1993
New Orleans, Louisiana

with

JOSEPH T. CATALANO RN, BSN, MSN, PhD, CCRN
Professor
Department of Nursing
East Central University
Ada, Oklahoma

F. A. DAVIS COMPANY • Philadelphia

F. A. Davis Company
1915 Arch Street
Philadelphia, PA 19103

Printed in the United States of America

Last digit indicates print number: 10 9 8 7 6 5 4 3 2 1

Publisher, Nursing: Robert G. Martone
Developmental Editor: Melanie Freely
Production Editors: Rose Gabbay, Arofan Gregory
Cover Design By: Donald B. Freggens, Jr.

As new scientific information becomes available through basic and clinical research, recommended treatments and drug therapies undergo changes. The author(s) and publisher have done everything possible to make this book accurate, up to date, and in accord with accepted standards at the time of publication. The authors, editors, and publisher are not responsible for errors or omissions or for consequences from application of the book, and make no warranty, expressed or implied, in regard to the contents of the book. Any practice described in this book should be applied by the reader in accordance with professional standards of care used in regard to the unique circumstances that may apply in each situation. The reader is advised always to check product information (package inserts) for changes and new information regarding dose and contraindications before administering any drug. Caution is especially urged when using new or infrequently ordered drugs.

Library of Congress Cataloging-in-Publication Data

Legal, ethical, and political issues in nursing / [edited by] Tonia
    Dandry Aiken, with Joseph T. Catalano.— 1st ed.
        p.   cm.
    Includes bibliographical references and index.
    ISBN 0-8036-0081-X (pbk. : alk. paper)
    1. Nursing—Law and legislation—United States.   2. Nursing
ethics—United States.   I. Aiken, Tonia D.   II. Catalano, Joseph T.
    [DNLM: 1. Ethics, Nursing.   2. Legislation, Nursing—United
States.   3. Jurisprudence—United States.   4. Malpractice—United
States—legislation.   5. Politics—United States.   WY 33 AA1 L47
1994]
KF2915.N8L34   1994
362.1'73—dc20
DNLM/DLC
for Library of Congress   93-46312
                                                                  CIP

PREFACE

In today's world, the nurse is not only a caregiver and patient advocate, but may also be placed in the role of defendant in a lawsuit. In our litigious society, patients are no longer afraid or unwilling to sue healthcare providers.

This book's purpose is to educate students and practicing nurses about the legal, ethical, and political issues in nursing that affect their practice and profession. It was also written as a resource for nurses who are pulled into the legal arena as defendants, witnesses, and even plaintiffs. Practical information on the law, legal system, malpractice, negligence, and standards of care is provided. Potential exposure to liability involving negligence and intentional torts is also described.

Ethical issues are discussed in detail throughout the book; ethical cases are presented so that the nurse can relate ethical decision-making concepts to situations encountered in everyday work life. Other topics include supervisor liability, hospital liability, employment issues, nursing contracts, lobbying, sexual harassment, and the Americans with Disabilities Act.

Every chapter contains case studies and practical tips, points to remember, and boxes that highlight important information. A glossary provides easy access to legal, ethical, and political terminology.

The instructor's manual provides a wealth of information on topics that include educator and student rights and liabilities; copyright; recommendations on how to teach legal, ethical, and political issues; case examples with charts for class discussions; examples of legal pleadings; and test questions for each chapter.

The material in this book must not be used as a substitute for legal advice. This textbook is a resource. If legal advice is warranted, the nurse should find a nurse attorney or attorney that is qualified and competent in the appropriate area of law.

Tonia D. Aiken, RN, BSN, JD

ACKNOWLEDGMENTS

I want to thank the knowledgeable and experienced contributors who gave so willingly of their time to accomplish this monumental task. I also wish to express my gratitude and thanks to James Aiken, my parents, family, and friends, and to Melanie Freely, all of whom provided support and assistance in accomplishing my goal—a textbook for nurses on legal, ethical, and political issues.

Tonia D. Aiken, RN, BSN, JD

CONTRIBUTORS

James B. Aiken, MD, FACEP
Chief of Emergency Services
Touro Infirmary
Assistant Associate Professor
Louisiana State University
Department of Medicine
Division of Emergency Medicine
New Orleans, Louisiana

Tonia Dandry Aiken, RN, BSN, JD
President/CEO
Aiken Development Group, Inc.
President of TAANA, 1993
New Orleans, LA

Mary Powers Antoinc, RN, JD
Partner
Health Law Section
McDonough, Holland and Allen
Attorneys at Law
Sacramento, CA

Julia W. Aucoin, RN, MN
Manager
Nursing Education and
  Development
Duke University Medical Center
Durham, North Carolina

Linda M. E. Auton, RN, BS, JD
Attorney and Counselor at Law
President of TAANA, 1994
Rockland, MA

Patricia Gauntlett Beare, RN, PhD
Professor
School of Nursing
Graduate Program
Louisiana State University
  Medical Center
New Orleans, LA

Sandra Lee Berkowitz, BSN, JD
Vice President
Johnson & Higgins of
  Pennsylvania, Inc.
Philadelphia, PA

D. M. Boulay, RN, JD
Health Law Consultant
Minneapolis, MN

Julia G. Bounds, BSN, CRNA
Private Practitioner
American Association of Nurse
  Anesthetists
President, Louisiana Association
  of Nurse Anesthetists
Jefferson, LA

Joseph Catalano, RN, BSN, MSN, PhD, CCRN
Professor of Nursing
East Central University
Ada, OK

Tamara Todd Cotton, BSN, JD
Nurse Attorney
Hardy, Logan, Priddy & Cotton
Louisville, KY

Mical De Brow, RN, MSN, CCRN
Division Director
River Region Home Health
    Services
New Orleans, LA

**Michele L. Deck, RN, BSN, MEd,
    ACCE-R**
President
Gimies and Mania Educate Staff
    (GAMES)
Senior Training Consultant
Creative Training Techniques
    International, Inc.
Nursing Education Consultant
Tool Thyme for Trainers
Metairie, LA

**Thania Savole Elliot, RN, MSH,
    JD**
Nursing Consultant for
    Compliance
Louisiana State Board of Nursing
Formerly Assistant Professor of
    Nursing
Loyola University—Nursing
    Program
New Orleans, LA

**Jean M. Farquharson, ASN, RN,
    BA, JD**
Attorney and Counselor at Law
Gretna, LA

Anne Goldman, RN, BSN
Special Representative
Federation of Nurses/UFT,
    NYSUT, AFT
New York, NY

Nancy S. Jecker, PhD
Associate Professor
School of Medicine
Department of Medical History &
    Ethics
Adjunct Associate Professor
School of Law
Department of Philosophy
University of Washington
Seattle, Washington

**Elizabeth Bowyer Malacoff, RN,
    BSN, JD**
Attorney and Counselor at Law
Bethlehem, PA

Melinda Mercer, MSN, RN, CS
Associate Director
Governmental Affairs
American Nurses Association
Washington, DC

**Katherine J. Pohlman, RN, MS,
    JD**
Associate Counsel North
Central Law Department
The Prudential Insurance
    Company of America
Minneapolis, MN

Felice Quigley, RN, JD
Warlick & Quigley, P.C.
St. Croix, VI

June Smith Tyler, RN, JD
Dinsmore & Shohl
Cincinnati, OH

Ann Verderber, BSN, RPN
Federation of Nurses/UFT
Local #2, AFT, AFL-CIO
New York, NY

**Diane Trace Warlick, BSN, RN,
    JD**
Warlick & Quigley, P.C.
St. Croix, VI

CONSULTANTS

Barbara Bell
New Mexico Jr. College
Hobbs, NM

Helen Connors, RN, PhD
University of Kansas Medical
  Center
Kansas City, KS

Lillian Del Papa, RN, EdD
University of Central Arkansas
Conway, AR

Jane Fotos
Marshall University
Huntington, WV

Lucille I. Gallegher
Community College of Rhode
  Island
Warwick, RI

Katie L. Kochanowsky, RN, MSN
Vinson & Elkins
Attorney at Law
Houston, TX

Lois J. Vice
Nursing Administrator
Memorial Hospital
The Woodlands, TX

Carol Petrosky Vozel, RNC, PhD
Western Pennsylvania School of
  Nursing
Greensburg, PA

CONTENTS

CHAPTER 10 LIABILITY OF NURSING SUPERVISORS 173

CHAPTER 11 HOSPITAL LIABILITY—EMPLOYMENT
   ISSUES 189

CHAPTER 12   THE NURSE AND THE CONTRACT 212

CHAPTER 13   DOCUMENTATION 234

APPENDIX A   LOBBYING: HOW TO IMPLEMENT CHANGE 253

APPENDIX B   THE AMERICANS WITH DISABILITIES ACT 267

CHAPTER

The Law

ETHICAL CONSIDERATIONS

▼ One sure way to invoke high levels of fear and anxiety in most health care providers in general, and nurses in particular, is to utter the word "lawsuit." To many nurses, the legal system is an incomprehensible monster poised to devour the nurse the first time a mistake in patient care is made. Although the legal system is imposing to those who have not been initiated into its complexities, in reality it is just one part of the total health care picture.

Laws are rules made by human beings to guide society and regulate human interactions. Laws usually have a sanctioned method of enforcement, such as the police. The goal of all laws is (or should be) to preserve the species and promote peaceful and productive interactions between individuals or groups of individuals.

Ethics is the science that deals with the rightness and wrongness of actions. The goal of ethics is similar to that of the legal system, except that in most cases there is no system of enforcement for ethical guidelines. Ideally, the ethical system is more inclusive and usually exceeds the legal system in the situations it covers. In reality, there can be and are laws that are unethical.

In practice, particularly where health care is concerned, law and ethics overlap in many areas. These areas include, but are not limited to, such issues as death, dying, birth, abortion, genetics, quality of life, breach of duty, and violations of others' rights. In health care, ethical and legal issues transect each other at every point. Each interaction with a patient produces an ethical and legal situation. Although anyone can make a mistake at any given time, nurses who have a thorough understanding of the ethical code, follow that code, and stay within the guidelines for practice set by standards of care and the Nurse Practice Act, are much less likely to have a lawsuit filed against them.

1

OBJECTIVES

Upon completing this chapter, the reader will be able to:

1 Define law and explain how society influences the development of law.
2 Identify the four major sources of law.
3 Differentiate between substantive law and procedural law, and between common law and civil law.
4 Distinguish between contract law and tort law.
5 Describe the judicial system, including the state and federal court systems.
6 Discuss how criminal law violations apply to nursing.
7 Define the criminal procedure process.

INTRODUCTION

The expanded scope of nursing practice has brought increased responsibility and, along with it, increased exposure to liability. Nurses practicing in the health care system must stay informed about changing laws, regulations, and public policies and be aware of the ethical dilemmas they may confront. This chapter introduces the reader to basic legal concepts vital for understanding the principles and ideas that underlie health care laws.

LEGAL STATUS OF NURSING

The status of nursing has evolved through the years as changing roles and economic forces have affected health care. Nursing has become a profession requiring increased education, competence, and technical skills.

The Nurse Practice Act, which defines nursing practice and establishes the standards for nurses in each state, is the most important legal statute or legislative act for regulating nursing practice. Nurse practice acts vary in scope from state to state; they tend to be worded generally and to follow, to some extent, the American Nurses' Association (ANA) model published in 1980 or the model act of the National Council of State Boards of Nursing, Inc., published in 1982 and revised in 1988. The practice acts are designed to safeguard people by defining and establishing standards for nursing practice. Most states now regulate the areas of advanced and specialized nursing practice to provide standards for nurses with increased skills[1] (see Chapter 3). Violation of the Nurse Practice Act can result in criminal prosecution.

As professional responsibility has increased, so has legal accountability. Historically, nurses were not named as defendants in malpractice suits because hospitals and physicians were considered the primary defendants. Today, however, a growing number of nurses are being held

accountable for their indi   s or omissions and are being named
in malpractice cases, pri   ospital settings.[2]

In malpractice cas   atutes, and case law determine such
things as when the law   e filed, the value of the damages suffered,
and how and where the claim must be filed.

DEFINITION OF LAW

Law is the body of rules and regulations that governs people's behavior as well as their relationships with others in the society and with the
state. Laws promote order by resolving conflicts and disputes nonvio-
lently, defining responsibilities, and protecting the health, safety, and welfare of the state's citizens.

Although some laws are constant, most are evolving to adapt to society's changing values, customs, and demands. The changing legal rights of
minorities and women in the United States during the past century provide a dramatic example of how laws evolve to meet the political, economic, and social values of society.

Both federal and state governments have the constitutional authority
to create and enforce laws. The U.S. Constitution, as the supreme law of
the land, grants certain powers to the federal government. Powers not
expressed in the Constitution are reserved for the state government. The
legal basis for federal government involvement in health care is found in
Article 1, Section 8, of the Constitution under the provision of general welfare and the regulation of interstate commerce.

States and local governments constitutionally possess the most
authority to regulate health care through the state's police power, which
allows states to protect the health, safety, and welfare of their citizens. An
example of a state's police power is the right to regulate the professional
practice of nurses, physicians, and other health care providers in the
health care industry.

SOURCES OF LAW

There are many different sources of law affecting health care providers and their practices. Some laws affect nurses personally, such as the
constitutional amendments that guarantee freedom of speech, whereas
other laws such as administrative laws regulate the nurse's professional
acts.

The four types of law in the United States are:

1. Constitutional law
2. Statutory law

3. Administrative law
4. Common law

Table 1–1 summarizes the role of government in developing laws.

Constitutional Law

The **Constitution** guarantees individuals certain fundamental freedoms. Very little constitutional law affects health care and nursing practice directly except for the personal rights protected by the Bill of Rights in the constitutional amendments. These amendments guarantee such rights as privacy, equal protection, and freedom of speech and religion. The Constitution does not protect individuals from the private acts of other individuals. For individuals to allege constitutional violations, a state action or statute must be involved. For example, nurses who work in state or federal hospitals may have more constitutional protection for employee rights than do nurses who work for private employers.

Statutory Law

Statutory laws are formal written laws enacted by federal, state, and local legislative branches. Federal statutes are published in the *United States Code* (U.S.C.); state statutes are published in various state publications, such as *Revised Statutes* or *Revised Codes Annotated.* The Medicare and Medicaid amendments to the Social Security Act of 1965 are examples of federal laws that have dramatically affected health care in a number of areas, including hospital admissions and discharges, available services, and level of care provided.

Table 1–1   ROLE OF GOVERNMENT IN DEVELOPING LAWS

Governmental Source	Role in Lawmaking	Types of Law
Constitution	Establishes supreme law	Constitutional law, Bill of Rights
Legislative branch House Senate	Creates laws Approves executive appointments	Statutes
Executive branch	Executes and administers laws	Administrative law, rules and regulations
President or governor	Vetoes bills	
Judiciary branch	Interprets laws	Common law or judge-made laws
Supreme Court Appellate courts Trial courts	Adjudicates disputes	

On the state level, state legislatures have broad powers to provide for the public's health. Nurse practice acts, in particular, are specific state statutes passed by the legislatures to define and regulate the practice of nursing within each state. Statutes that deal with acquired immunodeficiency syndrome (AIDS), other communicable diseases, child or elder abuse, consent for medical treatment, health care for the indigent, and Good Samaritan laws are other examples of state health care regulation.

Administrative Law

Administrative laws are created by administrative agencies under the direction of the executive branch. Once the legislature creates a statute or law, it delegates the authority to implement and establish new regulations to meet the intent of the statute. For example, although state legislators created the nurse practice acts in states, the acts in turn created state boards of nursing as administrative agencies with the authority to develop and enforce regluations concerning nursing practice. Regulations of nursing practice are within the delegated authority of the state boards and are considered administrative laws that are legally binding.

Common Law

Common law evolves from the judiciary branch through court decisions. Common law is the most frequent source of law for malpractice issues. When there is no written statute or regulation, the courts are asked to resolve legal disputes; over time, these decisions take on the force of law.

Precedent

Common law is based on earlier decisions of the court and follows a concept of precedent or *stare decisis,* which literally means "to stand by things decided." This concept allows courts to refer to previously decided similar cases and apply the same rules and principles to existing laws. Precedent, or prior law, then becomes law, and courts follow their prior decisions or those of courts of higher jurisdictions.

Organization of the Court System

A knowledge of the organization of the court system sheds light on how common law decisions are made. There are two separate court systems in the United States: the federal system and the state system. According to Article III, Section 1, of the U.S. Constitution, judicial power is vested in the U.S. Supreme Court and in lesser federal courts as dictated by Congress. Both state and federal courts have trial courts, appellate courts, and one supreme court, which in some states is called the "court of appeals" or the "supreme judicial court."

TYPES OF LAW

There are a number of ways to classify laws. Classifications are based on whether the laws are substantive, procedural, common, civil, or criminal. All types of law are intermingled in various ways and in different areas of litigation and practice.

Substantive versus Procedural Law

Substantive law determines the specific wrong, harm, duty, or obligation that causes an action to be brought to trial. In contrast, **procedural law** determines the form or process that regulates the legal right that is violated. Procedural law includes the various legal procedures required to bring a dispute to trial and determines the rules that parties must follow to litigate a matter before a court.

Box 1–1   SUBSTANTIVE VS. PROCEDURAL LAW

1. Substantive law determines the specific wrong, harm, duty, or obligation that causes the action to be brought to trial.
2. Procedural law determines the form or process that regulates the legal right that is violated.

Statute of Limitations

The **statute of limitations** is a procedural law that specifies the time during which a plaintiff may bring a lawsuit. This limitation varies with the different types of substantive law. For example, in most instances, malpractice suits must be filed sooner than suits alleging violations of contract or criminal laws. In addition, there may be great variation among the states. If the petition for damages or complaint is not filed within the statutory time limit, the plaintiff is prohibited from filing a lawsuit for that particular action.

Both procedural and substantive laws enter the picture when a lawsuit is filed. For example, in a medical malpractice case, substantive laws specify the elements of negligence that must be proved (duty, breach of duty, causation, and damages), while procedural laws regulate the statute of limitation and the process for admitting evidence at trial.

Common versus Civil Law

Laws can be further classified according to whether they originated from English common laws or written civil code. The federal courts and 49 of the state courts in the United States follow common law rules and legal principles developed in England from the days when the king pronounced rules according to his "divine right."[3] Common law developed from the practice of accumulating case decisions based on justice and reason. After the American Revolution, most of the states adopted the English common law system and have continued to use it. However, because individual states adopted different statutes and judicial interpretations, variations in common law exist among states today.

Louisiana is the only state in the United States that has adopted a **civil code** based on the Napoleonic Code. The Louisiana Civil Code developed from the civil laws of the Romans, Spanish, and French.[4] The difference between the civil code and common law is that in the civil code the law is authorized by the legislature rather than the judiciary; the code is a comprehensive written organization of general rules and regulations, rather than a case-by-case analysis of specific legal issues. The other distinguishing feature is that the original basis of civil law is Roman law rather than English law.

Contract Law

Contract law is concerned with agreements between two parties that involve an obligation or duty. The elements of a contractual agreement are the offer, acceptance, and consideration between two or more competent persons.[6] Although some contracts must be written in specified forms, others can be oral, and duties can be either overtly expressed or implied. The most common contractual issue that nurses encounter in practice relates to employee/employer agreements (see Chapter 12).

Tort Law

Tort law is the area of law with which nurses are most familiar because it involves negligence and medical malpractice. A **tort** is a wrongful act committed by one person against another person or against a property. The purpose of tort law is to make the injured person whole again primarily through monetary compensation or damages.

Torts are divided into two main categories:
1. Unintentional tort or negligence
2. Intentional tort

Unintentional Tort

An **unintentional tort** is an unintended, wrongful act against another person that produces injury or harm. Negligence and malpractice, which is a particular form of negligence, are considered unintentional torts.

Negligence

By law, every person is responsible for behaving in a reasonable way; an unreasonable or careless act that causes injury to another can provide the basis for a negligence suit. Likewise, the omission of an act that could have prevented harm is also considered negligence. For example, a nurse can be held liable for improper administration of a drug that causes sciatic nerve injury (commission) or for failure to give a prescribed medication (omission).

Box 1–2 CONTRACT LAW VS. TORT LAW

1. Contract law is private law involving an agreement between two persons that gives rise to an obligation or duty to do something for consideration. Example: contract between nurse employee and employer.
2. Tort law is law that makes the injured person whole again primarily through monetary damages. A tort is a wrongful act committed by one person against another or against another's property.

Malpractice

Malpractice is a specific type of negligence that occurs when the standard of care that can be reasonably expected from such professionals as lawyers, accountants, nurses, and physicians is not met; hence, it is also known as "professional negligence." Only a professional can be sued for malpractice; any other misconduct would be classified as negligence. To be liable for malpractice, a professional must fail to act as other reasonable and prudent professionals who have the same knowledge and education would have acted under similar situations."[5] A negligent act is considered malpractice, however, only if it was committed by a professional carrying out professional duties, not under other circumstances. For example, a nurse involved in a car accident is held only to a negligence standard, not to a higher malpractice standard. However, if a nurse infuses intravenous solution into an infant at the rate used for an adult, which causes brain damage, the malpractice standard applies.

To prove liability for malpractice, the plaintiff must prove four elements of negligence: (1) a duty owed to the plaintiff, (2) a breach of duty or standard of care by the professional, (3) a proximate cause or causal connection between the breach and the harm or damages, and (4) actual harm or damages suffered by the plaintiff.

Although anyone can be sued for almost any reason in today's litigious society, for the nurse or other health professional to be held liable under a malpractice claim, each of the four elements must be proved by the plaintiff in a court of law. The plaintiff must prove the case by a "preponderance of evidence,"[6] which means that the plaintiff must convince the jury that all allegations applying to the four elements are more probably true than not.

Damages suffered by the plaintiff include "hard" and "soft" damages. **Hard damages** are damages that are evident through bills, for example, medical or hospital bills, medication costs, and funeral expenses. **Soft damages** are more intangible and include compensation for such things as loss of love and affection, pain and suffering, mental anguish, and loss of consortium.

Box 1–3 THE FOUR ELEMENTS NEEDED TO PROVE LIABILITY FOR MALPRACTICE

1. A duty owed to the plaintiff
2. A breach of duty or standard of care by the professional
3. A proximate cause or causal connection between the breach and the harm or damages
4. Actual harm or damages suffered by the plaintiff

Intentional Tort

An **intentional tort** is a willful or intentional act that violates another person's rights or property (see Chapter 8).

JURISDICTION

Jurisdiction is the authority by which courts and judges accept and decide cases. Jurisdictional authority flows from federal and state constitutions and statutes. The federal court jurisdiction extends to cases involving federal questions or disputes between citizens from different states. Certain courts have general jurisdication, whereas other courts are more specialized, such as the U.S. Customs Courts, state juvenile courts, or local traffic courts. If both the state and federal court have jurisdiction over a particular case, then the parties may select which court system will try the case.

TRIAL COURTS

Trial courts are the first courts to hear legal controversies or disputes. The **plaintiff,** the party alleging harm, files a complaint or petition for damages in either the state local court or the U.S. Federal District Court. In some cases, the plaintiff is the person actually harmed or damaged by the defendant. In other cases, the plaintiffs are the person harmed and the immediate family members (or *only* the immediate family members). For example, if the injured party is married, the spouse may be added as a plaintiff because he or she may have "suffered" losses too. If the injured party dies as a result of malpractice, one of the immediate family members (e.g., the husband or wife) files a lawsuit on behalf of the deceased person and that person's estate, with the immediate family member then becoming the plaintiff in the suit. The **defendant,** the party being sued, must answer the complaint within a specified period of time. Pretrial activities include procedures that discover information about the case, such as **depositions, interrogatories, admissions of fact,** and **requests for production of documents** and specific items (see Chapter 5). If the parties cannot settle the dispute, the trial begins with both sides arguing their cases, using attorneys, witnesses, and evidence.

The initial trial can be decided by a judge or jury. In a medical malpractice case, the judge or jury decides whether the facts of the case prove that the defendant breached a standard of care, which caused damage or injury to the plaintiff. The standard of care is a "measuring scale" with which the health care provider's conduct is compared to determine whether there is any professional negligence. The judge supervises the court and interprets questions of law. Once the verdict is reached, the judge announces the judgment and the trial ends. The losing party has a right to request an appeal of the case to a higher court.

APPELLATE COURTS

The state appeals court and the U.S. Court of Appeals have the authority to review and alter the decisions of state or federal district courts that are under their authority and jurisdiction. In the federal system, 12 circuit courts hear cases from the lower federal courts within their circuit. Each circuit, except for Washington, DC, consists of three to nine states. Appellate courts can review only the trial court decisions in the state or federal district in their jurisdiction.

In appellate courts, the case is tried on the trial record alone. There are no witnesses, no new testimony, and no juries. The appellate court judges review the trial transcripts and the briefs filed by each party's attorney. The opposing attorneys may occasionally present oral arguments to the court; however, because the trial judge has heard the witnesses' testimony, great deference is given to his or her decision, based on a majority vote of participating judges. The appellate court renders a decision to either affirm or reverse the trial court's decision or remand the case back to the trial court with special instructions.

The appellate court decisions are written and published in state or regional books called *reporters,* which are distributed to public and private subscribers, including law libraries. Precedents are established through these written appellate decisions.

SUPREME COURTS

The state supreme court may hear appeals from the state appellate courts. Unless an important federal issue or a constitutional right is involved, the state supreme court is the final authority for state issues. Decisions from the state supreme court are binding on all other courts in that state.

The U.S. Supreme Court is the court of final decision for both the federal system and the state system in matters involving constitutionally protected rights, such as freedom of speech. Appeals are brought to the Supreme Court under a **writ of certiorari,** which is a written petition by the losing party requesting that the Supreme Court hear the case. Because the Supreme Court receives requests from thousands of cases annually, only those involving questions of substantial federal importance are selected for review. Once a case is heard by the U.S. Supreme Court, the decision becomes binding on all state and federal courts in the nation.

CRIMINAL LAW

Medical negligence is a tort or civil wrong that causes harm to a person, as opposed to a criminal wrong. **Criminal law** is concerned with violations of criminal statutes or laws. Violations of civil law are offenses against society as spelled out in the written criminal statute or code. The plaintiff in a criminal suit is a governmental body. Depending on the seriousness of the offense, crimes are generally divided into felonies or misdemeanors. **Misdemeanors** are considered lesser crimes, generally punishable by fines of less than $1000 or imprisonment of less than 1 year, or both. **Felonies** are more serious crimes than misdemeanors, with harsher punishments, which may include fines of over $1000, prison terms of over 1 year, and death. In many states, a felony conviction is grounds for denying, revoking, or suspending a nursing license.[7] In civil proceedings, the injured party receives monetary damages from the defendant. In criminal procedures, the defendant may lose life or liberty if found guilty. At trial, in order to find the defendant guilty, it must be proved beyond a reasonable doubt that the defendant committed the crime.

Although criminal law violations are uncommon in the health care field, nurses may risk being charged with a crime for such actions as withholding life support for terminally ill patients or defective newborns, falsifying narcotic records, or failing to renew their licenses. Nurses may also be called as witnesses in criminal cases when they have cared for a victim or perpetrator of a criminal act. Violation of nurse practice acts may also precipitate criminal charges, as reported in a Missouri court involving nurse practitioners:

Two nurse practitioners employed by a nonprofit family planning service in Missouri provided services according to specific physician-developed written standing orders and protocols. A complaint was filed with the medical board in Missouri alleging that the nurses were practicing medicine without a license. After investigation, the Board recommended criminal prosecution, and added that the nurses were practicing beyond the scope of professional nursing as it was defined in the Missouri Nursing Practice Act. The trial court found the nurses' activities constituted the unlawful practice of medicine. However, on appeal, the Missouri Supreme Court overturned the ruling and held that the nurses' practice was authorized by the Nurse Practice Act. The court further noted that when working under medical standing orders, the nurses were making nursing diagnosis and not medical diagnosis, and that nurses could assume new responsibilities for practice as long as they were consistent with the professional's specialized education and skills.

Sermchief v. Gonzales, 660 S.W.2d 683 (Mo. 1983).

THE CRIMINAL PROCESS

The following are steps usually followed if a case is brought to federal or state court. The federal system of criminal law is created by statutes. State criminal law is a combination of statutory law and common law. In criminal cases, the right to a jury is a constitutional right for felony cases but not for misdemeanor cases.

1. **Indictment or complaint.** The first step in criminal procedure is to issue an **indictment,** also known as a **complaint.** This written document is issued to the defendant and describes the allegations of wrongdoing.
2. **Grand jury.** If the crime is a federal felony, usually a **grand jury** is convened to determine whether evidence is sufficient to indicate

"probable cause" that a crime has been committed by the defendant. Various states also use the grand jury system.

3. **Arrested prior to indictment or complaint**
   - The person is brought before the judge, pleads guilty or not guilty, and has bail set. This process is called the **arraignment.**
   - If bail is refused or the person cannot make bail, then he or she is taken into custody.
4. **Arrested after indictment or complaint.** The state issues a **warrant** that allows the person to be taken into custody by law enforcement officers.
5. **Discovery stage.** If the defendant pleads not guilty, then the discovery stage is the next step in the process. Evidence is discovered through a variety of means, depending on the state.
6. **Pretrial motions.** These are legal documents filed in court and used to shorten the trial process. For example, motions can be made to suppress or exclude evidence that is improperly seized.
7. **The trial.** At the trial, evidence and witnesses are presented to prove the prosecution's position beyond a reasonable doubt and to defend the accused of the alleged crime. Common defenses used are insanity, self-defense, defense of others from danger, intoxication, duress, ignorance, necessity under the circumstances, and entrapment by the government or its agents.

If the defendant is found innocent, the matter cannot be tried again or appealed by the prosecution. If the defendant is convicted, the judge imposes a sentence for the crime. An appeal of the ruling of the court may also be made.

If the person is sent to prison, parole may be allowed after the prison sentence is served.[8]

CRIMINAL CASE EXAMPLES

RIGHT TO DIE, EUTHANASIA, AND ASSISTED SUICIDE

The right of an individual to die with dignity is generally accepted by society. The right of an individual to take his or her own life is also generally accepted. However, the right of others to assist and actively or passively participate in the death of a person is an extremely controversial area of law and medicine. Passive or negative euthanasia, in which a person dies without assistance, is acceptable, whereas many consider active or positive euthanasia, also called "mercy killing," to be an act of murder.

Both Washington and California have unsuccessfully tried to

pass "death with dignity" legislation legalizing voluntary or active euthanasia. Other states are expected to attempt to pass such legislation in the near future.[9]

Because of Dr. Jack Kevorkian's "suicide machine," the right-to-die cases have added a new dimension to the ethical arena. Dr. Kevorkian's assistance in suicides has resulted in the filing of first-degree murder charges against him; these have later been dismissed. Recently, Michigan passed a law making assistance of suicides a felony punishable with not more than 4 years in prison or with a fine of not more than $2000, or both. The law prohibits a person from knowingly or intentionally assisting a person in committing suicide or attempting to commit sucide. However, a licensed health care professional is not prohibited from with-drawing or withholding medical treatment from a terminally ill patient.[10,11]

After the Michigan law was passed, Dr. Kevorkian attended the suicide of a man with cancer who died of carbon monoxide poisoning. Kevorkian was arrested but released for lack of evidence that he assisted in the suicide. The ACLU has challenged the Michigan law, and a judge recently struck down the law, citing a technicality. The judge ruled that two terminally ill patients in an ACLU case had a right to die and a right to self-deter-mination.[12]

NEGLIGENT HOMICIDE

In *State of Utah v. Warden,* 813 P.2d 1146 (Utah 1991), a jury found a physician criminally liable for negligent homicide.[13]

The mother's due date was questionable, and she began having cramps and bleeding. Her physician delivered the infant at home. At birth, the infant weighed approximately 4 pounds. Soon after birth, the infant began experiencing respiratory problems, that is, periodic grunting and purplish-blue skin color.

The physician knew the condition was progressive and could end in death; however, he did nothing and gave no instructions to the family. During the night the infant became worse. At 8:00 A.M. the mother attempted to call her physician but was unsuccessful. Her clergyman and a pediatrician then came to the home and rushed the child to the hospital, where the infant died shortly after arrival. The physician lived only five blocks away, was up at 6:00 A.M., but did not attempt to contact the mother until noon, when he learned of the infant's death.

The evidence was sufficient to establish beyond a reasonable doubt that his treatment created a substantial and unjustifiable risk that the infant would die. The physician failed to perceive the risk to the infant whom he knew was suffering from prematurity and respiratory distress syndrome. Failure to perceive the risk constituted gross deviation from the standard of care.

PATIENT ABUSE

A nurse's aide received concurrent prison sentences of 3 years at hard labor, which were suspended for a 9-month imprisonment. The nurse's aide had physically assaulted three elderly patients by pinching and slapping them. She had also attempted to choke a patient.[14]

In the *State of Louisiana v. Brenner*,[15] nursing home staff members were charged with cruelty, neglect, and mistreatment of the infirm for the following reasons:
1. Failure to adequately feed and care for the patients
2. Failure to properly train the staff
3. Failure to provide adequate medical supplies
4. Failure to supply adequate staff
5. Failure to maintain a sanitary nursing home
6. Failure to maintain patients' records
7. Failure to see that the appropriate and necessary health services were performed

In Illinois, an aide was indicted on seven counts of aggravated battery, one count of abuse, and two counts of intimidation. In one incident, she slapped a patient on the head and face and punched him in the chest. The nurse's aide was convicted and sentenced for abuse of a resident of a long-term care facility.[16]

MURDER

A registered nurse was convicted of first-degree murder and sentenced to death in California. The registered nurse worked on the night shift in the cardiac care and intensive care units. Over a period of 3½ weeks, 13 patients suffered seizures and respiratory and cardiac arrests during the night shift. Nine of the 13 patients died.

The nurse was hired at another local hospital after the previous hospital closed. Three days later a patient died with the same signs, that is, seizures and cardiorespiratory arrest. The nurse was arrested shortly after the patient's death.

The nurse killed the patients by giving them massive doses of lidocaine, a drug that all of the patients took routinely, but on a therapeutic basis. Some of the evidence presented consisted of syringes with high concentrations of lidocaine that were found in the hospital. Lidocaine was also found in the nurse's home.[17]

MEDICAID FRAUD

Physicians were convicted of numerous counts of Medicaid fraud and found guilty of the following:

1. Improperly billing telephone calls to their patients as consultations
2. Overbilling for office visits
3. Making telephone calls to the emergency room and billing them as emergency room visits
4. Billing for follow-up visits that never occurred

Nurses testified at trial that they were instructed by the physicians to always bill office visits as comprehensive office visits, even though they informed the physicians that this was not the proper procedure. Nurses also testified that if a physician came to the emergency room to see a patient, their nurses' notes would indicate this fact. Testimony by the nurses refuted the physicians' claims that they had seen the patient on a consultation; the nurses testified that the physicians had only made a phone call to the emergency room.[18]

Box 1–4   CRIMINAL CATEGORIES

1. **Misdemeanor.** A lesser crime usually punishable either by fines or by imprisonment of less than 1 year, or by both.
2. **Felony.** A more serious crime with punishments greater than those of the misdemeanor level. A felony can be grounds for nursing license denial, revocation, or suspension.

SUMMARY

The legal system in the United States is a complex combination of laws, rules, and regulations that are created at both the federal and state levels. Nurses should stay informed regarding the legal scope of their nursing practice as society and the profession changes. A basic knowledge of the law and how it works can help nurses avoid litigation while giving them the confidence to practice more competently.

Points to Remember

▶ The state legislature creates the Nurse Practice Act and grants authority for a board of nursing to administer and enforce the Act.

- The Nurse Practice Act creates the legal boundaries for the scope of professional nursing practice.
- Both substantive law and procedural law affect the legal process.
- Substantive law defines specific rights, duties, obligations, or prohibitions that are imposed by authorities.
- Procedural law determines the method or process for legally enforcing these rights and obligations.
- Civil law refers to both the written law from Roman origin and the law relating to relationships between private persons.
- Suits for criminal law violations can only be brought by a government entity.
- Torts consist of negligence and intentional torts.

Study Questions

1. Describe the four major sources of law.
2. What effect do societal values and customs have on the development of laws?
3. How does civil law differ from common law and from criminal law?
4. Discuss the steps in a trial process.
5. Explain the concept of precedent or stare decisis.
6. Explain the functions of the trial courts, appellate courts, and supreme courts at the state and federal levels.
7. Discuss the differences between a misdemeanor and a felony.
8. Explain the types of torts.
9. List the four elements of negligence that must be present to prove liability for malpractice.
10. Discuss the differences that exist between intentional and nonintentional torts.

REFERENCES

1. Fiesta, J: The Law and Liability, ed 2. Wiley Medical, New York, 1988, pp 15, 24.
2. Guido, WG: Legal Issues in Nursing. Appleton & Lange, Norwalk, Conn, 1988, p 124.
3. Creighton, H: Law Every Nurse Should Know, ed 5. WB Saunders, Philadelphia, 1986, p 1.
4. Cazales, MW: Nursing and the Law. Aspen, Germantown, Md, 1978, p 3.
5. Catalano, JT: Ethical and Legal Aspects of Nursing. Springhouse, Springhouse, Pa, 1991, p 69.
6. Bernzweig, EP: The Nurse's Liability for Malpractice, ed. 5. CV Mosby, St. Louis, 1990, p 287.

7. Ford, RD (ed): Nurse's Legal Handbook. Springhouse, Springhouse, Pa, 1987, pp 32–39.
8. Northrup, C, and Kelly, M: Legal Issues in Nursing. CV Mosby, St. Louis, 1987.
9. Kamisar, Y: Active v. passive euthanasia: Why keep the distinction? Trial, March:32, 1993.
10. Wayne State University: Can a suicide machine trigger the murder statute? Specialty Digest: Health Care. Wayne Law Review 1921–1950, 1991.
11. Assisted suicide for the terminally ill: The inadequacy of current legal models to rationally analyze voluntary active euthanasia. Criminal Justice Journal 13:303, 1992.
12. Gibbs, N: Rx for death. Time, May 31, 1993.
13. *State of Utah v. Warden*, 813 P.2d 1146 (Utah 1991).
14. *State of Louisiana v. Pratt*, 573 So. 2d 607 (La. App. 2 Cir. 1991).
15. *State of Louisiana v. Brenner*, 486 So. 2d 101 (La. 1986).
16. *People of the State of Illinois v. Johnson*, 595 N.E.2d 1381 (Ill. App. 2d 1992).
17. *The People v. Diaz*, 834 P.2d 1171 (Cal. 1992).
18. *State of Louisiana v. Romero*, 574 So. 2d 330 (La. 1990).

▶ **ETHICS IN PRACTICE**

Mrs. J., 84 years old, was an active member of a local senior citizens group. One day at a group-sponsored picnic, Mrs. J. experienced an episode of acute chest pain, followed by collapse and cardiac arrest. A member of the group who had taken a cardiopulmonary resuscitation (CPR) course performed CPR on Mrs. J. for approximately 20 minutes, during which time an ambulance was called and the paramedics arrived. Mrs. J. never regained consciousness, although a cardiac rhythm was re-established by the paramedics. She was admitted to the intensive care unit (ICU) of a local hospital, intubated, and connected to a ventilator. Her two daughters and a son, all of whom lived out of state, were notified of her condition.

Over the several days it took her children to arrive at the hospital, Mrs. J.'s condition gradually deteriorated to the point at which vasoactive medications were required to maintain her blood pressure and urinary output. Although she did not meet all the criteria of brain death, owing to some reflex reactions that remained, her primary physician believed that because of the extended period of anoxia she had suffered before she was intubated by the paramedics, she had suffered irreversible brain damage.

When the situation was explained to her children, Daughter A and the son agreed that to attempt any further resuscitation on their mother would be futile and cruel. Daughter B, however, disagreed and demanded that "everything" be done to keep her mother alive. After a rather spirited discussion involving the three children, the physician, and the head nurse of the ICU, a compromise was reached. Mrs. J. was to be assigned a "medication-only" code, which meant that antiarrhythmic, vasopressor, and cardiotonic agents would be used to keep the heart beating. The family signed the appropriate form for this procedure, and the physician wrote a medication-only code on the physician order sheet.

The following day, with the family members at the bedside, Mrs. J. went into a sustained episode of ventricular fibrillation. The nurse who was caring for Mrs. J. gave the appropriate medications for the condition. Without chest compressions to circulate the medications, however, there was no change in her cardiac pattern. After approximately 5 minutes into the medication-only code, Daughter B began to yell loudly, "You better do something else, or I'm going to sue you and this hospital for everything you're worth!"

What should the nurse do at this point? Start chest compressions? Tell the family that she cannot do so because of the order? Would Daughter B actually be able to file a lawsuit in this situation?

Ethics in Nursing

ETHICAL CONSIDERATIONS

▼ Nurses in today's health care system, where major technological advances are almost a daily occurrence, often face ethical dilemmas they may be ill prepared to resolve. Rapid advancements in health care research, as well as fundamental changes in society's values and cultural norms, have outpaced the health care system's ability to solve complicated ethical issues. As a result, judges and juries are being asked to resolve ethical questions that concern life-and-death issues between patients, their families, physicians, and nurses.

The legal system is particularly ill prepared to resolve sensitive ethical issues. In many ethical conflicts, no laws deal specifically with the issues at hand. In other types of conflicts, general legal principles and/or laws can be cited that offer guidelines; however, ethical dilemmas are often complicated by circumstances not addressed by the legal system. When the legal system does make decisions concerning ethical dilemmas, those cases can be cited later as precedents. They then take on the force of law under the common-law principle found in this country.

OBJECTIVES

Upon completing this chapter, the reader will be able to:

1 Discuss the difference between law and ethics.
2 Define the key terms used in ethics.
3 Discuss the important ethical concepts.
4 Distinguish between the two most commonly used systems of ethical decision making.

5   Name the steps in the ethical decision-making process.
6   Demonstrate the use of the ethical decision-making process in the analysis of an ethical case study.

INTRODUCTION

As the health care system moves from the 20th to the 21st century, any nurse providing care for patients must understand the steps involved in ethical decision making. Sound ethical decisions are based on an understanding of:

- the underlying ethical principles
- the key ethical theories or systems that can be used
- the profession's code of ethics

Ethical decision making is a skill that can be learned by any nurse. However, as with all skills, it requires mastering the theoretical material and practicing the skill itself.

This chapter presents the basic information necessary to understand ethics, the code of ethics, and ethical decision making. The fundamental definitions and principles involved in understanding ethics, two key ethical systems or theories often used by health providers in resolving ethical dilemmas, and an ethical decision-making model based on the nursing process are discussed.

IMPORTANT DEFINITIONS

The study of ethics is a specialized area of philosophy, the origins of which date back to ancient Greece. In fact, ethical principles enunciated by Hypocrites still serve as the underpinnings of many of today's ethical issues. Like most specialized areas of study, ethics has its own language and terminology, which are used in very precise ways. The following are some key terms that are necessary for understanding health care ethics:

1. **Values** are ideals or concepts that give meaning to the individual's life. Values are most commonly derived from societal norms, religion, and family orientation and serve as the framework for making decisions and taking certain actions in everyday life. Although values are usually *not* written down, at some time in their careers, it may be important for nurses to make a list of their own values and attempt to rank them by priority. *Value conflicts* often occur in everyday life and can force an individual to select a higher priority value over a lower priority value. For example, nurses who value

both their career and their family may be forced to decide between going to work or staying home with a sick child.

2. ***Morals*** are the fundamental standards of right and wrong that an individual learns and internalizes, usually in the early stages of childhood development. An individual's moral orientation is generally based on religious beliefs, although societal influence plays an important part in this development. Moral behavior is often manifested as behavior in accordance with a group's norms, customs, or traditions. For example, in the Mormon tradition, polygamy was an accepted (therefore, morally correct) practice, whereas most Christian religions consider polygamy an immoral activity.

3. ***Laws*** are generally defined as rules of social conduct devised by people to protect society. Laws are based upon concerns for fairness and justice. The fundamental goal of society's laws is the preservation of the species, which can be achieved by the promotion of peaceful and productive interactions between individuals and groups of individuals. Laws achieve this goal by preventing the actions of one citizen from infringing on the rights of another citizen. One important aspect of laws is that they are enforceable through some type of police force.

4. ***Ethics*** are declarations of what is right or wrong, and what ought to be. Ethics, which are usually presented as systems of valued behaviors and beliefs, serve the purpose of governing conduct to ensure the protection of an individual's rights. Ethics exist on several levels, ranging from the individual or small group to the society as a whole. The concepts of ethics and morals are similar in both their development and purposes. In one sense, ethics can be considered a system of morals for a particular group. There are usually no systems of enforcement for ethics or ethical statements.

5. ***A code of ethics*** is a written list of a profession's values and standards of conduct. The code of ethics provides a framework of decision making for the profession and should be oriented toward the day-to-day decisions made by members of the profession. Codes of ethics are presented in general statements and do not give specific answers to every possible ethical dilemma that might arise. However, these codes do offer guidance to the individual practitioner in making decisions. Ideally, codes of ethics should undergo periodic revision to reflect changes in the profession and society as a whole. While codes of ethics are not legally enforceable as laws, consistent violations of a professional code of ethics indicate an unwillingness by the individual to act in a professional manner, which often results in disciplinary actions ranging from reprimands and fines to suspension and revocation of licensure.

Although similar, there are several different codes of ethics that nurses may adopt. In the United States, the American Nurses' Association Code of Ethics is the generally accepted code. However, there is a Canadian Nurses' Association Code of Ethics and even an International Council of Nurses Code of Ethics for Nurses.

6. *An ethical dilemma* is a situation that requires an individual to make a choice between two equally unfavorable alternatives. When ethical dilemmas are reduced to their elemental aspects, conflicts between one individual's rights and those of another, or between one individual's obligations and the rights of another, or a combination of obligations and rights conflicting with others' obligations and rights, usually form the basis of the dilemma. By the very nature of an ethical dilemma, there is no one good solution, and the decision made often has to be defended against those who disagree with it.

KEY CONCEPTS IN ETHICS

In addition to the terminology used in the study and practice of ethics, there are several important concepts, or principles, that often underlie ethical dilemmas. Although the following list is by no means comprehensive, it does present several key principles that often serve as the underpinnings for ethical dilemmas.

1. *Autonomy* is the right of self-determination, independence, and freedom. Autonomy in the health care setting involves the health care provider's willingness to respect patients' rights to make decisions about and for themselves, even if the provider does not agree with those decisions.

   As with most rights, autonomy is not an absolute right. Under certain conditions, limitations can be imposed upon it, such as when one individual's autonomy interferes with another's rights, health, or well-being. For example, patients generally can use their right to autonomy by refusing any or all treatments. However, in the case of contagious diseases that affect society, such as tuberculosis (TB), the individual can be forced by the health care and legal systems to take medications to cure the disease. The individual can also be forced into isolation to prevent the spread of the disease.

2. *Justice* is the obligation to be fair to all people. The concept is often expanded to what is called **distributive justice,** which specifically states that individuals have the right to be treated equally regardless of race, sex, marital status, medical diagnosis, social standing, economic level, or religious belief. The principle of justice underlies the first statement in the ANA Code of Ethics for Nurses. Distributive justice

is sometimes expanded to include ideas such as equal access to health care for all. As with other rights, limits can be placed upon justice when it interferes with the rights of others.

3. **Fidelity** is the individual's obligation to be faithful to commitments made to self and others. In health care, fidelity includes the professional's faithfulness or loyalty to agreements and responsibilities accepted as part of the practice of the profession. Fidelity is the main support for the concept of accountability, although conflicts in fidelity might arise because of obligations owed to different individuals or groups. For example, a nurse who is just finishing a very busy and tiring 12-hour shift may experience a conflict of fidelity when asked by a supervisor to work an additional shift because of "call-ins." The nurse would have to weigh fidelity to the employing institution against fidelity to the profession and patients to do the best job possible, particularly if the nurse feels that fatigue would interfere with the performance of those obligations.

4. **Beneficence** is a very old requirement for health care providers that views the primary goal of health care as doing good for patients under their care. In general, the term "good" includes more that just technically competent care for patients. Good care requires that the health care provider approach the patient in a holistic manner, including the patient's beliefs, feelings, and wishes as well as those of the patient's family and significant others. However, the difficulty that sometimes arises in implementing the principle of beneficence lies in determining what exactly is good for another and who can best make the decision about this good.

5. **Nonmaleficence** is the requirement that health care providers do no harm to their patients, either intentionally or unintentionally. In a sense, it is the opposite side of the coin of beneficence, and in fact, it is difficult to speak of one term without mentioning the other. In current health care practice, the principle of nonmaleficence is often violated in the short run in order to produce a greater good in the long-term treatment of the patient. For example, a patient may undergo a very painful and debilitating surgery to remove a cancerous growth in order to prolong his life in the future.

By extension, the principle of nonmaleficence also requires that health care providers protect those from harm who cannot protect themselves. This protection from harm is particularly evident in such groups as children, the mentally incompetent, the unconscious, and those who are too weak or debilitated to protect themselves. For example, very strict regulations have developed around situations involving child abuse and the health care provider's obligation to report suspected child abuse.

6. **Veracity,** or "truthfulness," requires that the health care provider tell the truth and not intentionally deceive or mislead patients. As with other rights and obligations, there are limitations to this principle, for example, in situations where telling patients the truth would seriously harm (principle of nonmaleficence) their ability to recover or would produce greater illness. Many times health care providers feel uncomfortable giving patients the "bad news" and have a tendency to avoid answering questions truthfully. Feeling uncomfortable is not a good enough reason to avoid telling patients the truth about their diagnosis, treatment, or prognosis. The patient has a right to know this information.

7. **The standard of best interest** is a decision made about individual patients' health care when they are unable to make an informed decision for their own care. The standard of best interest is based upon what the health care providers and/or the family decide is best for that individual. It is very important to consider the individual's expressed wishes, either formally in a written declaration (such as a living will) or informally in what may have been said to family members.

   The standard of best interest should be based on the principle of beneficence. Unfortunately, in situations where patients are unable to make decisions for themselves, the resolution of the dilemma often appears to be a unilateral decision made about the individual's health care by the health care provider(s). This type of unilateral decision by health care providers, which implies that they know what is best, disregarding the patient's wishes, is called **paternalism.**

8. **Obligations** are demands made upon individuals, professions, society, or government to fulfill and honor the rights of others. Obligations are often divided into two categories:
   a. **Legal obligations** are those obligations that have become formal statements of law and are enforceable under the law. For example, nurses have a legal obligation to provide safe and adequate care for patients assigned to them.
   b. **Moral obligations** are those obligations that are based upon moral or ethical principles, but are *not* enforceable under the law. For example, in most states there is no legal obligation for a nurse on a vacation trip to stop and help an automobile accident victim.

9. **Rights** are generally defined as just claims or titles, or as something that is owed to an individual according to just claims, legal guarantees, or moral and ethical principles. Although the term "right" is frequently used in both the legal and ethical systems, its meaning is often blurred in everyday usage. Those things that individuals tend to claim as "rights" are really privileges, concessions, or freedoms. There are several classification systems for "rights" in which different types of rights

are delineated. The following three types of rights cover the range of definitions:

a. *Welfare rights* (also called *legal rights*) are rights that are based upon a legal entitlement to some good or benefit. These rights are guaranteed by laws (such as the Bill of Rights) and, if violated, can be punished within the legal system. For example, citizens of the United States have a right to equal access to housing regardless of race, sex, or religion.

b. *Ethical rights* (also called *moral rights*) are rights that are based upon a moral or ethical principle. Ethical rights usually do not have the power of law to enforce the claim. In reality, they are often privileges allotted to certain individuals or groups of individuals. Over time, popular acceptance of an ethical right can give it the force of a legal right. For example, the right to health care is really a long-standing privilege for Americans that is sometimes viewed as a right.

c. *Option rights* are based upon a fundamental belief in the dignity and freedom of human beings. Option rights are particularly evident in free and democratic countries and much less evident in totalitarian and restrictive societies. Option rights give individuals the freedom of choice and the right to live their lives as they choose, as long as they stay within a set of prescribed boundaries. For example, people may wear whatever clothes they choose, as long as they wear some type of clothing.

TWO ETHICAL SYSTEMS

An ethical situation exists every time a nurse interacts with a patient in a health care setting. Nurses are continually making ethical decisions in their daily practice, whether or not they recognize it. The type of ethical decisions they make are what is known as **normative decisions.** Normative decisions deal with questions and dilemmas requiring a choice of actions where there is a conflict of rights or obligations between the nurse and the patient, the nurse and the patient's family, the nurse and the physician, or any other combination. In resolving these ethical questions, nurses often use one of, or perhaps a combination of, the ethical systems.

A detailed, comprehensive presentation of all the existing systems of ethics is beyond the scope of this chapter. The two fundamental and predominant systems that are most directly concerned with ethical decision making in the health care professions will be addressed. These systems are utilitarianism and deontology. The following discussion of these two systems of ethics is undertaken within the context of **bioethics**—the ethics of life, or death in some cases. Bioethics, a word that is in common use, has become synonymous with health care ethics. It includes not only questions concerning life and death, but also questions of quality of life, life-sustaining and altering technologies, and bioscience in general.

Utilitarianism

The Ethical Precepts

Utilitarianism (also called teleology, consequentialism, or situation ethics) is referred to as the ethical system of utility. As a system of normative ethics, utilitarianism defines "good" as happiness or pleasure. It is based on two underlying principles. The first principle is stated as: "The greatest good for the greatest number." The second principle is: "The end justifies the means." Because of these two principles, utilitarianism is sometimes subdivided into **act utilitarianism** and **rule utilitarianism.** According to rule utilitarianism, the individual draws upon past experiences to formulate rules that are the most useful in determining the greatest good. With act utilitarianism, the particular situation that an individual finds himself or herself in determines the rightness or wrongness of a particular act. In practice, the true follower of utilitarianism does not believe in the validity of any system of rules because the rules can change depending on the circumstances surrounding the decision to be made.

Situation ethics is probably the most publicized form of act utilitarianism. Joseph Fletcher, one of the best known proponents of act utilitarianism, outlines a method of ethical thinking in which the situation determines whether an act is morally right or wrong. An act, then, is good to the extent that it promotes happiness, and wrong to the degree that it promotes unhappiness. Although happiness is the happiness of the greatest number of people, the happiness of each person weighs equally.

Based upon the concept that moral rules should not be arbitrary but should serve a purpose, ethical decisions derived from a utilitarian framework weigh the effect of alternative actions that influence the overall welfare of present and future populations. As such, this system is oriented toward the good of the population in general and the individual as a member of that population.

Advantages

The major advantage of the utilitarian system of ethical decision making is that many individuals find it easy to apply to most situations because it is built around their own need for happiness, in which they have an immediate and vested knowledge. Another advantage is that utilitarianism fits well into a society that shuns rules and regulations. The follower of utilitarianism can justify almost any decision based upon the "happiness" principle. Also, its utility orientation fits well into western society's belief in the work ethic and the behavioristic approach to education, philosophy, and life. For example, the follower of utilitarianism would agree with a general prohibition against lying and deceiving because, ultimately, the results of truth telling lead to more happiness than the results of lying. Yet truth telling is not an absolute requirement for the follower of utilitarianism. If telling the truth would produce widespread unhappiness for a great number of people and future generations, then it would be ethically better to tell a lie that would yield more happiness than to tell the truth that would lead to unhappiness. While such behavior might appear to be unethical at first glance, the follower of strict act utilitarianism would have little difficulty in deriving this as a logical conclusion of utilitarianistic ethical thinking.

Disadvantages

There are some serious limitations to utilitarianism as a system of health care ethics or bioethics. For example, does "happiness" refer to the average happiness of all or to the total happiness of a few? Because individual happiness is also important, how does one make decisions when the individual's happiness conflicts with the larger group's happiness. Perhaps more important are the basic questions of what constitutes "happiness" or "the greatest good for the greatest number"? Who determines what is "good" in the first place? Society in general? The government? Governmental policy? The individual? In health care delivery and the formulation of health care policy, the general guiding principle often seems to be the greatest good for the greatest number. Yet where do minority groups fit into this taxonomy? And what happens when the minority group becomes the majority group as is happening in parts of this country today?

In addition, the "ends justify the means" principle has been consistently rejected as a method of achieving ideals. This aphorism has been invoked to justify brutal and repressive acts that are difficult to view as "good." It is generally not considered acceptable to do whatever you want just as long as the final goal or purpose is good. When dealing with health care issues that involve individuals' lives, quantifying such concepts as "good," "harmful," "beneficial," or "greatest" is especially difficult.

Because of these difficulties, pure utilitarianism is a poor decision-making system to use in the resolution of health care dilemmas. The decisions made under pure utilitarianism tend to be egocentric and more concerned with the decision maker than with the individuals who are being affected by the decision. In day-to-day health care situations, individuals who espouse utilitarianism as their primary system of ethical decision making usually combine it with the principle of *distributive justice*.

Distributive justice has several levels of meaning. In the broadest sense, distributive justice is an ethical principle that advocates equal allocation of benefits and burdens to all members of society. At this level, the main concerns of distributive justice become (1) how the country as a whole should allocate its resources, and (2) who should pay for these resources. The U.S. Tax Code, to some degree, is based on the principle of distributive justice. It is easy to see that utilitarianism and distributive justice share some common goals at the theoretical level.

Most nurses have little time or desire to consider all the broad theoretical underpinnings and implications of their daily patient care decisions. At this more practical level, distributive justice simply means treating all patients equally, regardless of their backgrounds, beliefs, or diagnoses. The principle of distributive justice presumes that people are very similar in the most important aspects of life, such as basic needs (food, housing, health care), freedoms, (self-determination, self-expression, self-government), and goals (life, liberty, and the pursuit of happiness). These basic presumptions of distributive justice constitute relatively fixed and unchanging rules. When the principle of distributive justice is combined with utilitarianism as a system of ethical decision making, the decisions made will more often than not approximate the decisions made by the follower of the deontological system.

Unfortunately, using the principle of distributive justice with utilitarianism contradicts the most basic principle of pure utilitarianism, namely that there are no fixed or unchanging rules. Pure utilitarianism, while easy to use as a decision-making system, does not work well as an ethical system for decision making in health care because of its arbitrary, self-centered nature. In the everyday delivery of health care, utilitarianism is often combined with other types of ethical decision making in the resolution of ethical dilemmas.

Deontology

The Ethical Precepts

Deontology is a system of ethical decision making that is based on moral rules and unchanging principles. This system is also referred to as the formalistic system, the principal system of ethics, or duty-based ethics. A follower of a pure form of the deontological system of ethical decision making would believe in the ethical absoluteness of principles regardless of the consequences of the decision. This strict adherence to an ethical theory in which the moral rightness or wrongness of human actions is considered separately from the consequences is based upon a fundamental principle called the **categorical imperative.** It is not the results of the act that make it right or wrong, but the principles upon which the act is carried out. These fundamental principles are ultimately unchanging and absolute and are derived from the universal values that underlie all major religions. Focusing on a concern for right and wrong in the moral sense, the system is based on the need for survival of the species and social cooperation.

While the deontological system is sometimes divided, like the utilitarian system, into act deontology and rule deontology, act deontology is a contradiction in terms. By definition, *act deontology* is based on the personal moral values of the individual making the ethical decision, and not on hard-and-fast, unchanging principles. There would be no major conflict if the individual's personal values and principles were identical to the unchanging principles upon which the deontological system is based. Given the nature of the human animal, there is minimal likelihood of that symmetry of values and principles occurring.

Rule deontology is based upon the belief that there are standards for the ethical choices and judgments that an individual makes. These standards are fixed and do not change when the situation changes. While the number of standards or rules is potentially unlimited, in reality, and particularly in dealing with bioethical issues, many of these principles can be grouped together into a few general or cover principles. These principles can also be arranged into a type of hierarchy of rules including such maxims as: "Humans should always be treated as ends and never as means"; "Human life has value"; "One is always to tell the truth"; "Above all in health care, do no harm"; "The human person has a right to self-determination"; "All persons are of equal value"; and so on. The similarity among these principles and fundamental documents, such as the Bill of Rights and the Hospital Patient's Bill of Rights, is immediately evident.

Advantages

Nurses who espouse the deontological system of ethical thinking believe that duties and obligations, rather than mere actions, bring about the best ends. When the concepts of rights and duties are added to moral and ethical thinking, the result is a decision-making process that also takes into account a larger and often interwoven system of duties. These guiding principles affect nurses' behavior and consequently their relationships with patients. The deontological system is useful in making ethical decisions in health care because it holds that an ethical judgment based upon principles is the same in a variety of similar situations regardless of time, location, or particular individuals involved.

The terminology and concepts used in the deontological approach to ethics are similar to those used by the legal system. Like the deontological system, the legal system stresses rights and duties, principles and rules. However, it is important to remember that there are significant differences between the two. Legal rights and duties are enforceable under the law;

ethical rights and duties usually are not. In general, ethical systems are much wider and more inclusive than the system of laws to which they relate. An ethical perspective on law by health care professionals ultimately leads to an interest in making laws that govern health care and nursing practice. Evaluating and revising laws from an ethical perspective prevents professional nurses from being placed in practice situations where there is no legal support for their ethical practice.

Disadvantages

The deontological system of ethical decision making is not free from imperfection. Some of the more troubling questions include: What do you do when the basic guiding principles conflict with each other? What is the source of the principles? Is there ever a situation where an exception to the rule will apply? Although various approaches have been proposed to circumvent these limitations, it may be difficult for the nurse to resolve situations where duties and obligations conflict, particularly where the consequences of following a rule may end in harm or hurt to a patient. In reality, there are probably few followers of pure deontology because most people do consider the consequences of their actions in the decision-making process.

THE APPLICATION OF ETHICAL THEORIES

When ethical theories are applied to information the nurse already possesses, they form an essential structure for the practicing nurse to use as a means of resolving a particular ethical dilemma. Depending on which theory or system of ethics is used, similar or different decisions for an action may be reached. Ethical theories do not provide cookbook solutions for ethical dilemmas. Instead, they provide a framework for decision making that the nurse can apply to a particular ethical situation.

At times, ethical theories may seem too abstract or general to be of much use to specific ethical situations. Without them, however, ethical decision making often becomes an exercise in personal emotions. In reality, most nurses attempting to make ethical decisions combine the two theories presented here. Using the theories helps pinpoint the important aspects of the ethical decision-making process.

THE DECISION-MAKING PROCESS IN ETHICS

Nurses, by definition, are problem solvers. The primary focus of nursing education is to learn to solve patient nursing care problems. One of the important problem-solving tools is the nursing process itself, which is a systematic, step-by-step approach to resolving problems that arise when dealing with a patient's health and well-being.

Despite this ability to deal with patients' physical problems, many nurses feel inadequate when dealing with ethical dilemmas associated with patient care. These feelings may stem from their unfamiliarity with a systematic problem-solving technique for ethical dilemmas. However, nurses in any health care setting can develop the decision-making skills necessary to make sound ethical decisions if they learn and practice using an ethical decision-making process.

The ethical decision-making process provides a method for nurses to answer key questions about ethical dilemmas and to organize their thinking in a more logical and sequential manner. The problem-solving method presented here, unlike some others, is based upon the nursing process. It should be relatively easy for the nurse to move from the nursing process used in resolving patient physical problems to the ethical decision-making process used in resolving ethical problems.

The chief goal of the ethical decision-making process is determining right from wrong in situations where clear demarcations do not exist or are not apparent to the nurse faced with the decision. The ethical decision-making process also presupposes that the nurse making the decision knows that a system of ethics exists, knows the content of that ethical system, and knows that the system applies to similar ethical decision-making problems despite multiple variables. At some point, nurses need to undertake the task of clarifying their own values, if this has not been done or has not been done recently. The nurse should also have an understanding of the possible ethical systems that may be used in making decisions about ethical dilemmas.

The following five-step ethical decision-making process is presented as a tool for resolving ethical dilemmas:

Step 1   Collect, Analyze, and Interpret the Data

Obtain as much information as possible about the particular ethical dilemma to be decided. Unfortunately, information is sometimes limited, which complicates the analysis and interpretation. Among the things that are important to know are the patient's wishes, the family's wishes, and the extent of the physical or emotional problems causing the dilemma.

A common ethical situation that many nurses must face at some time is whether or not to resuscitate a hospital patient with a terminal disease. Physicians often leave instructions for the nursing staff not to code or resuscitate the patient, but to go through the motions to make the family feel better. The nurse's dilemma is whether to seriously attempt to revive the patient in the event of cardiac and/or respiratory cessation.

Some of the questions nurses need answered in these cases include how mentally competent the patient is to make a no-resuscitation decision, what the patient's desires are, what the family thinks about the situation, and whether the physician has sought input from the patient and the family. Many institutions have policies concerning no resuscitation, and it is wise to consider these in the data collection stage. After collecting information, the nurse needs to bring the pieces of information together in a manner that gives the clearest and sharpest focus to the dilemma.

Step 2   State the Dilemma

After collecting and analyzing all available information, the nurse needs to state the dilemma as clearly as possible. In the majority of ethical dilemmas, the dilemma can be reduced to a statement or two that revolves around the key ethical issues. These ethical issues often involve a question of conflicting rights or basic ethical principles.

In the resuscitation case just posed, where the situation is a question of slow resuscitation or no resuscitation, the statement of the dilemma might be: "The patient's right to death with dignity versus the nurse's obligation to preserve life and do no harm." In general, the principle that the competent patient's wishes must be followed is unequivocal. If the patient has become unresponsive before expressing his or her wishes, then the family members' wishes must be given serious consideration. Additional questions can arise if the family's wishes conflict with those of the patient.

Step 3   Consider the Choices of Action

After stating the dilemma as clearly as possible, list all the possible courses of action that can resolve the dilemma without considering their consequences. This undertaking needs to be a real brain-storming activity in which *all* possible courses of action are considered. The consequences of the different actions are considered later. This process of idea development may require input from outside sources such as colleagues, supervisors, or even experts in the ethical field.

Some of the options for the nurse who is dealing with the patient who is a questionable resuscitation candidate include:

- resuscitating the patient to the nurse's fullest capabilities despite what the physician has requested

- not resuscitating the patient at all, just going through the motions without any real attempt to revive the patient
- seeking another assignment so as to avoid dealing with the situation
- reporting the problem to a supervisor
- attempting to clarify the question with the patient
- attempting to clarify the question with the family
- confronting the physician about the question

Step 4   Analyze the Advantages and Disadvantages of Each Course of Action

Some of the courses of action developed during the previous step in the process are more realistic than others. That will become readily evident during this step, when the advantages and the disadvantages of each action are considered in detail. Along with each option, the consequences of taking each course of action must be thoroughly evaluated.

In the above ethical dilemma, discussing the decision with the physician might lead to an angry physician who will no longer trust the nurse involved. Any of the other choices has the potential to make practicing nursing at that institution difficult. A nurse who successfully resuscitates a patient despite orders to the contrary may face disciplinary action ranging from a reprimand to termination. Not resuscitating the patient at all has the potential to produce a lawsuit if there is no clear order for a no resuscitation. Presenting the situation to a supervisor may, if the supervisor supported the physician, cause the nurse to be labeled a troublemaker and have a negative effect on future evaluations. The same process, enumerating the advantages and disadvantages, could be applied to the other courses of action.

By considering the advantages and disadvantages, the nurse should be able to reduce the realistic choices of action. Other relevant issues need to be examined while attempting to weigh the choices of action. A major factor would be the appropriate code of ethics. The ANA Code of Ethics is an important source for guidance when making many patient care decisions where ethical dilemmas exist.

Step 5   Make the Decision

The most difficult part of the process is actually making the decision and then living with the consequences. By their nature, ethical dilemmas produce differences of opinion. Not everyone will be pleased with the decision. The best decision that can be hoped for is one that is based on a sound ethical decision-making process.

In the attempt to solve any ethical dilemma, there will always be a question of the correct course of action. The patient's wishes almost always supersede independent decisions on the part of health care professionals. Collaborative decision making among the patient, physician, nurses, and family about resuscitation is the ideal and tends to produce fewer complications in the long-term resolution of such questions.

PRACTICING THE ETHICAL DECISION-MAKING PROCESS

As in learning all skills, practice is necessary. The case study at the end of this chapter presents an ethical dilemma. By applying the ethical decision making process to this case study, and using the ethical theories discussed, an increased level of skill in ethical problem-solving ability may be achieved. Other ethical case studies are presented throughout this book. Attempt resolving the ethical dilemmas presented using the ethical decision-making process.

Points to Remember

▶ Ethics deals with the rightness and wrongness of certain situations and has no mechanism of enforcement, while laws are manmade rules that regulate society and are enforceable.
▶ Ethical dilemmas often have no clear or ideal solution, and differences of opinion often exist.
▶ Autonomy is the right to choose one's own health care and is the most important principle to consider in resolving ethical dilemmas.
▶ Beneficence, the obligation to do good for patients, and nonmaleficence, the obligation to do no harm to patients, are the minimal ethical requirements for nurses.
▶ Rights are just claims or titles to something. Many times individuals claim something as a "right" that may really be a privilege, concession, or freedom. Only legal rights have the force of law behind them.
▶ Utilitarianism is a system of ethics that is based on the the "greatest good" principle. As a system, utilitarianism may not be appropriate for some health care decisions.
▶ Deontology is a system of ethics that is based on unchanging principles. This system parallels the legal and moral systems most people grew up with.
▶ The ethical decision-making process is a step-by-step approach for making ethical decisions. These steps are:
  ▷ Collect, analyze, and interpret the data.
  ▷ State the dilemma.
  ▷ Consider the choices of action.

▷ Analyze the advantages and disadvantages of each choice of action.
▷ Make a decision about the action to resolve the dilemma.

Study Questions

1. Compare and contrast ethics with law by delineating the purposes, scopes, and methods of enforcement.
2. Define and explain ethics, law, values, morals, ethical code, and ethical dilemma.
3. Define and explain the concepts of autonomy, justice, fidelity, beneficence, nonmaleficence, veracity, obligations, and rights.
4. Distinguish between the two types of obligations.
5. Distinguish between the three categories of rights.
6. Define "utilitarianism" and list its advantages and disadvantages as an ethical decision-making system.
7. Define "deontology" and list its advantages and disadvantages as an ethical decision-making system.
8. Name and explain the steps in the ethical decision-making process.
9. Analyze an ethical dilemma case study using the ethical decision-making process.

BIBLIOGRAPHY

American Nurses' Association: Code for nurses with interpretive statements. Kansas City, Mo, 1985.

Davis, AJ, and Aroskar, MA: Ethical Dilemmas and Nursing Practice. Appleton-Century-Crofts, New York, 1978, pp 34, 204.

Doheny, M, Cook, C, and Stopper, C: The Discipline of Nursing. Appleton & Lange, Norwalk, Conn, 1987.

Elias, JL, and Merriam, S: Philosophical Foundations of Education. Robert E. Krieger, Malabar, Fla, 1980.

Ellis, RE, and Hartley, CL: Nursing in Today's World. JB Lippincott, Philadelphia, 1988.

Fletcher, J: Situation Ethics. Westminster, Philadelphia, 1966.

Jameton, A: Nursing Practice: The Ethical Issues. Prentice-Hall, Englewood Cliffs, NJ, 1984, pp 7–12.

Quinn, CA, and Smith, MD: The Professional Commitment: Issues and Ethics in Nursing. WB Saunders, Philadelphia, 1987.

Thelan, LA, Dave, JK, and Urden, LD: Critical Care Nursing. CV Mosby, St. Louis, 1990, pp 14–25.

Thompson, JE, and Thompson, HO: Teaching ethics to nursing students. Nursing Outlook 37(2):84–88, 1989.

Thompson, JE, and Thompson, HO: Bioethical Decision Making for Nurses. Appleton-Century-Crofts, Norwalk, Conn, 1985, pp 29, 95.

Veatch, RM, and Fry, ST: Case Studies in Nursing Ethics. JB Lippincott, Philadelphia, 1987, pp 37–42.

▶ ETHICS IN PRACTICE

Ruth Rigid, RN, began her career in home health care some 7 years ago after having worked as an assistant head nurse on a busy medical-surgical unit for almost 10 years at a Veterans' Administration (VA) hospital. Ruth has proved to be a hard-working, very responsible and reliable home health care nurse with excellent assessment and nursing skills. In general, she communicates well with patients and provides a high level of care to the patients she is assigned. Ruth has a reputation among the other nurses working in the agency as being competent and hard working, but rather inflexible when it comes to the interpretation of protocols, procedures, and standing orders. This "by-the-book" philosophy is an essential part of Ruth's psychological makeup and pervades all aspects of her life including her religious beliefs and value system.

This past week a new patient has been referred to the agency for home care. He is a 38-year-old admitted homosexual male who is HIV positive and in the terminal stages of acquired immunodeficiency syndrome (AIDS). He (along with his mother and father) had decided to spend his final days at home rather than in a hospital intensive care unit (ICU). Because of the rural location of this agency, this is the first AIDS patient referral it has received.

After consideration of the various qualifications and experience levels of the nurses available, as well as their patient loads, the director of the agency decides that Ruth would be the most qualified nurse to care for this patient. The agency director places the referral form and chart on Ruth's desk with a note to see the patient before the end of the week.

Later that day when Ruth returns from her morning visits, she discovers the referral and chart on her desk. After reviewing the chart and referral form, she storms into the director's office, throws the chart down on the director's desk and states in a loud voice: "I cannot take care of a patient who has AIDS. My religion teaches that homosexuality is a sin against nature and God and I believe that AIDS is a punishment for that sin!"

If you were the director, how would you handle the situation? Use the ethical decision-making model in solving this problem.
- What are the important data in relation to this situation?
- What is the ethical dilemma? State it in a clear, simple statement.
- What are the choices of action, and how do they relate to specific ethical principles?
- What are the consequences of these actions?
- What decision can be made?

Other factors to consider:
- Are there ever any situations when a nurse can ethically (and legally) refuse a work assignment?
- What effect will the final decision have on the other staff members?

CHAPTER

Nursing Practice

ETHICAL CONSIDERATIONS

▼ Today's elaborate and complicated system for licensing and credentialing nurses is a recent development of the health care system. Prior to the early 1900s, a willingness to care, a strong back, and a rudimentary understanding of the treatments used by Florence Nightingale were all that was required to be called a nurse. As nursing became more independent and began to be recognized by the public as a separate occupation, if not profession, some type of guarantee was needed to protect the public from unqualified practitioners. The processes of licensure and credentialing developed out of this concern with protecting the public.

Although licensure laws have been in place in one form or another since 1903, it was not until the 1950s that the various nursing organizations began developing standards to regulate the profession. The first step in developing standards of care for nurses was the American Nurses' Association's (ANA) "Code of Ethics of Nursing." Although this code only presented general guidelines, it forms the basis for most of the standards of care that are used today.

One of the primary functions of state boards of nursing is to protect the public from unqualified persons who may wish to practice the profession of nursing. Through such mechanisms as the Nurse Practice Act, standards of care, and the code of ethics, the state boards of nursing are able to guarantee a degree of public safety where nursing care is involved. The Nurse Practice Act is a legal document, and although stated in very general terms, does have the force of law and the mechanisms for enforcement. Standards of care and codes of ethics are *not* laws and have no means of enforcement. However, when a nurse violates either the standards of care or the code of ethics (or both) frequently and with disregard, this generally indicates that person is not acting in a professional manner. Most state boards of nursing have the authority to discipline nurses who are not acting in a professional manner. This discipline can range from a reprimand to licensure suspension or even revocation.

OBJECTIVES

Upon completing this chapter, the reader will be able to:

1 Discuss the relationship between the state nurse practice act and the requirements for entry into practice.

2 Describe how state nurse practice acts define the scope of nursing practice.

3 Describe the role of state boards of nursing.

4 Discuss licensure and disciplinary issues.

INTRODUCTION

Nursing practice has changed considerably over time and will continue to change as health care delivery evolves. As technology advances and the profession responds to societal needs, the regulatory agencies and professional associations continue to redefine the roles, functions, and responsibilities of nurses.

This chapter discusses nursing practice—specifically, the relationship between the state nurse practice act and entry into practice requirements and the scope of practice. The chapter also outlines the role of state boards of nursing and discusses licensure and disciplinary issues.

LICENSURE

Licensure is the process by which an agency of a state government grants permission to an individual to engage in a given occupation. There must be evidence that the applicant has attained the minimal degree of competency to ensure that the public health, safety, and welfare are reasonably protected.[1] Licensing can be described as either permissive or mandatory. **Permissive licensing legislation** regulates the use of a title and requires compliance with the licensing statute only if an individual intends to use the title granted by the licensing authority. **Mandatory licensure** regulates the practice of a profession such as nursing and requires compliance with the licensing statute if an individual engages in the activities defined within the scope of that profession.

> ## Box 3–1   LICENSURE
>
> **Permissive licensing** legislation regulates the use of a title and requires compliance with the licensing statute only if an individual intends to use the title granted by the licensing authority.
>
> **Mandatory licensure** regulates the practice of a profession such as nursing and requires compliance with the licensing statute if an individual engages in the activities defined within the scope of that profession.

Prior to the early 1900s, anyone could provide care to those in need. The first nursing licensure laws regulated the use of the title "nurse," allowing anyone to practice provided they did not use that title. North Carolina was the first state to adopt a nurse practice act. Eventually, licensure laws regulated not only the use of the title "nurse," but also the practice of nursing. The laws defined the scope of practice and created requirements for entry into practice, as well as penalties for proscribed actions or practice without the requisite license.

Licensing can be contrasted with **credentialing,** which is a voluntary form of self-regulation seen in many health care disciplines. While licensure implies that an individual has met the minimum competency levels set by the state for the public's protection, credentialing implies that the individual has met higher standards than licensure. Usually, the profession sets credentialing standards that serve the purposes of protecting the public and advancing the profession. In many health care professions, credentialing standards exist for the various subspecialties within that profession. The professional association that represents the subspecialty often contributes to or sponsors the development of the standards for the certification programs for practitioners.[2]

Educational programs and institutions also often seek some type of credentialing certification, such as the accreditation granted to hospitals by the Joint Commission for the Accreditation of Healthcare Organizations (JCAHO) or the accreditation granted to nursing programs by the National League for Nursing (NLN). As in professional subspecialties, educational or institutional accreditation implies that the program or facility has met standards that exceed those of the licensing agency.

Source of the State's Authority

In areas unregulated by the federal government, each state remains free to exercise control over its citizens, provided that state decisions do not conflict with federal laws. Each state possesses *parens patriae* power (literally translated as "parent of the country" power), which allows it to create laws designed to protect the public's health, safety, and welfare.[3] When it creates laws necessary to carry out its responsibility for public protection, a state can reasonably limit individual rights by virtue of its police power.[4]

Licensure laws represent an example of a state's exercise of its police power. In addition to state restrictions, the federal government can also enact legislation that affects a nurse's practice, as discussed later in this chapter.

Most state nurse practice acts define the scope of practice, establish the requirements for licensure and entry into practice, create and empower a board of nursing to oversee licensees, and identify grounds for disciplinary actions.[5] Requirements for entry into practice typically include graduation from an accredited nursing education program, successful completion of an examination, and payment of a fee to the state.

Box 3–2 NURSE PRACTICE ACTS

1. Define the scope of practice
2. Establish the requirements for licensure and entry into practice
3. Create and empower a board of nursing to oversee licensee
4. Identify grounds for disciplinary actions

BOARDS OF NURSING

Composition

In order to enforce its nurse practice act, each state creates a board of nursing or board of registration (the board). Most boards function in a manner typical of a governmental or administrative body, exercising only powers conferred by statute or reasonably implied as necessary to carry out their authority.[6] The board usually exercises rule-making power over regulatory and disciplinary matters involving licensees. The authority of boards varies across the states from fully autonomous to advisory power only.[7] Similarly, the composition of boards varies from all-professional boards to those composed of registered nurses (RNs), licensed practical nurses (LPNs) or licensed or vocational nurses (LVNs), and representatives of the public.

Legal representation of the boards also varies. Some boards share legal counsel with other administrative agencies, while boards in densely populated states may enjoy counsel dedicated solely to representing health care boards. The increased attention paid to impaired professionals has led to more administrative activity for many boards and a reason to have competent legal counsel. (For example, a hospital and board that know a nurse is using drugs or alcohol but allow the nurse to continue to practice can be held liable if a patient is injured by the nurse because they failed to protect the public.) Also, if it can be shown that the intervention program was below the standards and ineffective in helping impaired nurses, liability and exposure may ensue. An attorney dedicated solely to a health care board offers better representation of the board, more efficient and fairer proceedings, and, presumably, fewer successful challenges to board decisions.

Regulation of Educational Institutions

Most state boards of nursing also regulate nursing education programs. Many require those programs to obtain accreditation, often from the NLN. Accreditation by any objective organization is usually granted only after that organization conducts a thorough evaluation to determine whether the applicant program meets the standards established by the accrediting body. Accreditation may affect a program's ability to obtain funding or an individual graduate's chances of later admission for advanced study or the armed services.

In addition to the NLN accreditation required by a state board of nursing, other state agencies (such as the department of education) may require that the nursing education program obtain accreditation from its official body. To the extent that accrediting bodies publish criteria that must be met before accreditation status is granted, those criteria represent standards for nursing education.

Regulation of Practice

Entry-into-Practice Requirements

Long a source of controversy within the profession, entry-into-practice requirements may differ from state to state. Historically, most state licensure laws created two categories of nurses—licensed practical (or vocational) nurses (LPNs or LVNs) and registered nurses (RNs). LPN licensure requirements usually include successful completion of a 1-year education program and the LPN examination.

RN licensure requirements usually include completion of either a 2-year community college program (associate degree), 3-year hospital-based program (diploma), or 4- or 5-year university (baccalaureate degree) program and successful completion of the RN examination. Despite the variability of the RN educational preparation, most state laws require RN applicants to complete the same examination and grant all successful candidates an identical RN license. Many within the nursing profession have lobbied for standardization of entry requirements. Citing other health care professions as an example, some nursing leaders have proposed the baccalaureate degree as a requirement for entry into prac tice for professional nurses and the associate degree as a requirement for entry into practice for associate or technical nurses. The struggle to accomplish that objective has been long and complicated.

In 1964, the American Nurses' Association (ANA) passed a resolution which specified that all states require a bachelor of science degree in nursing (BSN) for entry into professional practice by 1985.[8] In 1984, the ANA adopted a more realistic timetable, calling for all states to achieve the goal by 1995.[9] In 1985, the ANA urged the state nurses' associations to establish a BSN as the minimum entry level for professional nurses and the associate degree (AD) as the minimum entry level for associate (technical) nurses.[10]

Although opinions differ within the profession, many who support the BSN for entry into professional nursing practice also support abolishment of the traditional LPN role. They propose expanding LPN educational and licensure requirements to equal associate degree requirements for entry into practice as an associate or technical nurse. Others advocate the elimination of LPN programs but support the licensing of AD graduates as associate or technical nurses. Still others advocate a single category of licensure as a professional nurse with a BSN as the entry requirement. Supporters of the latter position advocate elimination of all LPN, AD, and diploma nursing programs. Despite the fact that all states plan to grandfather currently licensed RNs into the professional category, those prepared at the AD level often speak out against the BSN as the entry requirement, citing the lack of data in support of that position.[11]

Regardless of the reasons, efforts to standardize the entry-into-practice requirements have met with limited success. By 1988, 30 state nurses' associations (SNAs) had formally addressed the issue, and 28 had adopted resolutions advocating the BSN as the entry requirement.[12] Twenty-seven state legislatures introduced 29 BSN legislative proposals (25 in favor, 4 opposed). Of those 25 proposals, 3 BSN entry proposals were approved and 3 rejected. Of those opposed to change, two were approved and two rejected.[13]

However, by 1991, only two states (North Dakota and Maine) had succeeded in changing entry requirements.[14] North Dakota became the first state to require a BSN for entry into professional nursing practice as an RN when the North Dakota Board of Nursing changed its administrative regulations in March 1986.[15]

Aided by an ANA grant, Maine's efforts to change the entry requirement met with success in 1986, although the legislation does not require implementation until 1995. Maine's approach included a legislative amendment that created two categories of nursing—the registered professional nurse with a BSN as the entry requirement and the associate nurse with an AD as the entry requirement.[16]

Other states actively involved in efforts to mandate a BSN as the entry requirement include Oregon, Montana, Illinois, and Massachusetts. Factors cited as responsible for the delay include division among nurses, lack of the necessary commitment from organized nursing, failure to mobilize nursing's natural allies, and the legislature's desire to maintain the safety of the status quo.[17]

Scope of Practice—Advanced Nursing Practice and Expanded Role

Many social factors, including limited resources and the increasing complexity of health care delivery, have affected the evolution of nursing practice and other health care disciplines. In its Nursing Social Policy Statement, the ANA describes the scope of nursing practice as multidimensional and characterized by four major elements.[18] Those elements include a core of professional practice common to all members of nursing, dimensions or characteristics of nursing practice, intraprofessional and interprofessional relationships between nursing and other disciplines, and boundaries of nursing practice.

Box 3–3   ANA'S SOCIAL POLICY STATEMENT:
ELEMENTS OF SCOPE OF NURSING
PRACTICE

1. Core of professional practice common to all members of nursing
2. Dimensions or characteristics of practice
3. Intraprofessional and interprofessional relationships
4. Boundaries

Historically nursing has struggled with boundaries, particularly with respect to the overlap between nursing and medical practice. Physicians' assistants and registered care technicians represent two relatively recent types of "physicians' extenders" that further cloud any clear boundary between the scopes of the respective practices. That historical overlap has led to the development of "advanced nursing practice" or "expanded nursing roles." As health care delivery has changed, many of the functions originally defined as expanded practice have been legally absorbed into the scope of professional nursing practice.

Nurse midwifery and nurse anesthesia, two disciplines usually considered representative of expanded nursing practice, actually developed prior to the regulation of nursing.[19] As early as 1912, the literature proposed training nurse midwives, and by the 1920s nurse anesthetists were relatively common. Clinical specialization dates back to 1936, while history traces the nurse practitioners' movement back to 1965. After a report by the U.S. Department of Health, Education, and Welfare in 1971, Congress made available federal funding to train nurse practitioners as primary care providers.[20]

Not all states have adopted the same approach to regulation of the expanded role. Some states control advanced nursing practice through specific statutes separate from the state's nurse practice act. In some states, the nurse practice act authorizes advanced nursing practice, but the board of nursing has established regulations which define and control that practice. Those expanded roles usually include nurse midwives, nurse anesthetists, nurse practitioners, and clinical nurse specialists. The latter category often includes nurse administrators, as well as nurses practicing in subspecialties (such as pediatrics, mental health, etc.).

Such expanded role regulations usually require that a nurse demonstrate evidence of additional education or experience and, in some cases, the existence of a supervisory relationship with a physician. Many state boards require that the nurse obtain certification through the ANA. The ANA offers certification programs in various expanded roles, usually at initial and advanced levels. Other specialty nursing organizations may offer certification programs, such as the National Certification Board for School Nursing or the American Association of Nurse Anesthetists.

In some states, nursing has met with success in legal challenges related to the control of practice. In a landmark case, *Sermchief v. Gonzales,*[21] the Missouri court recognized the actions of certified nurse practitioners as the legal practice of nursing rather than the illegal practice of medicine. The nurse practitioners were providing routine gynecological care (including such things as Pap smears and pregnancy testing) pursuant to protocols developed jointly by the nurses and supervising physicians. The Missouri Nurse Practice Act did not require direct physician supervision or identify nurse practitioners separately, but instead defined professional nursing as:

> The performance of any act which requires substantial specialized education, judgment and skill . . . including, but not limited to: . . . teaching health care and the prevention of illness . . . assessment, nursing diagnosis, nursing care and counsel . . . the administration of medications and treatments as prescribed by a person licensed in this state to prescribe.[22]

Sermchief represented a significant victory in the struggle for nursing autonomy. That struggle continues in many states, supported by the ANA and its strong belief that nurse practice acts should broadly define nursing.[23] A broad definition allows flexible boundaries and minimizes the need for frequent legislative amendment in response to changes in health care delivery.

NONTRADITIONAL NURSING ROLES

In addition to the expanded roles discussed above, many nurses have become involved in professional activities that require nursing expertise, but that do not clearly fall within the scope of practice as defined by most nurse practice acts. Health promotion and managed health care represent two of these nontraditional areas. Although no formal certification programs exist for these fields, specialized training is available. The ANA joined forces with the Group Health Association of America to develop a 3-day managed care nursing curriculum at the University of Kansas City. Sponsors of that program hope to eventually expand it into a master's degree program.[24] As the health care delivery system continually evolves to meet society's changing needs and financial limitations, more nontraditional roles may emerge.

Although state boards of nursing have not actively attempted to exercise authority over nurses practicing in nontraditional roles, some state boards of medicine have attempted to do so with physicians practicing in similar roles. The American Medical Association has proposed model legislation that defines the practice of medicine to include activities currently outside the scope of many practice acts, such as rendering a clinical opinion based upon review of medical records without direct examination of a patient. Such legislation would allow the board to regulate physicians conducting insurance examinations. As health care delivery continues to evolve, state boards of nursing may take similar steps.

Recently, several states have introduced legislation to require state certification of health care professionals practicing in cost-containment positions within the managed health care system. Much of that legislation requires certification of the cost-containment program rather than the individual practitioner. However, some states have proposed individual certification, arguing in favor of bringing the cost-containment positions within the practice of the health care profession as a subspecialty.[25]

Prescriptive Authority

Prescriptive authority is the limited authority to prescribe certain medications according to established protocols. Certain medications or devices incidental to routine health or family planning can also be dispensed.

Box 3–4 PRESCRIPTIVE AUTHORITY

Prescriptive authority is the limited authority to prescribe certain medications according to established protocols. Certain medications or devices incidental to routine health or family planning can also be dispensed.

Two issues emerge when discussing prescriptive authority for nurses: (1) Does the state recognize the prescriptive authority of nurses? (2) Does the state regulate that authority within the context of professional nursing practice? As with scope-of-practice issues, the board of nursing rather than state agencies should retain control of professional nursing issues.

California was the first state to grant prescriptive authority to nurses.[26] Since 1991, nurse practitioners (as distinguished from registered nurses) in several states have had limited authority to prescribe certain medications pursuant to protocols, often developed jointly by a nurse and physician.[27]

California allows a nurse practitioner to furnish medications or devices incidental to routine health care or family planning pursuant to standardized procedures.[28] The statute states that the prescriptive authority is pursuant to physician supervision but specifies that the physician need not be present.[29] The statute does not allow the nurse practitioner to prescribe controlled substances.[30] It also requires that the nurse complete a pharmacology course and a 6-month practicum under physician supervision.[31]

Many of the prescriptive authority provisions also allow nurses to dispense certain medications, although comments accompanying the ANA suggested legislation on prescriptive authority urge caution in the area of dispensing.[32] The comments accompanying the ANA suggested legislation recommend that legislation limit dispensing authority to no more than the doses of medication necessary until a client can obtain a full prescription from a pharmacist.[33] Presumably, such limited authority represents a balance among such variables as the additional liability associated with dispensing, as well as the overlapping boundaries between nursing and pharmacy.

Hospital Privileges

As more and more nurses enter independent practice in the expanded role, hospital privileges become an increasingly controversial issue. In many subspecialties, such as mental health, without privileges a nurse cannot practice to the fullest scope of the profession.

For the most part privileges are handled by the granting facility rather than the state legislature. The extent of the privileges varies widely among facilities. At some facilities, the "privileges" include merely the opportunity to visit the client outside regular visiting hours, whereas at others privileges allow the nurse to make entries in the medical record. Few facilities consider privileges to include the right to admit a client without a supervising physician. Nurses have obtained some assistance from the courts in their efforts to secure privileges.[34]

Third-Party Reimbursement

Many of the issues discussed above, including the expanded role, prescriptive authority, and hospital privileges, have had an indirect effect on the nursing profession's efforts to obtain third-party reimbursement (e.g., payment from the patient's insurance carrier for services rendered). As nurses legally assume increased responsibility for the primary care of patients, third-party reimbursers have been forced to provide benefits for services. In some states, the legislature has forced the issue by adopting laws that require reimbursement of nurses to the extent that they provide services identical to those for which other providers receive reimbursement. Nurse psychotherapists have benefitted most often from such legislation.

Unfortunately, certification and third-party reimbursement requirements sometimes limit direct reimbursement to nurses practicing in expanded roles as nurse practitioners.[35] When such requirements rely on broadly worded language, a nurse may successfully challenge the provisions through administrative channels. In some states that have not passed such legislation, third-party reimbursers have voluntarily offered coverage for such services, realizing that reimbursement for the less costly nursing services eliminates the need for the more costly services of a physician.

Mandatory Continuing Education

The last decade has seen a trend toward mandatory continuing education for nurses. Most states that have adopted such legislation require nurses to have a specific number of continuing education units (CEUs) or contact hours as a condition for license renewal.[36] Requirements for maintaining current specialty certifications are dictated by the certifying organization.

ADMINISTRATIVE PROCEEDINGS

Traditional Disciplinary Provisions

All nurse practice acts provide a traditional disciplinary system. Such systems empower the state board to take action against a nurse's license for certain grounds which are specifically outlined by the board or defined by regulations. In addition to granting the power to take action against a licensee, the nurse practice act also empowers the board to reinstate licenses.

Traditionally, the board can deny, revoke, suspend, limit, or other-wise condition a license for grounds that often include substance abuse, negligence, incompetence, criminal activity, or violation of the nurse practice act. Some acts include broad language that allows the board to discipline for unprofessional conduct, a term interpreted differently in various states. Often, the interpretation of broad language such as unprofessional conduct is accomplished by regulation or case law.

Box 3–5   DISCIPLINARY ACTIONS AND GROUNDS FOR DISCIPLINING

1. Disciplinary actions by a board of nursing: Deny, revoke, suspend, limit, or condition a nurse's license
2. Grounds
   a. Substance abuse
   b. Negligence
   c. Incompetence
   d. Criminal activity
   e. Violation of the Nurse Practice Act
   f. Unprofessional conduct

Although each state's administrative procedure act (or its equivalent) specifically defines the manner in which the board must proceed when disciplining a licensee, most involve a similar process. The board usually must investigate a complaint prior to taking any action, unless the law provides for summary suspension, a rare action reserved for situations involving extreme danger to the public. Even where the law permits summary suspension, after the action the licensee has the right to exercise due process rights similar to those available to all licensees subjected to disciplinary charges.

Unless waived, a nurse is entitled to notice of the time and place of the investigatory hearing conducted by the board or a body acting at the board's direction, such as a committee or hearing officer.[37] The nurse is also entitled to a clear statement of the charges, the right to confront and produce witnesses, the right to an attorney, the right to a record of the proceedings, and the right to a fair determination by the presiding body based upon the evidence presented. Finally, the nurse is entitled to some type of appeal or judicial review, whether by the full board or the state court.

Despite the variability among states, the rules of evidence applied by most administrative proceedings are less formal than those used in civil or criminal cases. The "burden of proof," or amount of evidence required to support a particular board decision, also varies from state to state. Many states apply a variation of the substantial evidence test, a burden defined by Arkansas as "evidence which is valid, legal and persuasive and such relevant evidence as a reasonable mind might accept as adequate to support a conclusion."[38]

The development of a defense against disciplinary charges involves the same principles applicable in any administrative, civil, or criminal case. Perhaps the most critical variable is retaining a knowledgeable attorney who can assist with preparation of the defense. While many attorneys may offer such assistance, nurse attorneys often serve as particularly well qualified advocates based upon their understanding of the profession and its regulations. Regardless of the nurse's choice of advocate, thorough investigation and the ability to persuade the board to adopt the nurse's position form the foundation of any defense.

While the Nurse Practice Act may empower a state board of nursing to discipline a licensee for negligence, that administrative action remains separate from a civil action. Any individual who believes that he or she has suffered an injury as a result of a nurse's professional negligence can file a lawsuit against that nurse for damages. Unlike a criminal conviction, a finding of negligence in a civil action, that is, a medical malpractice claim, does not usually serve as the basis for disciplinary action. The board can conduct an investigation at the same time as the civil lawsuit or after the suit has ended. If the board is empowered by the Nurse Practice Act, the board can take action against the licensee.

Disciplinary Diversion Acts

Over the last decade, the nursing profession has demonstrated a commitment to the rehabilitation of nurses impaired by psychological dysfunction or substance abuse. That commitment has been seen through legislative efforts to establish rehabilitative programs under the state board of nursing to divert impaired nurses from traditional disciplinary procedures.

A 1989 study reveals significant variation in board actions toward impaired nurses.[39] The study focused on the specific disciplinary procedures that board members would use on physical, mental, and substance abuse impairments. Significantly higher percentages of board members would use specific disciplinary actions for criminal abuse impairments versus physical impairments, which seems to indicate that the rehabilitative philosophy for psychological dysfunction or substance abuse has not spread widely among boards.

When determining whether to reinstate a nurse's license, the criteria judged most significant among board members include active treatment and an ability to function in the workplace.[40] Whether these two criteria are met is determined by the results of a board evaluation and the persuasiveness of a physician's statement of support. These same criteria represent the conditions required by many of the nursing disciplinary diversion acts—with one critical difference. That is, as long as a nurse is able to meet these two conditions, at least one act would allow the nurse to retain a limited nursing license which would permit the rehabilitative benefits of employment and associate financial resources.

In 1990, the ANA published suggested state legislation which included a Nursing Disciplinary Diversion Act.[41] That suggested legislation provides a diversion procedure as a voluntary alternative to traditional disciplinary action, creates a rehabilitative evaluation committee, and defines the powers and duties of that committee.

Failure to comply with the voluntary rehabilitation program can result in reversion to the traditional disciplinary procedures. The model diversion program allows a nurse to avoid traditional disciplinary actions such as license revocation, providing that the nurse complies with the rehabilitative program overseen by the committee. Records of rehabilitation and board action remain confidential and, unless a relapse occurs, may be destroyed after 5 years. Immunity provisions exist for those providing information related to a nurse's functioning or rehabilitation.

National Practitioner Data Bank

Although public attention has focused predominantly on its effect upon the practice of medicine, the **National Practitioner Data Bank** (NPDB) does impact the nursing profession. Created by the Health Care Quality Improvement Act of 1986,[42] the NPDB became operational on September 1, 1990. Congress enacted the Health Care Quality Improvement Act (HCQIA) based upon a belief that the need to improve the quality of care and slow down the increasing malpractice litigation could no longer rest solely with the licensing bodies in the states.[43] The intent of the HCQIA is to provide "positive incentives" for participation in peer review, predominantly in the form of good faith immunity for those providing information to the NPDB.[44]

NPDB information is available upon request to hospitals and health care entities engaged in credentialing. Ideally, the information should "restrict the ability of incompetent practitioners to move from state to state."[45] The NPDB addresses three types of data: (1) information relating to medical malpractice payments made on behalf of health care practitioners; (2) information relating to adverse actions taken against clinical privileges of a physician, osteopath, or dentist; and (3) information concerning actions by professional societies that adversely affect membership.

Box 3–6   NATIONAL PRACTITIONER DATA BANK

1. NPDB addresses three types of data:
   a. Information relating to medical malpractice payments made on behalf of health care practitioners.
   b. Information relating to adverse actions taken against clinical privileges of physicians, osteopaths, or dentists.
   c. Information concerning actions by professional societies that adversely affect membership.
2. Types of information reported:
   a. *Required reporting*—adverse professional review actions against physicians, osteopaths, and dentists.
   b. *Optional reporting*—adverse professional review actions against other health care providers (including nurses).
   c. *Required reporting*—medical malpractice payments made on behalf of all health care providers.

Reporting of information relating to adverse professional review actions against physicians, osteopaths, and dentists is required. Reporting regarding other health care providers (including nurses) is optional as contrasted to the broader reporting requirement associated with medical malpractice payments, which requires reporting payments made on behalf of all health care providers. Optional reporting most likely will affect nurse midwives, nurse anesthetists, and nurse practitioners, since those professionals often are subject to credentialing procedures similar to those associated with granting clinical privileges.

As you might expect, failure to report to the NPDB carries fines and penalties for those identified as mandatory reporters. Although health care providers receive notice of reports filed, requests of copies of any report filed against them can be made to the NPDB and sent without charge. Appeal procedures exist for those wishing to challenge the validity or accuracy of reported information.

FINANCIAL RESPONSIBILITY FOR PRACTICE

The financial burden of defending against an administrative or civil proceeding can be significant. As a result, many nurses arrange for professional liability insurance as protection against such burdens. Many do so regardless of the coverage available through an employer. The American Association of Nurse Attorneys maintains that financial responsibility for practice is a fundamental component of professional accountability.[46] Given the increasing incidence of litigation against health care professionals and the costs to the health care system and society, many states have undertaken tort reform. In an attempt to reverse that trend, some states have explored state compensation pools for individuals injured by a professional with inadequate insurance or financial resources to otherwise compensate the injured party. A nurse should be familiar with the various sources of financial relief for injured clients and consider those when making a decision regarding insurance and accountability for professional practice.

Points To Remember

▶ Licensure is the process by which an agency of a state government grants permission to an individual to engage in a given occupation.
▶ Credentialing implies that the professional has met higher standards than licensure.
▶ Nurse practice acts define the scope of practice, establish licensure requirements and entry into practice, empower a board to oversee licensees, and identify grounds for disciplinary actions.
▶ Prescriptive authority allows limited authority for nurses to prescribe medications.
▶ Third-party reimbursement requirements may limit direct reimbursement to nurses.
▶ Mandatory continuing education for nurses is a trend that is increasing throughout the states.
▶ Several grounds for state board of nursing disciplinary actions include substance abuse, negligence, incompetence, criminal activity, unprofessional conduct, or violation of the Nurse Practice Act.
▶ The National Practitioner Data Bank was created by the Health Care Quality Improvement Act of 1986.

Study Questions

1. Discuss the source of the state's authority for licensure and its purpose in exercising that authority.
2. Discuss the source of the board's disciplinary authority.
3. Discuss at least three "grounds" for disciplinary action, the potential

defenses to each, and the actions available to the board of registration for each.

4. Discuss the differences between entry requirements for practice as a professional nurse and as an associate nurse and the history of the development of the different requirements.

5. Discuss the implications of separate "expanded role" licensure for nurse practitioners.

6. Discuss the purpose of your state Nurse Practice Act.

7. Discuss the functions of the state board of nursing.

8. What is licensure, and what are the general requirements for licensure?

9. What is credentialing?

10. Discuss third-party reimbursement and how it can affect the nursing profession.

REFERENCES

1. Shimberg, B: Occupational Licensing: A Public Perspective. Center for Occupational and Professional Assessment, Educational Testing Service, Princeton, 1982.
2. Driscoll, VM: Legitimizing the Profession of Nursing: The Distinct Mission of the New York Nurses' Association. Foundation of the New York Nurses' Association, New York, 1976.
3. *Parens patriae,* literally "parent of the country," refers traditionally to the role of the state as sovereign and guardian of persons under legal disability. *State of W.Va. v. Chas. Pfizer & Co.,* C.A.N.Y., 440 F.2d 1079, 1089. *Parens patriae* originates from the English common law where the king had a royal prerogative to act as guardian to persons with legal disabilities such as infants, idiots, and lunatics. In the United States, the *parens patriae* function belongs with the states. See Black's Law Dictionary, ed 5. West Publishing Co, St. Paul, Minn, 1979, p 1041.
4. *Police power* is the power of the state to place restraints on the personal freedom and property rights of a person for the protection of the public safety, health, and morals or the promotion of the public convenience and general prosperity. Police power is subject to the limitations of the federal and state constitutions, and especially to the requirements of due process. Police power is the exercise of the sovereign right of a government to promote order, safety, health, morals, and general welfare within constitutional limits and is an essential attribute of government. See Black's Law Dictionary, ed 5. West Publishing Co, St. Paul, Minn, 1979, p 1041.
5. Kelly, LY: Dimensions of Professional Nursing. Macmillan, New York, 1991, pp 437–471.
6. Northrop, CE: Licensure revocation. In Northrop, CE, and Kelly, ME (eds): Legal Issues in Nursing. CV Mosby, St. Louis, 1987, pp 405–422.
7. *Id.*
8. Pohlman, KJ, et al: Should Nursing Implement the 1985 Resolution? In McCloskey, J, and Grace, HK (eds): Current Issues in Nursing. Blackwell Scientific Publications, Boston, 1981, pp 149–159.
9. Hood, G: At Issue: Titling and licensure. American Journal of Nursing 85(5):592–594, 1985.
10. Lewis, E: Taking care of business: The ANA house of delegates. Nursing Outlook 33(5):239–243, 1985.

11. *Id.*
12. Velsor-Friedrich, B, and Hackbarth, DP: A house divided. Nursing Outlook 38(3):129–133, 1990.
13. George, S, and Young, WB: Baccalaureate entry into practice: An example of political innovation and diffusion. Journal of Nursing Education 29(8):341–345, 1990.
14. *Id.*
15. *Id.*
16. *Id.*
17. Velsor-Friedrich, B, and Hackbarth, DP: A house divided. Nursing Outlook 38(3):129–133, 1990.
18. American Nurses' Association: Nursing Social Policy Statement (Publ. No. NP-68A). American Nurses' Association, Kansas City, Mo, 1980, pp 3–4.
19. Kelly, ME: Control of the practice of nurse practitioners, nurse midwives, nurse anesthetists, and clinical nurse specialists. In Northrop, CE, and Kelly, ME (eds): Legal Issues in Nursing. CV Mosby, St. Louis, 1987, pp 469–485.
20. *Id.* at 469.
21. *Sermchief v. Gonzales,* 660 S.W.2d 683 (Mo., banc., 1983).
22. Mo. Rev. Stat. Sec. 335.016.8(A)–(E), 1975.
23. Mechanic, HF: Redefining the expanded role. Nursing Outlook 36(6):280–284, 1988.
24. Wood, M: Personal communication, April 1991.
25. Group Health Association of America, Inc: GHAA State Legislative & Regulatory Issues Digest. GHAA, 1991, pp 1–30.
26. George, S, and Young, WB: Baccalaureate entry into practice: An example of political innovation and diffusion. Nursing Outlook 29(8):341–345, 1990.
27. Minnesota 148.235. Subd 2 and North Dakota 43.12.1-08.1.
28. West's Ann. Cal. Bus. & Prof. Code Sec. 2836.1(a)–(b) (1991).
29. West's Ann. Cal. Bus. & Prof. Code Sec. 2836.1(d) (1991).
30. West's Ann. Cal. Bus. & Prof. Code Sec. 2836.1(f).
31. West's Ann. Cal. Bus. & Prof. Code Sec. 2836.1(g).
32. American Nurses' Association: Suggested State Legislation: Nursing Practice Act Nursing Disciplinary Act, Prescriptive Authority Act (Publ. NP-78). American Nurses' Association, Kansas City, Mo, 1990, pp 1–46.
33. *Id.*
34. *Wrable v. Community Memorial Hospital,* 205 N.J. Super. 428 (1985), *aff'd,* 517 A.2d 470 (10/22/86), *cert. denied,* 526 A.2d 210 (4/28/82).
35. Mechanic, HF: Redefining the expanded role. Nursing Outlook 36(6):280–284, 1988.
36. Massachusetts Minnesota C.M.R. 112 St. 74.
37. Northrop, CE: Licensure revocation. In Northrop, CE, and Kelly, ME (eds): Legal Issues in Nursing. CV Mosby, St. Louis, 1987, pp 405–422.
38. *Arkansas State Board of Nursing v. Long,* 651 S.W.2d 109 (Ark., 1983).
39. Swenson, I, Havens, B, and Champagne, M: State Boards and Impaired Nurses. Nursing Outlook 37(2):94–96, 1989.
40. *Id.*
41. American Nurses' Association: Suggested State Legislation: Nursing Practice Act, Nursing Disciplinary Diversion Act, Prescriptive Authority Act (Publ. No. NP-78). American Nurses' Association, Kansas City, Mo, 1990, pp 1–46.
42. Health Care Quality Improvement Act of 1986 (Title IV of P.L. 99-660) (11/14/86), 42 U.S.C. 11101 et. seq., as amended by Sec. 402 of P.L. 100-177, Public Health Service Amendments of 1987 (12/1/87) and Sec. 6103(e)(6) of P.L. 101-239 Omnibus Budget Reconciliation Act of 1989 (12/19/89) amending Sec. 402 of P.L. 100-177.
43. Culbertson, RA: National Practitioner Data Bank has implications for nursing. Nursing Outlook 39(3):102–103, 142, 1991.

45. *Id.*

46. American Association of Nurse Attorneys: Demonstrating Financial Responsibility for Nursing Practice. American Association of Nurse Attorneys, Baltimore, 1989.

▶ **ETHICS IN PRACTICE**

After her initial 6-week orientation period, Patty N., a new graduate RN, was beginning her first job on the 11 to 7 shift in a busy surgical unit of a city hospital. Patty enjoyed the busy pace of the unit, the development of new skills in the care of complicated postoperative patients, and the spirit of cooperation and comraderie with the other nurses on the shift. She particularly liked to see the patients recover and resume a normal life.

Because of the nature of the surgical unit and the fact that most of the patients were in pain to some degree, large quantities of narcotics and other pain medications were used. Occasionally the narcotic count was "off" at the end of the shift, but the nurses were usually able to track down who forgot to "signout" a medication. After several weeks of working on the unit, Patty began to notice that the narcotic count was always wrong when Vickie L., an older RN who had worked on the unit for 5 years, was on duty. Patty also noticed that Vickie signed out pain medications for her patients at the *minimal intervals* ordered all through the shift, even if the patient had not received any medication for the previous 24 hours.

Patty asked one of the other nurses about Vickie. Patty was told by the nurse that Vickie was an excellent nurse, a hard worker, and would be virtually impossible to replace if she were to leave or be fired. Patty was also reminded that she was the newcomer to the unit and that she really should not "make waves." If Patty really wanted to help, she was informed that she could "cover" for Vickie, as the other nurses did, when she was "sick," which was often.

After observing Vickie more closely, Patty recognized the symptoms of drug abuse that she had been taught in school, including moody and erratic behavior, frequent absences because of "illness," forgetting to give scheduled medications on time, and frequent and prolonged "bathroom" breaks throughout the shift. Patty felt that Vickie's behavior and problem were dangerous to the patients she was caring for at the hospital.

What should Patty do? What are the key elements in this ethical dilemma? What does the Code of Ethics for Nurses say about incompetent practitioners? Are there any legal and/or ethical obligations that apply to Patty's actions?

Standards of Care

ETHICAL CONSIDERATIONS

▼ Although most nurses probably give little thought to standards of care, these standards are used daily in all aspects of nursing care. Standards of care form the basis for competent, high-quality nursing care. The basic purpose of these standards is to protect and safeguard the public. Standards of care are the "yardstick" that the legal system uses to measure the actions of a nurse in a malpractice suit.

However, standards of care have an ethical component that exceeds the narrow legal definition of the term. In the ANA Code of Ethics for Nurses, statement 5 simply states: "The nurse maintains competence in nursing." Although this statement can be interpreted in different ways, the generally accepted interpretation is that nurses can best maintain the patient's optimum well-being by providing nursing care that reflects and incorporates the latest techniques, knowledge, and practices as they develop. The only way a nurse can maintain this high level of competency is by knowing the standards of care and seeking the knowledge required to meet these standards. Quite apart from the legal demands, the ethical principle of fidelity to the profession underlies this obligation on the part of nurses.

Statement 8 of the ANA Code of Ethics states: "The nurse participates in the profession's effort to implement and improve standards of nursing care." The profession of nursing is based upon understanding and using a body of knowledge, some of which is borrowed from other disciplines, some of which is unique to nursing. This body of knowledge is reflected in the various standards of care that have been adopted by professional organizations representing nurses To be most effective, standards of care need to change as technology progresses, society changes, and the demands of the profession are altered. Under the Code of Ethics, nurses have a responsibility to monitor these standards and to improve the standards through an ongoing effort at all levels.

This responsibility means that nurses must be active, participating members on the many committees that deal with standards of care. These committees range from local institutional committees on standards of care, to state-level committees, and even to national-level committees and they may meet and make decisions with or without the participation of nurses. If nurses are not active in this process, then others who do not necessarily have nurses' best interests in mind will decide the standards of care that nurses will be held to in the future.

OBJECTIVES

Upon completing this chapter, the reader will be able to:

1 Define the term "standards of care."
2 Describe how sources of standards of care are used in a disciplinary proceeding and in a malpractice case.
3 Describe the role of an expert in establishing the standard of care in a malpractice case.
4 Distinguish between standards and guidelines.
5 Understand the process used to develop standards.
6 Understand the importance of defining the scope and purpose of documents that may be used as evidence of standards of care.
7 Distinguish between a national and local standard of care.
8 Describe how the "error-in-judgment rule" and the "two-schools doctrine" relate to standard of care.

INTRODUCTION

This chapter reviews sources of standards of care and discusses the points to remember in developing standards of care. It also focuses on the legal implications of standards in a disciplinary proceeding and a nursing malpractice case including the role of expert testimony in establishing deviations in the standard of care.

STANDARDS OF CARE

Standards are created to provide guidelines and to define appropriate levels of quality patient care that must be implemented to protect the patient. In the context of a malpractice case, the **standard of care** is a measuring scale based on negligence and means the average degree of skill, care, and diligence exercised by members of the same profession under the same or similar circumstances. In the context of a disciplinary proceeding, the standard of care is assessed in terms of incompetency or gross negligence, rather than ordinary negligence.

Sources of Standards

Joint Commission on Accreditation of Health Care Organization Requirements

The **Joint Commission on Accreditation of Healthcare Organizations** (JCAHO) annually publishes the **Accreditation Manual for Hospitals** (AMH). The purpose of the manual is twofold: first, it serves as a basis for the Joint Commission's evaluations; second, it is used internally to develop policies and procedures and to assess whether health care providers and services in the institution or facility are measuring up to the AMH standards.[1] The manual provides standards for the various services rendered by hospitals, and many of the chapters in the AMH relate to nursing care, for example, emergency services, ambulatory care services, and surgical and anesthesia services.

The standards are drafted in a general way to evaluate nursing care in a variety of settings. Along with the standards, the AMH includes *required characteristics* specific to each standard of care. (See Appendix 4–1 at the end of this chapter.) The required characteristics focus on the processes necessary to comply with the standards of nursing and patient care.

State Statutes and Regulations

Nursing licensure is regulated on a state-by-state basis. The criteria for credentialing, the grounds for disciplinary action, and the scope of practice are contained in state statutes and regulations. **Statutes** are laws passed by the state legislature in accordance with recommendations and lobbying by such groups as the state nurses' association, special interest groups, or specialty nursing organizations. Nurse practice acts also take the form of statutes. **Regulations,** on the other hand, are rules or orders issued by various regulatory agencies, such as state boards of nursing. From a practical perspective, regulations have the force and effect of law because their intent is to carry out the law.

Statutes and regulations are the standards required of nurses to be licensed to practice. While statutes and regulations do not always directly pertain to patients, they dictate standards of practice for nurses and affect the delivery of health care. Generally, nurses are required to demonstrate *competent* practice; however, there may be different levels of standards, in addition to competency, in licensing legislation. For example, in Pennsylvania, licenses can be revoked or suspended for incompetency or repeated acts of negligence.[2] The Maryland Nurse Practice Act predicates disciplinary action on incompetency or gross negligence.[3]

The American Nurses' Association's (ANA) Suggested State Legislation recommends disciplinary action when the nurse negligently *and* willfully acts in a manner inconsistent with the health or safety of the patient or negligently *and* willfully practices nursing in a manner that fails to meet generally accepted standards of such nursing practice.[4] As the ANA's comments make clear, the incorporation of the term *willful* in their suggested language makes it clear that disciplinary action should not be based on ordinary negligence alone, but rather on gross negligence; in other words, the subjective component of willfulness is required. The difference between these two terms is significant. **Ordinary negligence** implies carelessness or omission of care; it can be seen as a failure to take the precautions that any ordinary person would in a similar situation. **Gross negligence,** on the other hand, involves an intentional, reckless disregard of the consequences to a person or property.

Because licensing laws differ from state to state, nurses must be familiar with those statutes and regulations that apply to their nursing practice. In fact, some states' nursing regulations require knowledge of statutes and regulations governing nursing and other topics related to nursing;[5] failure to possess such knowledge may result in disciplinary action on the grounds of incompetency. For example, some boards of nursing deny, revoke, suspend, and take other actions to restrict a nurse's license upon a finding of professional incompetency.[6]

American Nurses' Association

The American Nurses' Association published its first standards of practice in 1973. Since then, the ANA, in collaboration with speciality nursing organizations, has adopted standards that apply to many different fields of nursing. (See Appendix 4-2 for a list of standards available from the ANA).[7] Nursing does not have a national data base of information on standards development. Because the contributions of nursing to health care will be effective only if there is a consensus among those in the profession on standards of practice, the ANA Cabinet on Nursing Practice appointed a special task force on nursing practice standards in 1989 to explore these issues. The ANA was approached by the Agency for Health Care Policy and Research for assistance in developing and updating clinical guidelines, standards of quality, performance measures, and medical review criteria. The purpose was to improve health care by better understanding the effect of health care practices on patient outcomes. To ensure that the nursing component is included in the evaluation of health care generally, the task force developed a framework for drafting and updating standards. Included in that framework is a plan for establishing a centralized collection system of guidelines and standards that have already been developed by nursing speciality groups.[8]

The ANA Congress of Nursing Practice adopted the Standards of Clinical Nursing Practice.[9] Included are generic standards based on nursing process (assessment, diagnosis, outcome identification, planning, implementation, and evaluation) and criteria to measure compliance with the standards.[10] The ANA Standards contain both standards of care and standards of professional performance.[11]

Standards of professional performance are professional activities such as continuous quality improvement, education, research, ethics, and peer review. Standards of care and standards of performance are both described in terms of competency, rather than in terms of reasonable care or optimal level of performance.[12] According to the ANA, the standards remain stable; however, the criteria used to measure compliance with the standards of practice may change as dictated by technological advances.[13] It is expected that specific criteria will be developed in conjunction with nurse specialty organizations to assess compliance with standards in particular fields of nursing.

In addition to the standards and criteria, the ANA Standards address the development of *practice guidelines.* The ANA makes a clear distinction between standards and guidelines; a **standard** is an authoritative statement, whereas a **guideline** is a recommended course of action.[14] This distinction certainly has important legal implications. Guidelines suggest or recommend practices by which standards of care can be met; however, the standards do not mandate compliance with the guidelines. The ANA is attempting to prevent the guidelines being used as evidence of standards of care in legal proceedings.

Although the ANA standards are based on competency, they recognize that a nurse's ability to provide care depends on the working environment.[15] The ANA Standards specifically delegate responsibility to the employer for providing adequate resources and working conditions.

Treatises and Publications

Standards of care are also found within nursing texts and articles. To be a competent source of standards, the text or publication must be recognized as an authoritative work in the field.[16] The legal implication of using texts and articles as evidence in a proceeding is important and is discussed below.

Bylaws, Rules and Regulations, Policies and Procedures

Bylaws are rules that are adopted to regulate practice and privileges. Bylaws affect the medical, surgical, and nursing staff. Bylaws may incorporate standards for credentialing as well as other aspects of professional conduct like staff privileges and patient care.

Health care facilities may have **rules and regulations** relating to speciality practice areas, such as obstetrics and gynecology. Although their primary purpose is to regulate the care provided by physicians, rules and regulations can also set standards of care for nursing.

A mother gives birth to a baby 32 hours after her membranes ruptured. The infant develops sepsis several days after birth. The parents file suit against the nurses and the obstetrician. The grounds are: (1) failure to perform a caesarean section and (2) failure to advise the parents that the cesarean birth is the recommended treatment (when labor fails to progress 24 hours after the membranes rupture). In addition, the plaintiffs allege that the nurses are negligent because they performed too many internal examinations on the mother. The theory of liability is that the number of internal examinations, combined with the delay in delivery, caused or increased the risk that infection would be introduced.

The rules and regulations of the obstetrical and gynecological staff state that a caesarean birth should be performed 24 hours from the time the membranes ruptured; this information can be used by the plaintiff's attorney to prove there was a breach in the standard of care that caused damage to the infant.

In the preceding case, the plaintiff's attorney may also argue that the standard of care required the nurses to notify their supervisor and the supervising physician when the attending obstetrician failed to take action 24 hours after the mother's membranes ruptured. It is important for nurses to be familiar with all rules and regulations pertinent to their area of practice since these may be used as a source of evidence regarding the standard of care.

It is also essential that nurses have a good working knowledge of the policy and procedure manual. A **policy** is an overall plan to accomplish general goals. **Procedures** are the tools used to implement the policies.

Policies, which are broader than procedures, may deal with many different services within the health care facility. For example, a policy on fire safety includes all individuals regardless of their job or profession within the hospital. In addition to the policy on fire prevention, a hospital will likely have procedures that specifically outline particular responsibilities, such as evacuation plans and safety equipment maintenance.

Health care facilities must have policies and procedures covering all aspects of patient care. They must address everything from how to deal with staffing shortages to how to change intravenous tubing. The manuals that contain these policies and procedures are an important source of standards and are often introduced as evidence in legal proceedings. (*Note:* A word of caution—policy and procedure manuals should not be thrown away when new policies are created.) Policy and procedure manuals should be maintained for a period of time based on the statute of limitation and state or federal laws. If a facility has created standards that are based on the highest level of care available rather than reasonable standards, the facility may be held to the higher level of care even though legally, only reasonable care is required. For example, if your national specialty nursing organization requires "level one" standards which are reasonable standards, but your institution guarantees the "highest level of nursing care in the world," the hospital has created a higher standard that the nurse will be held to in a court of law.

The sophistication of rules, regulations, policies, procedures, and standards of care may depend on the level of the health care facility. Major university teaching institutions tend to be more progressive; their standards may be higher than those reflected in the policies or rules of a small community hospital. If procedures and rules have not been properly revised, the nurses working in the facility could be practicing under parameters that are not acceptable standards of care. Following hospital policy does not automatically excuse a nurse from liability.[17] If the conduct at issue is not consistent with the appropriate standard of care, adherence to an outdated hospital procedure may be grounds for holding a nurse negligent. It is especially important that the nursing profession take an active part in developing standards and in reviewing, evaluating, and updating policies and procedures.

Standards Development

Using Other Sources

The many sources of standards of care—nurse practice acts, rules and regulations, policies—should be used not only to develop standards but also as the criteria by which to evaluate compliance. Nurses should take advantage of the lobbying efforts and expertise demonstrated by associations drafting standards of care and obtain the documents on standards by writing to the associations who created them, such as the ANA. Nursing administration or staff development offices should have these standards available, as well as copies of state statutes and regulations pertinent to the nursing profession. The state nursing associations, boards of nursing, and national specialty nursing organizations and associations are also resources for information on standards.

How Standards Vary

In developing standards, it is important to remember that they vary according to the level of care being measured and as to whether their purpose is to dictate general or more specific aspects of patient care.

A standard of care that is framed broadly to address general aspects of patient care affects a large segment of patient care and health care providers. For example, a standard of care on disaster safety (e.g., a hurricane or flood) involves every person who is responsible for patient care—administrators, medical staff, nurses, and biomedical engineers. Achieving that standard depends on compliance with procedures, guidelines, or criteria by many individuals, all of whom may have different positions within the health care setting.

Standards that dictate specific aspects of patient care are restricted to a particular segment of health care providers or to a subspecialty within that segment. They should be drafted incorporating the practitioner's education, training, and experience. Standards that evaluate a particular clinical aspect of patient care and have significance for a smaller segment of practitioners are referred to as *profession specific* because they are tailored only to those whose conduct they are dictating. For example, a standard assessing intravenous placement may only apply to perivascular nurses.

Standards vary according to the *type of care involved* and *who is delivering* the care. They also differ regarding the *level of practice* being measured. As with any profession, levels of practice may be categorized in a number of ways. Legally, the most frequent terms used to describe levels of practice are *reasonable care* and *competence,* and the terms used to describe breaches of those standards of care are *incompetence, negligence,* and *malpractice.*

Understanding the Terms

In developing standards, it is important to have a clear understanding of such terms as incompetency, gross negligence, negligence, and malpractice. It is also important to understand the distinction between standards and the criteria used to assess compliance with standards.

Competency is a level of care used to determine whether grounds exist for disciplinary action by a state licensing board. Competency is also used to assess civil liability against a nurse in a malpractice case. Under the theory of corporate liability, a health care facility can be held liable for damages caused by its employees or staff when it has reason to know that a nurse rendering care is incompetent to do so.[18]

Box 4–1   DEFINITIONS

The American Nurses' Association Task Force on Nursing Practice Standards and Guidelines Working Paper contains the following definitions:

Guidelines: A process of client care management which has the potential of improving the quality of clinical and consumer decision making; includes assessment and diagnosis, planning, intervention, evaluation, and outcome.

Criteria: Variables known to be relevant, measurable indicators of the standards of practice.

Procedures: A series of recommended actions for the completion of a specific task or function. Procedures may be either specific to an institution or applicable across settings.

The ANA's task force defines *standard* as an "authoritative statement enunciated and promulgated by the profession by which the quality of practice, service, or education can be judged."[19] The task force also specifically defines "standards of nursing practice," "standards of care," and "standards of professional performance." In framing any document that incorporates standards or criteria, it is important to remember that the document may someday be presented to a judge or hearing board to determine whether it should be used as evidence against a nurse. It is essential to articulate the definition and purpose of the standard carefully so that its scope and intent are clearly understood.

Legal Implications

Standards as Evidence

A nurse can be held liable under a number of different legal theories. Depending on the proceedings, liability can result in civil judgments, criminal penalties, imprisonment, and restrictions on licenses to practice. In a judicial or administrative proceeding, a nurse defendant is almost always faced with the question of whether his or her conduct is consistent with a particular standard. State statutes, regulations, ANA standards, criteria, and guidelines, state nurse practice acts, JCAHO standards, and hospital policies and procedures can all be used as evidence of standards of care. The nurse's attorney argues that the nurse was following a particular standard and that the judge, jury, or hearing board should not hold the nurse liable. The opposing counsel presents evidence of other standards and argues that the nurse defendant failed to comply with those practices.

Whether evidence of standards is admissible depends on the legal theories involved, the standard, the type of proceeding, and the jurisdiction.

Standards in Disciplinary Proceedings

Issues involving licensing violations are decided by a state board of nursing administrative proceeding. State statutes and regulations indicate the grounds on which the disciplinary action is based, such as drug addiction, criminal conduct, or incompetency. Administrative procedure along with other statutes or regulations set parameters for disciplinary action. Both types of provisions affect how standards are used in an administrative proceeding. The statutes and regulations determine whether the alleged conduct constitutes a licensing violation. In addition to serving as evidence of standards, statutes and regulations also determine whether other sources of standards are admissible because they provide procedural guidelines that indicate what will be allowed.

A nurse's attorney should prevent the indiscriminate introduction of standards that dictate levels of care which are more stringent than the grounds for disciplinary action. The attorney should argue that the purpose of the Nurse Practice Act is to discipline nurses who are incompetent, not those who are negligent or practicing less than the highest level of care. The nurse's attorney can refer to the other provisions of the Nurse Practice Act, which base violations on fraud, drug abuse, criminal convictions, and gross negligence. The attorney could also refer to the regulations of the state board of nursing, which specifically define competency and provide a basis for incompetency.

The rules of evidence that apply to disciplinary proceedings are not as stringent as those used in a malpractice case.[20] A hearing board is more likely to admit documents that are subject to objections in a trial such as relevancy (meaning that the document should not be allowed to be presented because it is irrelevant to the case).

Standards as Evidence in a Malpractice Case

Overview To establish malpractice or professional negligence against a nurse, the plaintiff must prove the four elements of **negligence:** (1) duty, (2) breach of duty, (3) proximate cause, and (4) damages.

The Role of the Expert The standard of care in a malpractice case is most often determined by expert testimony. The role of the expert is to describe the "reasonable" care that is required under the circumstances. Expert testimony is needed to educate judges and jurors who do not have the training, education, and experience to make decisions about health care practices. The purpose of the expert is to assist the court in determining the applicable standard of care.[21]

The plaintiff and defendant usually present expert testimony on the issues of standard of care, breach of the standard, causation, and dam ages. In many cases, there is disagreement between the experts concerning what standard of care is required. For example, in a wrongful death and survival action brought by the parents on behalf of their stillborn infant, it is likely that there would be contradictory expert testimony focusing on whether the standard of care required the nurse to institute and to continue fetal monitoring, or whether the failure to do so contributed to the death of the fetus.

Standards, hospital procedures, treatises, and forms of documentary evidence, along with expert testimony, may be used in a malpractice case to establish the standard of care. However, the effect of those documents and their admissibility as evidence depend on the rules of evidence and case law of the jurisdiction. The judge makes a preliminary determination concerning whether evidence should be admitted in a case. The two issues that the judge must decide before admitting documents into evidence are whether they are *relevant* and whether they are *hearsay*.

Relevancy Evidence is **relevant** when it tends to either prove or dis prove a contested matter.[22] Documents containing standards that are introduced into evidence must be relevant to the factual issues involved. The documents must relate to both the subject matter and the time period at issue in the case; they must also contain information that is generally recognized as the acceptable standard of care by the profession.

In a case involving a specialty area of practice, documents incorporating standards that generally relate to nursing may be relevant; however, in a case involving general aspects of nursing care, standards relating to a specialized field of nursing are probably not relevant.

To be relevant, documents must contain acceptable standards of the profession. A guideline that simply promotes the *best* patient care is not relevant and should not be used to decide whether a nurse exercised the skill and judgment that are routinely exercised by nurses under similar circumstances. For a text to be relevant, the party must prove, usually by means of expert testimony, that the text is an authoritative work in the profession and that it is recognized by members of the profession as containing well-established and accepted principles.

Hearsay In addition to relevancy, a judge must also decide whether documents introduced as evidence of the standard of care should be excluded as hearsay. **Hearsay evidence**[23] is evidence that is derived from sources other than witnesses testifying at the hearing. Documents containing standards are likely to be considered hearsay evidence if the author of the documents is not in court. Since the opposing side has no opportunity to cross-examine the author and challenge the credibility of the statements made in the documents, it may be unfair to admit that evidence into trial. However, if the documents contain the type of information that an an expert would rely on, then the expert may be allowed to read that information into evidence.[24]

The Effect of Standards as Evidence   Even if documents are admitted as evidence of the standard of care, they are not necessarily *conclusive* evidence.[25] That is, just because a judge permits a procedure to be introduced as evidence does not necessarily mean that a nurse's failure to follow the procedure automatically amounts to malpractice. The judge will instruct the jury on the law regarding the use of that evidence. Depending on the judge's instructions, the impact of the evidence on the issue of malpractice is decided by the jury.

Case Study on the Use of Standards as Evidence

Facts of the Case

The defendants are a surgeon, a scrub nurse, a circulating room nurse, and a hospital. The allegation is failure to remove a sponge during a laparoscopy procedure, which caused peritonitis to develop. The sponge count is performed twice and is documented as being correct. The circulating room nurse testifies at her deposition that the counts were in fact correct and that the retained sponge may have been an extra one in the package. The procedure at the defendant hospital did not include provisions to count the sponges before they were used. The defense experts for both the surgeon and the nurses testify that the standard of care at the time of the surgery did not call for them to make preliminary counts when removing sponges from packages. The nurses' experts also testify that the standard of care for scrub nurses did not dictate that they be involved with the counts.

Plaintiff's Argument

The attorney for the plaintiff attempts to introduce procedures from other hospitals to demonstrate that the defendant hospital is negligent for failing to include a preliminary sponge count in their procedure. The hospital's attorney objects to the introduction of that evidence, arguing that the procedures from other hospitals are not *relevant* to the defendant hospital's negligence. The plaintiff's attorney also attempts to introduce the Recommended Practices for Sponge, Sharp and Instrument Counts issued by the Association of Operating Room Nurses (AORN).[26] The recommended practices specifically indicate that counts of sponges, sharps, and instruments should be done concurrently by the circulating room nurse and the scrub nurse. Although the recommended practices do not state that preliminary counts have to be performed, the Guidelines, which are included at the end of the practices, do state: "Incorrectly numbered packages of sponges and sharps should be isolated and not used during the procedure." The plaintiff's attorney argues that the AORN Guidelines establish that sponges should be counted when they are removed from the package.

Defendant's Argument

The attorney for the hospital argues that the AORN-recommended practices are not *relevant* because they are not evidence of the standard of care; rather, they are *recommendations* and *guidelines*. The attorney argues that the recommended practices from AORN represent what is believed to be an *optimal* level of practice and that AORN recognizes when drafting the recommended practices and guidelines that procedures vary among institutions.

How Will the Judge Rule?

The judge in this case will probably rule that the AORN practices and guidelines are *not* admissible as evidence of the standard of care. The standard of care in a malpractice case is reasonable care, not optimal care, so that the AORN-recommended practices are *not relevant* to the issues in the case. Since the recommended practices do not say anything about preliminary counts and since the guidelines are not clear on the issue, they should be excluded because they have *no relevance* to the subject matter involved in the case; their introduction into evidence would only confuse and mislead the jury.

Legal Theories and Standards of Care

National Versus Local Standards

Standards of care can be based on a local or national standard. In a medical malpractice case, the standard of care is based on reasonableness and is the average degree of skill, care, and diligence exercised by members of the same profession. With increased specialization, courts in many jurisdictions are holding health care practitioners to a national rather than a local standard of care.[27] However, in a state following the locality rule, a nurse defendant's conduct is evaluated based on the care required by nurses in that geographic area[28] or in a similar community.[29] On the other hand, states following the national standard of care doctrine evaluate a nurse's conduct based on the care required by nurses practicing throughout the country. The national standard is most often applied in cases dealing with specialty fields of nursing. Applying a national standard holds a nurse in a rural community hospital to the same standard of care as a nurse working in a university medical center.

Standard for Nurses in Training

Some jurisdictions hold licensed physicians and nurses to a higher standard of care than practitioners who are still involved in the training process. In those jurisdictions, a malpractice case against someone in training may be successfully defended by applying a less stringent standard of care.

Error-in-Judgment Rule

Another theory regarding standard of care is the *error-in-judgment rule*. The error-in-judgment rule can be used successfully to defend a claim of malpractice by arguing that the standard of care was met by the nurse even though a mistake was made.[30]An error in judgment, including a mistaken diagnosis, does not necessarily prove malpractice if a nurse follows the standard of care required by using the skill, knowledge, and care routinely exercised by nurses with the same background and experience.

Two-Schools Doctrine

The *two-schools-of-thought doctrine* may also be used to defend a malpractice claim. When there is more than one method of treatment recognized among nurses as being proper, a nurse is not considered negligent for adopting any of these modes of treatment.[31] A nurse may choose to follow a school of thought that differs from the majority—as long as the nurse treats the plaintiff according to a method or school of thought deemed proper by a considerable number of nurses.

Conclusion

There are many different sources of standards of care. A familiarity with these sources improves patient care and promotes awareness of legal responsibilities. All nurses should have a working knowledge of the state statutes, regulations, and the various legal theories in their jurisdiction regarding standards of care. Failure to adhere to standards of care may result in a disciplinary action or a malpractice trial. Understanding the purpose and concepts of standards of care is an important step in the process of standards development. Since various sources of standards may be used as evidence in a legal proceeding, it is essential that all nurses be familiar with this process.

Points to Remember

▶ "Standard of Care" in a malpractice case is based on negligence and means the average degree of skill, care, and diligence exercised by members of the same profession under the same or similar circumstances.

▶ Depending on the law of each jurisdiction, "standard of care" in a disciplinary proceeding may be assessed in terms of incompetency, gross negligence, or negligence.

▶ The American Nurses' Association's suggested state legislation recommends that standard of care in a disciplinary proceeding be assessed in terms of whether the nurse negligently *and* willfully acted in a manner inconsistent with the health or safety of the patient or negligently *and* willfully practiced nursing in a manner that fails to meet generally accepted standards of such nursing practice.

► Standards are created by accreditation bodies, by state and federal legislatures, by professional associations, and by health care facilities.

► Standards may be used for evidentiary purposes to determine whether the standard of care has been violated in any given case.

► The JCAHO's Accreditation Manual for Hospitals (AMH) and the ANA's standards of clinical nursing practice both dictate competency as the level of care required by nurses.

► Adherence to an outdated hospital procedure that is a standard at a facility may leave a nurse open to liability.

► Standards are drafted for different purposes and vary in the level of practice they dictate. In drafting standards, it is important to clearly identify to whom the standard should apply and whether it is meant to dictate optimal, competent, reasonable, or minimally acceptable parameters of care.

► A standard is not automatically admissible as evidence in a malpractice case. It must be relevant and must overcome any hearsay objections.

► The standard of care in a malpractice case is primarily established by expert testimony. The expert may rely on documents containing standards, such as hospital procedures or treatises, *if* the expert establishes that such documents contain principles which are accepted by the profession.

Study Questions

1. Discuss where you can find the various sources of standards of care.
2. Develop standards of care for: (a) a nursing treatment, and (b) a risk management problem.
3. Why are standards of care developed by nursing facilities and institutions?
4. Discuss two state statutes or regulations that affect nursing practice standards of care in your state.
5. Develop policies and procedures for an area of nursing practice that you see as a "problem" area.
6. Develop a list of resources for standards available to you in your facility, institution, or nursing school.
7. Discuss various standards of care that your state nurse practice act requires.

8. Identify and discuss the role of standard of care in: (a) a malpractice case, and (b) a disciplinary proceeding.

9. Discuss the two factors that a judge in a malpractice case must consider in deciding whether standards are admissible evidence in a malpractice case.

10. Discuss common breaches of the standards of care by nurses.

APPENDIX 4–1

The JCAHO AMH Chapter on nursing care contains six standards along with required characteristics for each standard. An example is[32]:

Standard

NC.4 The hospital's plan for providing nursing care is designed to support improvement and innovation in nursing and is based on both the needs of the patients to be served and the hospital's mission.

Required Characteristics

NC.4.1 The plan for nurse staffing and the provision of nursing care is reviewed in detail on an annual basis and receives periodic attention as warranted by changing patient care needs and outcomes.

NC.4.1.1 Registered nurses prescribe, delegate, and coordinate the nursing care provided throughout the hospital.

NC.4.1.2 Consistent standards for the provision of nursing care within the hospital are used to monitor and evaluate the quality of nursing care provided throughout the hospital.

NC.4.2 The appropriateness of the hospital's plan for providing nursing care to meet patient needs is reviewed as part of the established budget review process. **(LD.1.5.2)**

NC.4.2.1 The review includes **(scoring guideline for LD.1.5.2)**

NC.4.2.1.1 an analysis of actual staffing patterns; and **(scoring guideline for LD.1.5.2)**

NC.4.2.1.2 findings from quality assessment and improvement activities. **(scoring guideline for LD.1.5.2)**

NC.4.2.2 The allocation of financial and other resources is assessed to determine whether nursing care is provided appropriately, efficiently, and effectively. **(scoring guideline for LD.1.5.2)**

NC.4.2.2.1 The allocation of financial and other resources is designed to support improvement and innovation in nursing practice. **(scoring guideline for LD.1.5.2)**

NC.5 The nurse executive and other nursing leaders participate with leaders from the governing body, management, medical staff, and clinical areas in the hospital's decision-making structures and processes. **(LD.1.8)**

APPENDIX 4–2

The following standards pertaining to specialty practice areas in nursing are available from the American Nurses' Association:

Standards and Scope of Gerontological Nursing Practice
Standards and Scope of Hospice Nursing Practice
Standards for Psychiatric Consultation Liaison Nursing Practice
Standards of Addictions Nursing Practice with Selected Diagnoses and Criteria
Standards of Cardiovascular Nursing Practice
Standards of Child and Adolescent Psychiatric and Mental Health Nursing Practice
Standards of College Health Nursing Practice
Standards of Community Health Nursing Practice
Standards of Home Health Nursing Practice
Standards of Maternal-Child Health Nursing Practice
Standards of Medical-Surgical Nursing Practice
Standards of Neurological and Neurosurgical Nursing Practice
Standards of Nursing Practice in Correctional Facilities
Standards of Oncology Nursing Practice
Standards of Perioperative Nursing Practice
Standards of Practice for the Perinatal Nurse Specialist
Standards of Practice for the Primary Health Care Nurse Practitioner
Standards of Psychiatric and Mental Nursing Practice
Standards of Rehabilitative Nursing Practice
Standards of School Nursing Practice

RECOMMENDED READINGS

Ardoin v. Hartford Accident & Indemnity Co., 360 So.2d 1331 (La. 1978).
City of Somerset v. Hart, 549 S.W.2d 814 (Ky. 1977).
Cushing, M: A judgment on standards. American Journal of Nursing, 797, 1981.
Koeniguer v. Eckrich, 422 N.W.2d 600 (S.D. 1988)
Richardson v. LaBuz, 474 A.2d 1181 (Pa. Commw. Ct. 1984).
Rogers v. Kasdan, 612 S.W.2d 133 (Ky. 1981).
Synder, M: Unprofessional Conduct: Disciplinary Action by Boards of Nursing, in Brief. American Association of Nurse Attorneys, Winter, 1987, p 12.
Wood v. Roland, 592 P.2d 1322 (Colo. App. 1979).

REFERENCES

1. Joint Commission on Accreditation of Healthcare Organizations: The 1991 Joint Commission Accreditation Manual for Hospitals, Vol 1, Standards, 1990.
2. Pa. Stat. Ann., Title 63, Section 224, 95 (1991 Supp.)
3. Md. Code Ann., Title 7, Section 313 (1988).

4. American Nurses' Association: Suggested State Legislation. Kansas City, Mo, 24, 1990.
5. Md. Code Ann., Title 7, Section 313, 20 (1988).
6. Md. Code of Regulations, Title 10, Subtitle 27, Sections 10.27.09, 7 and 10.27.10, 5 (1989).
7. See: American Nurses' Association 1991 Publications Catalog.
8. American Nurses' Association Task Force on Nursing Practice Standards and Guidelines Working Paper, final paper (Dec. 11, 1990) and American Nurses' Association Task Force on Nursing Practice Standards and Guidelines Working Paper (June 1990).
9. American Nurses' Association: Standards of Clinical Nursing Practice, 1991.
10. *Id.* at 3.
11. *Id.* at 4.
12. *Id.* at 4, 5.
13. *Id.* at 5.
14. *Id.* at Glossary.
15. *Id.* at 5.
16. Graham: Handbook of Federal Evidence, ed 3, section 703.1, 1991.
17. *Vanstreenburg v. Lawrence and Memorial Hospital,* 481 A.2d 750 (Conn. 1984).
18. *Thompson v. Nason Hospital,* 535 A.2d 1177 (Pa. Supp. 1988), *aff'd on appeal.*
19. American Nurses' Association: Standards of Clinical Nursing Practice, Glossary, 1991.
20. Northrup, C, and Kelly, M: Legal Issues in Nursing. CV Mosby, St. Louis, Mo, 1987, p 412.
21. Graham: Handbook of Federal Evidence, sec. 702.1, ed 3, 1991.
22. Graham: Handbook of Federal Evidence, sec. 401.1, ed 3, 1991.
23. Graham: Handbook of Federal Evidence, sec. 801(c), ed 3, 1991.
24. *Id.* at sec. 803.18.1
25. *Darling v. Carlestown Community Hospital,* 211 N.E.2d 253 (Ill. 1965).
26. The Association of Operating Room Nurses, Inc: Recommended Practices for Sponge, Sharp and Instrument Counts, May 1976, revised March 1984.
27. Black's Law Dictionary, ed 5: West Publishing Co, St. Paul, Minn, 1979, p 1260.
28. *Katsetos v. Nolan,* 170 Conn. 637, 646, 368 A.2d 172 (1976).
29. *Gittens v. Christian,* 600 F.Supp. 146 (D.V.I. 1985), *aff'd* 782 F.2d 1028 (3rd Cir. 1986).
30. *Smith v. Yohe,* 194 A.2d 167 (1963).
31. *Furey v. Thomas Jefferson University,* 472 A.2d 1083 (Pa. Supp. 1984).
32. Joint Commission on Accreditation of Healthcare Organizations: The 1994 Joint Commission Accreditation Manual for Hospitals, Vol 1, Standards, 1994, p 145.

▶ ETHICS IN PRACTICE

Bill Z., a 6'3", 135-pound, 76-year-old retired college professor was admitted to a medical unit in a large metropolitan hospital. He had been diagnosed 6 months previously with metastatic cancer that had spread from his lungs to the liver, GI system, and bones. He had received some chemotherapy but with little effect. He was admitted to the hospital because he had become too weak to walk or care for himself at home and because the large doses of oral narcotic medications were having little effect on his generalized pain.

His physician had decided that further chemotherapy would be useless and ordered Mr. Z. to be kept comfortable with medications. A continuous morphine sulfate IV drip was started to help control the pain. Although he was talkative and friendly by nature, as Mr. Z.'s cancer spread, he would cry out and beg the nurses not to move him. Because he was very tall and underweight, his bony prominences quickly became reddened and showed signs of breakdown. The hospital standards of care for bedridden patients required that they be turned from side to side every 2 hours. Mr. Z. yelled so loudly when he was turned that the nursing staff wondered if they were helping him or hurting him.

To decide what should be done, a patient care conference was called by the nurses most often involved in providing care for Mr. Z. The head nurse of the unit stated very clearly that the hospital standards of care required that he be turned at least every 2 hours to prevent skin breakdown, infections, and perhaps sepsis. In his already weakened condition, an infection or sepsis would most likely be fatal. Melanie F., who had been an RN for some 15 years, disagreed with the head nurse. Her feeling was that causing this obviously terminal patient such extreme pain by turning him was cruel and violated his dignity as a human being. She stated that she could not stand to hear him yell anymore and refused to take care of him until some other decision was made about his nursing care. Susan B., a new graduate nurse, felt that the patient should have some say in his own care and that perhaps some type of compromise could be reached about turning him, even if less frequently. Ellen R., who had worked on the unit for 2 years, felt that the physician should make the decision regarding turning this patient and then all that the nurses would have to do was to follow the order. This last suggestion was met with strong negative comments by the other nurses present because patient comfort and turning are nursing measures.

What should they decide? Violation of a standard of care can leave a nurse open to a lawsuit. What about the patient's right to make a decision when this violates a standard of care? Are there ever any situations where a nurse might legally and ethically violate a standard of care? What are the consequences?

The Nurse and the Lawsuit

ETHICAL CONSIDERATIONS

▼ For many years those involved in nursing have strived to be recognized by medicine as belonging to a separate and distinct profession. During those years, nursing has gained a great deal of power, independence, and influence in the health care industry. However, these gains have been accompanied by an increase in, and stricter interpretation of, the legal accountability associated with nursing practice. Nurses cannot avoid professional accountability by seeking refuge in the past. Nurses have a professional obligation to use this long-sought-after power, independence, and influence to increase the quality of patient care as well as to promote the legal and ethical practice of nursing.

Because of the increased fears of many nurses about legal liability and legal actions against them, concern for the law has become a major preoccupation. Indeed, all practicing nurses must recognize what types of actions increase their risk of malpractice suits. Yet the law and the legal system have a narrow view of nursing practice.

Legally speaking, those aspects of patient care called nursing can be limited to activities that are specifically covered in the Nurse Practice Act and scope of practice. In reality, the practice of nursing involves all the activities, both tangible and intangible, that nurses do whenever they enter into a relationship with a patient. This broader view of the nurse-patient relationship is the concern of ethics.

In most situations, ethics includes or exceeds the law where questions of nursing practice are involved. Ethical nursing practice is almost always legal nursing practice. If nurses are aware of the ethics involved in nursing practice and follow the ethical code, then they should have little to be concerned with from the legal system.

OBJECTIVES

Upon completing this chapter, the reader will be able to.

1 Describe defenses to medical malpractice claims.
2 Discuss how to prepare for a deposition.
3 Outline the various types of discovery techniques.
4 Identify the stages of the trial process.
5 Discuss alternatives to lawsuits.

INTRODUCTION

This chapter discusses how the legal system operates and how nurses can best protect themselves if they are sued or called as material witnesses in a malpractice suit.

The **plaintiff** is the party initiating the lawsuit. In some lawsuits, the plaintiff can be either the person actually harmed or damaged by the defendant (person or entity, for instance, a hospital being sued) or the patient and family members of the injured patient. In cases where a patient has died, the family members of the decedent can sue on behalf of the estate of the deceased. Only one lawsuit can be brought on behalf of all family members who are damaged or injured by the act of malpractice.

TYPES OF DAMAGES

The plaintiff can sue for various types of damages. **Hard** and **soft damages** were discussed in Chapter 1. Other types of damages include the following:

Special damages are based on the actual monetary losses, such as lost wages, for the past, present, and future that were caused by the defendant's acts.

General damages are awarded for the plaintiff's pain and suffering caused by the defendant's acts.

Punitive damages are intended to punish the defendant for the egregious nature of the tort. The defendant's actions must be willful and wanton, and the damages are not based on the plaintiff's actual monetary loss. Usually the award is doubled or tripled to "punish" the defendant economically so that this type of behavior will never occur again.

NEGLIGENCE

In order to maintain a medical malpractice claim, the four elements of negligence must be present. The four elements of negligence are duty, breach of duty, proximate cause or causal connection, and damages. The plaintiff has the burden of proving two suppositions:

1. The defendant is liable by having breached a duty.
2. The defendant caused damages.

Box 5–1   THE LEGAL PROCESS: STAGES OF A MALPRACTICE CLAIM

1. Pretrial preparation (review of medical records by attorney and expert witness: retrieval of all medical and office records and patient bills)
2. Procedural process that may be required by state law: Prelitigation panels
   a. Medical review panel
   b. Medical tribunal
   c. Arbitration panel
3. Petition for damages or complaint filed in court
4. Complaint or summons sent to health care provider by certified mail or served by a sheriff or process service company
5. Health care provider contacts insurance company to notify of claim
6. Attorney or law firm assigned to health care provider
7. Answer to complaint or counterclaim filed by defendant—defenses alleged
8. Discovery stage (subpoenas and *subpoena duces tecum* may be used)
   a. Depositions
   b. Interrogatories
   c. Requests for production of documents and things
   d. Admissions of fact
   e. Physical or mental examination
9. Pretrial hearing
10. Settlement negotiations
11. Trial of lawsuit (may be a judge or a jury trial)
12. Jury selection
13. Opening statements by plaintiff and defendant
14. Case presentation by plaintiff
15. Case presentation by defendant
16. Motion by defendant for directed verdict against plaintiff
17. Closing statements by plaintiff and defendant
18. Jury instructions by the judge
19. Jury deliberations
20. Verdict
21. Appeal (optional)

To prove that the defendant is liable, the plaintiff must show that a duty owed to the plaintiff (for example, nursing care) was breached, causing damage. If all four elements of negligence are not proved, then the plaintiff does not receive an award for damages. If the judge or jury decides that the liability issue has been proved, then the specific amount of the award for the damages is decided.

PRELITIGATION PANELS

The majority of malpractice cases are tried in state courts. Prior to actually litigating the case in state court, the plaintiff may have to present the case to a prelitigation panel, medical tribunal, medical review panel, or arbitration panel. The filing process differs from state to state. If a prelitigation panel is required, the plaintiff usually submits evidence to a panel of health care providers and attorneys that demonstrates how the injury was caused by the defendant and the extent of the injury. Evidence includes medical records, affidavits, expert reports, treatises, authoritative texts, journal articles, photographs, medical illustrations, depositions, and a medical or legal memorandum.

Arguments are made for and against such panels or tribunals. Defendants contend that they reduce frivolous suits, while plaintiffs argue that they merely delay and prolong the legal process and increase expense by requiring a "trial" submission to the tribunal prior to actually litigating in court. Most malpractice cases take approximately 3 to 5 years before they are tried or settled. In those states with prelitigation panels, the process is usually delayed by 6 months to 1 year.

After the case goes through the panel or tribunal process, a lawsuit is then filed in court. If there is no requirement for a prelitigation panel, the case is filed directly in court. The petition for damages or complaint is filed by the plaintiff. Defendants named in the petition or complaint are served by a sheriff or process service company. The complaint outlines: (1) the names of the plaintiffs and defendants; (2) the allegations of breaches of the standard; (3) the damages or injuries; and (4) the demand for an award. (Some states do not allow specific amounts for damages to be specified in the petition. This practice avoids publicity for malpractice suits where huge awards are demanded.)

IF YOU ARE SUED

As soon as notification of a suit is received, the hospital administrator should be notified, and the nurse must contact the insurance company, which will contact the attorney or law firm who will represent the nurse. Usually attorneys or law firms are retained by insurance carriers and will handle all of the lawsuits filed against the insured person. Some nurses feel that if they have insurance, they are more likely to get sued. However, prior to filing a lawsuit, most attorneys do not check to see if a nurse has insurance. Also there is no central data bank that supplies information on nurses' insurance policies. The lawsuit filed against a nurse is usually based on nursing negligence found in the medical records. Unfortunately, some attorneys use the "shotgun" approach and sue everyone who was treating or caring for the patient, rather than limiting the number of defendants.

The nurse must refrain from consulting with anyone except his or her attorney, hospital attorney, risk manager, or supervisor. Staff members, the plaintiff's attorney, and the plaintiffs should not be spoken to about the circumstances surrounding the lawsuit.

After the petition is received by a defendant, the attorney files an answer on behalf of a defendant. The answer usually admits, denies, or declines to answer the allegations in the petition. Defenses to the allegations of negligence are then listed. Defenses can include: (1) contributory versus comparative negligence, (2) statute of limitations, (3) assumption of the risk, (4) Good Samaritan statute, (5) unavoidable accident, (6) defense of fact, or (7) sovereign immunity.

Box 5–2 DEFENSES TO A MALPRACTICE CLAIM

1. Contributory versus comparative negligence
2. Statute of limitations
3. Assumption of the risk
4. Good Samaritan statute
5. Unavoidable accident
6. Defense of fact
7. Sovereign immunity

DEFENSES TO A MALPRACTICE CLAIM

Contributory Negligence vs. Comparative Negligence

How or whether a claim is paid depends on the state where the case is tried. In a contributory negligence state, patients (plaintiffs) are not allowed to recover damages if they contributed to their injuries in any manner. For example, the physician performed the surgery procedure incorrectly; however, the plaintiff increased the damages by not taking the medication ordered by the physician and therefore contributed to the damages.

In a comparative negligence state, the award is based upon the percentage of fault if there is negligence on the part of both the plaintiff and the defendant. For example, if the award is $100,000 and plaintiff is found to be 40% negligent, he or she receives only $60,000 for damages. Usually, if the plaintiff is 50% or more at fault, no award will be given.

Statute of Limitations

The statute of limitation outlines when to file a lawsuit. If the malpractice suit is not filed within the time limits mandated by law, the plaintiff loses the right to sue the defendants. In most states, a suit must be filed within a specified period of time from the date of the act or omission of care and treatment, or from the date upon which the patient knew or discovered that malpractice caused the injury. Every state has different time limits and different guidelines for determining the time frame during which a lawsuit may be filed. Some states base the time period from the date of the last treatment, while others allow a minor or the child's parents or guardian to file a malpractice claim when the child reaches the age of 18 or 18 plus 2 years. Other states are very restrictive and do not allow minors or their parents or guardians the right to file a lawsuit when they reach their majority.

Assumption of the Risk

The assumption-of-risk defense argues that the plaintiff, by agreeing to have a procedure or treatment performed by a health care provider, has assumed either expressed, voluntary, or implied risks. This theory is based upon the informed consent of the patient (see Chapter 6).

Good Samaritan Statute

The Good Samaritan statute is enacted to protect those who render health care at the scene of an accident, emergency, or disaster. Good Samaritan laws usually cover nurses who are reasonable and who practice using the standards of nursing as guidelines. They will not cover the nurse for negligent acts that occur during the course and scope of employment. If a nurse receives a fee for services rendered, the Good Samaritan statute cannot be invoked. Also, if a nurse intentionally harms a patient or is grossly negligent (based upon accepted standards of care), then the Good Samaritan statute cannot be used as a defense. Depending on the state, laws may differ as to nurses and physicians and the coverage received by each from the Good Samaritan statute.

Unavoidable Accident

This defense is used when nothing other than an accident could have caused the plaintiff's injury. For example, a patient walks down a hall, slips, and hurts an ankle. Nothing on the floor caused the accident, and no one else is at fault. (Documentation in an incident report or chart that the floor is clean may save the hospital from exposure and a damage award.)

Defense of the Fact

This defense contends that the health care provider's treatment is not below the standard of care, and, furthermore, even if the standard were breached, it was not the *cause* of the damage to the plaintiff. For example, the plaintiff has a tonsillectomy performed and claims that she has numbness and tingling in the left leg as a result of the tonsillectomy, which is medically impossible.

Sovereign Immunity

Historically, the federal and state governments used the legal doctrine of sovereign immunity to prevent suits from being filed against them based on negligence. Likewise, however, the federal government can be sued under the Federal Tort Claims Act. Many states are also no longer immune from tort liability actions.

DISCOVERY

Discovery is the stage in a lawsuit in which all information, facts, and circumstances surrounding the alleged malpractice incident are "discovered" by plaintiff and defendant. Discovery techniques include interrogatories, requests for production of documents, admissions of facts, physical and mental examinations, and depositions.

The discovery stage is the most time consuming stage of litigation and can take years to complete. There are several methods used by trial attorneys to "discover" all the information surrounding the allegations of negligence and damages.

Interrogatories

Interrogatories are written questions sent by one party to the other requesting *information* about issues and witnesses surrounding the incident of alleged malpractice. The information requested can be very general, such as: "List all employers and reasons for leaving employment." Interrogatories can also seek very detailed and medically oriented information, such as: "What are the common signs and symptoms of sepsis?" Such information can later be used at the trial during cross-examination of the witnesses.

Interrogatories may request information that is privileged and confidential. The nurse's attorney should argue confidentiality and contend that some information is protected from disclosure to the plaintiff's attorney. Depending on the state laws, privileged information can include correspondence, notes, documents, incident reports, and conversations between the attorney and the client. This is considered "attorney work product." Clients have a right to speak freely without fear that information given to their attorney is available to the opposition.

Attorneys can make objections to interrogatories. For example, "Objection to Interrogatory No. 1 because it would cause undue hardship and burden to obtain the information." If the attorney refuses to answer interrogatories within the allowed time period, opposing counsel can file a Motion to Compel Answers to Interrogatories. A hearing is set in court and the judge decides whether the interrogatories must be answered and whether the party would be severely hindered in presenting the case without the requested information.

EXAMPLES

1. Please list names and addresses of all fact and expert witnesses that will be used at the trial of this matter.
2. What are the common signs and symptoms that may indicate fetal distress?
3. Please list all signs and symptoms of fetal distress exhibited by Baby Brett on June 6, 1993.

Requests for Production of Documents

Requests for production of documents and things are requests by the plaintiff or defendant for items from the other party, which pertain to the issues of the lawsuit and may lead to discoverable information. *Document requests* include such items as medical records, hospital and office records, unit and hospital policies and procedures, personnel files, continuing education records, logs, computer printout sheets, notes, letters, diaries, calendars, transcripts, contracts, minutes of meetings, X-rays, invoices, authorizations, appointment books, photographs, medical illustrations, budgets, charts, tables, microfilm, ledgers, memoranda, slides, videotapes, phonograph records, time charts, work sheets, call schedules, notebooks, magazines, data processing disks or tapes, mechanical or electrical sound recordings, hospital medical staff bylaws, patient acuity logs, and staffing records.

Routinely, when a request for a huge volume of documents is made, the material is provided so that opposing counsel can review and select the specific documents that must be produced.

EXAMPLE

Please produce at 10:00 A.M. on March 1, 1994, at the law offices of Dandry and Aiken any and all "documents," which include but are not limited to the terms: materials, outlines, memoranda, records, files, reports, phono records, microfilms, computer disks, computer printouts, budgets, analyses, medical records, hospital and office records, unit and hospital policies and procedures, personnel files, continuing education records, logs, computer printout sheets, notes, letters, diaries, calendars, transcripts, contracts, minutes of meetings, X-rays, invoices, authorizations, appointment books, photographs, medical illustrations, budgets, charts, tables, microfilm, ledgers, memoranda, slides, videotapes, phonograph records, time charts, work sheets, call schedules, notebooks, magazines, data processing disks or tapes, mechanical or electrical sound recordings, hospital medical staff bylaws, patient acuity logs, staffing records, and sound recordings regarding the following:

1. All policies and procedures in effect for 1989 to 1994 at J.B. Hospital regarding the care, treatment, and standards of nursing for patients with decubitus ulcers.
2. All personnel records of Jane Doe, RN, including but not limited to evaluations, raises, reprimands, continuing education reports on courses and in-service courses attended.

Plaintiff Examination

Plaintiff examination is another type of method that is used to "discover" information about the plaintiff's mental and physical condition. For example, if a person is claiming severe pain from a surgical procedure, an examination by the defendant's doctor of choice or by a physician selected by plaintiff and defendant may be ordered to get a second opinion as to the type and extent of injuries or to see if the patient is just a malingerer.

Admissions of Fact

Admissions of fact are written requests to admit or deny facts regarding issues of the lawsuit. This technique attempts to limit the number of facts that must be disputed and argued at trial.

EXAMPLES

1. Do you admit or deny that Mrs. Shirley Anthony was admitted to Health Hospital on October 4, 1993?
2. Do you admit or deny that the common signs and symptoms of fetal distress can be decelerations, meconium staining, and bradycardia?
3. Do you admit or deny that Mrs. Anthony had the following signs and symptoms of fetal distress: decelerations, meconium staining, and bradycardia?

DEPOSITIONS

Although most malpractice suits are settled prior to trial, many nurses have to endure the anxiety and tension of having their depositions taken. A **deposition** is a structured interview in which the person being interviewed (the **deponent**) is placed under oath and asked questions about issues of the lawsuit.

Why Are Depositions Taken?

The purposes of depositions are as follows:
1. To gather all available discoverable information about the case
2. To assist attorneys in assessing strengths and weaknesses in their cases
3. To assist attorneys in formulating settlement and trial strategies
4. To evaluate the credibility, knowledge, demeanor, and appearance of the witnesses
5. To determine the existence and substance of pertinent documents
6. To determine the availability and limits of insurance coverage
7. To discover the facts and circumstances of the alleged malpractice and breaches of the standard
8. To preserve the testimony of a witness who may be unavailable at the time of trial because of relocation or death (called a deposition for perpetuation of testimony)
9. To determine the cause of the plaintiff's injuries
10. To determine the extent of the injuries and types of injuries sustained by the plaintiff and his family

11. To be used prior to or during trial to refresh the witness's memory
12. To be used during trial to impeach a witness's credibility

Who Can Be Deposed?

Parties (plaintiffs or defendants) to a lawsuit are routinely deposed. **Fact** (or **material**) **witnesses** are persons having knowledge about the circumstances surrounding the events of the alleged malpractice; they may also be deposed. For example, a circulating nurse who is not a defendant may be deposed to determine if she knows anything about the events involving the birth of a brain-damaged infant.

In medical malpractice and personal injury cases, medical and nursing **expert witnesses** are used to assist the judge and jury in understanding causal connections between breaches of the standard and damages sustained by the plaintiff. This is one of the most common types of depositions taken because experts are crucial to sustaining a claim. Also, each side must understand the strengths and weaknesses of their cases according to expert opinions. Attorneys routinely retain expert witnesses to evaluate medical records to determine if a standard of care has been breached and, if so, what damages have been caused by the breach. Expert witnesses in a malpractice suit may be nurses, physicians, economists, physical therapists, hospital administrators, and so on, depending on the allegations of negligence. For someone to be considered an expert, attorneys look at the following points:

1. Is the nurse currently practicing? If not, is the nurse teaching students in the specialty area that is in issue in the lawsuit?
2. Has the nurse published journal articles or textbook chapters?
3. Is the nurse an officer in nursing organizations or associations?
4. Has the nurse testified previously in a deposition or trial? Has this testimony been primarily for plaintiffs or defendants?

Another type of deposition commonly taken is that of the *custodian of documents or evidence* related to a case, for example, an operating room director who is in charge of maintaining the operating room log. Remember, it is important to reserve the right to read and sign the deposition after it is taken. This gives the nurse an opportunity to review the deposition for accuracy.

How to Prepare for a Deposition

Prior to a deposition, all medical records or pertinent information must be reviewed. If you are a defendant and have kept a "diary" of the events surrounding the incident, notify your attorney. If you review this diary to prepare for your deposition, opposing counsel can request that a copy be attached to the deposition. If you are an expert witness, counsel can request that you list and produce all documents, that is, treatises, textbooks, journal articles, depositions, and any other material that you used to develop your expert opinion of the case. Also be careful about materials you bring to your deposition which may be discoverable.

Caution must be used if incident reports are reviewed prior to a deposition. Some health care providers avoid the potential of having the confidential or incident report produced at the deposition by discussing— rather than actually reviewing—the report with the attorney. The attorney-client privilege may then be invoked to prevent the production of the incident report. Some states allow the opposing counsel to obtain the incident report.

General Tips for Depositions

1. Do not volunteer information. Remember, the purpose of the deposition is to allow the opposing attorney to *discover* information.
2. Answer verbally since a court reporter is recording your answer verbatim.
3. Be familiar with the medical records.
4. Do not be intimidated.
5. Before answering, make sure you understand the question.
6. Do not make assumptions or exaggerations.
7. Take your time. Before answering, take 5 seconds to allow your attorney to make any objections that are needed to preserve the record for trial.
8. Be honest and straightforward and tell the truth.
9. If you do not understand a question, ask for clarification.
10. Do not speculate. Base your answers on the facts of the case.
11. Do not lie or exaggerate.
12. Speak slowly and clearly.
13. Maintain eye contact only with the questioning attorney.
14. If you do not know or cannot remember, simply state, "I don't know" or "I don't remember."
15. If you are an expert witness, be cautious if a hypothetical question is asked. Many times the hypothetical question does not state exactly the facts in the case being tried.
16. Think before answering the question. Take as much time as necessary. Remember, it is *your* deposition.
17. Provide a résumé or curriculum vitae, if requested.
18. Maintain your composure.
19. If you are tired or confused, take a break.

20. Do not argue, get angry, or be sarcastic with the opposing attorney.
21. Avoid using "absolutes," such as "I *always* take vital signs on a post-op patient every 30 minutes."
22. Do not make excuses for other people's actions.
23. If the question can be answered by "yes" or "no," then do so.
24. Be cautious of the "yes" or "no" trap. Attorneys who cross-examine witnesses do not want them to "explain away" problems in the evidence, so they will ask questions that look bad for the witness or party. Answer "yes" or "no" but always explain.

    For example: Q: Isn't it a fact that you failed to take vital signs every 15 minutes as ordered? A: Yes, but only one time because the nurse's aid took vital signs instead of me at 11:15 P.M.
25. If the same question is asked again, have the court reporter read back your previous answer.
26. Do not volunteer additional information if the attorney remains silent for a period of time after you answered. (This is a common attorney deposition tactic called the "pregnant pause.")
27. Listen to your attorney when she makes objections to questions. Follow her lead if you are instructed to answer the question.
28. If testifying in a deposition or at trial, arrive early so that you can become comfortable with the surroundings.
29. Be cautious of leading questions. For *example:* "Isn't it true that you really didn't check on the patient for 5 hours?"
30. *Caution:* Be sure you have read your deposition prior to testifying at trial. If you change your testimony at trial, the following type of scenario could occur:

    Attorney: "On March 31, 1993, your deposition was taken by me?"
    Nurse: "Yes."
    Attorney: "And you were sworn under oath to tell the truth. Isn't that correct?"
    Nurse: "Yes."
    Attorney: "On March 31, you stated that you contacted Dr. Candace about the patient's decreased pedal pulses, cyanotic skin coloring, and coldness to the extremity seven times during the 7–3 shift of July 31, 1993. Is that correct?"
    Nurse: "Yes."
    Attorney: "Today, you are again under oath to tell the truth. Is that correct?"
    Nurse: "Yes."
    Attorney: "Today, you are telling the jury that you only contacted the physician one time as documented in the record? When were you lying, March 31 or today?

Types of Questions Asked in a Deposition

Through depositions, attorneys attempt to elicit information from the *plaintiff, defendant,* or *fact witnesses* on:

1. General background and marital status of the deponent.
2. Educational background.
3. Professional and social organizations.
4. Employment history.
5. Basic medical and nursing knowledge information, such as common signs and symptoms of fetal distress or common nursing care and treatment given to alleviate pressure sores.
6. Continuing educational courses attended.
7. In-service courses attended.
8. Specific information related to the case at issue, such as: "What specific symptoms of lithium toxicity did Mr. Beam exhibit on October 26, 1993?"
9. Teaching positions.
10. What would be done differently, if anything.

If you are an *expert,* questions can be asked concerning:

1. General background.
2. Marital status.
3. Educational background.
4. Employment history.
5. Professional and social organizations.
6. Teaching positions.
7. Seminars, lectures, and presentations.
8. Textbooks, journal articles, treatises, or research papers written or authored.
9. Clinical experience in the areas of alleged malpractice.
10. Number of times you have testified in a deposition and at trial as an expert for plaintiff or defendant.
11. The fee for evaluating the case, testifying at a deposition, and testifying at trial.
12. How you were contacted by the attorney to review the case.
13. What texts you view as authoritative in the field.
14. Whether you personally examined the patient.
15. Your relationship with the attorney or law firm.
16. Your opinion on hypothetical situations.
17. Breaches of the standard by each defendant.
18. Causal connection between the breach and the plaintiff's injuries.
19. The elements of malpractice.
20. Whether any court has ruled that you are not qualified to testify as an expert in a case and in what specialty area.
21. The standard of care in effect at the time the patient received care.

22. The standard of care for other health care providers.
23. Whether you have ever had your license or privileges revoked, suspended, or limited.
24. You may also be asked questions attempting to discredit you: (a) When is the last time you actually worked as an OB nurse? (b) Why have you changed jobs so often? (c) When were you hired by the plaintiff to testify on his behalf?
25. You may be asked repetitive questions to see if you change your answer.

TRIAL PREPARATION AND TIPS

When meeting with your attorney:

1. Develop a chronology of events and circumstances, with times, dates, and important events.
2. Provide a list of nurse experts who can be used in your defense.
3. Ask how you "fit into" the entire picture, and what the allegations in the complaint are.
4. Ask about types of questions and information you can expect to be asked.
5. Ask about possible defenses to the lawsuit allegations.
6. Review statements or depositions previously taken from you or others involved in the lawsuit.
7. Review statements made by others in depositions or affidavits about actions taken by you.
8. Discuss allegations of negligence by each defendant in the lawsuit.
9. Review documents such as medical and office records, X-rays, videotapes, policies and procedures, national standards for your specialty, or authoritative texts and journal articles.
10. Know the "weak spots" in your testimony.
11. Be open and honest with your attorney about facts and circumstances surrounding the alleged malpractice.
12. Educate your attorney about nursing and medical terms or conditions, national standards, hospital and unit policies and procedures, job descriptions, and other information that can help your case.
13. In preparation for your trial, your attorney may videotape you in a mock direct or cross-examination. Review and study your demeanor, appearance, and presentation.

During the trial:

14. During the trial, write notes to your attorney if there is an impor-

tant point that is missed or information that should be brought out before the jury.

15. Do not express emotion in the form of fidgeting, rolling your eyes, nodding, pencil tapping, knuckle cracking, or verbally. Remember, the jurors are watching you on and off the stand.
16. Dress conservatively. Do not wear heavy makeup or excessive jewelry.
17. Wear a suit or dress. If you are a female defendant or witness, do not wear slacks.
18. When testifying, look at the jury or judge and not at your attorney.
19. When sitting at the trial table, sit up, look interested, and look at the witness who is testifying.
20. Do not talk about the case in hallways or elevators. Do not talk to the jurors or a mistrial may be declared.
21. If you are an expert witness, use demonstrative evidence to "teach" the judge or jury. Examples of demonstrative evidence include:
    a. Medical charts
    b. Medical illustrations
    c. Skeletons and anatomical body parts
    d. Videotape—with medical graphics
    e. Medical models
    f. Blow-up charts of policies, procedures, and standards
22. In most states, you have to convince the jury that *more probably than not* a breach of the duty owed caused damages to the plaintiff.

VIDEOTAPE DEPOSITION

If your deposition is being videotaped, your attorney should do a trial run prior to your actual deposition. Be very conscious of fidgeting, not looking at the camera, and your appearance (color and style of clothes, makeup, type of jewelry). If a glare bounces off your glasses, take your glasses off so that the judge or jury can see your eyes (it is very disturbing when you cannot see a person's eyes and facial expressions).

Practice so that your videotape is an asset to the case. This may be the only way that the judge or jury will see or hear you if you cannot be at trial for some reason (for example, you are teaching in England).

THE TRIAL

After the discovery stage is completed, the case should go to trial. The discovery process can take 1 to 3 years or longer, depending on the number of plaintiffs, defendants, fact or material witnesses, and expert witnesses.

To shorten the trial, pretrial hearings are set so that the judge can decide such issues as the qualifications of witnesses, what evidence should be allowed, and whether an expert is qualified to testify.

On the day of a jury trial, the first step is to select a jury. Jurors are selected from a jury pool of citizens from the area. The attorneys or court ask questions of the potential jurors to determine whether there are any biases, prejudices, or relationships between jurors and plaintiffs, defendants, attorneys, or significant others. This judicial process is called **voir dire,** which means "to speak the truth."

Each side has peremptory challenges or can challenge for cause. A **peremptory challenge** is a challenge of the juror, which does not require the attorney to show cause for removal from jury selection.

Challenge for cause means that an attorney can ask that a juror be dismissed from the jury because of bias or prejudice. For example, if one juror states that her daughter is a nurse and that she therefore would never find another nurse liable for medical malpractice, then this potential juror would be excused by reason of bias. In most malpractice claims, 12 jurors and one or two alternates are selected.

After the jury is selected, the opening statements are presented by plaintiff and defense counsel. The opening statements summarize what the parties will try to present and prove through evidence and witnesses during the trial. Since the plaintiff has the burden of proof, the plaintiff presents his or her case first. Evidence must be sufficient to meet the four elements of negligence in order to be successful: duty, breach of duty, causal connection, and damage.

The plaintiff presents evidence in the form of standards, policies, procedures, medical records, expert testimony, fact, material witnesses, and other means. To prove the case, the attorney directly questions witnesses. Defense counsel then has the opportunity to conduct a cross-examination to discredit the witness and "punch holes" in the testimony. The plaintiff's counsel can then do a re-direct examination to clarify new points brought out during the cross-examination or to rebuild his witness's credibility.

After the plaintiff has presented all of the evidence and witnesses, the plaintiff rests. Defense counsel then proceeds by presenting evidence and witnesses to refute the plaintiff's allegations and the evidence presented. Direct examination, cross-examination, and re-direct of a witness are also allowed during the defendant's presentation. After all the evidence, witnesses, and examinations are completed, the defendant rests. The defense may then make a motion for a directed verdict against plaintiff arguing that the plaintiff has not met the burden of proof. If the judge agrees, the trial ends. If not, the motion is denied and the trial continues. Plaintiffs may be allowed to present rebuttal evidence to any new evidence that was presented in defendant's case.

The jurors then hear the closing arguments. Each attorney summarizes the evidence presented, points out important testimony presented by fact and expert witnesses, and attempts to prove whether or not the four elements of negligence were met. Closing arguments are prepared by counsel and may be rehearsed to provide the most effective argument since it is the last chance for the attorneys to argue their cases to the judge or jury. The judge then instructs the jury on the laws pertinent to the case.

The jury retires to deliberate the evidence presented during trial. It selects a foreperson who maintains control of the deliberations. Jurors are not allowed to speak to anyone during deliberations. Material that was admitted into evidence during the trial can be taken into the deliberations to be reviewed by jurors. If the jury has questions, the foreperson sends a message to the judge for an answer. After jury deliberation is completed, the jurors return to the courtroom and the judge reads the verdict regarding liability and the award for damages.

If the trial is a judge trial, the judge renders a judgment immediately or takes the matter under advisement and renders a judgment after reviewing trial materials or trial briefs submitted by counsel.

In many courts, judges allow the attorneys to speak to the jurors about how they decided the verdict, concentrating on the strong and weak points of the case, the credibility of the witnesses, and other issues related to the trial presentation.

The plaintiff or defendant may then appeal the verdict. This process can take several years if it goes to the court of appeals and supreme court levels.

Box 5-3   DEFENSIVE NURSING PRACTICE TIPS

1. Avoid blaming or criticizing other health care providers in the presence of the patients.
2. Recognize the problem patient and troubleshoot. Use thorough documentation for the noncompliant patient or complainer.
3. Maintain thorough and accurate documentation.
4. Send only copies and never the originals of records or X-rays requested.
5. Know the charting policies and procedures of the facility and your unit.
6. Know the accepted abbreviations for the facility.
7. Maintain thorough documentation of telephone calls between you, physicians, or other health care providers.
8. Maintain good communication and rapport with the patient and family. Many lawsuits are pursued because the patients did not like the way that they were treated by hospital staff.

Points to Remember

▶ Four elements of negligence are duty, breach of duty, proximate cause or causal connection, and damages.
▶ In some states prelitigation panels must be completed prior to pursuing the claim in court.
▶ Several defenses to malpractice claims are: contributory or comparative negligence, statute of limitations, assumption of the risk, Good Samaritan statute, unavoidable accident, defense of the fact, and sovereign immunity.
▶ Discovery is the stage in a lawsuit where facts and information are "discovered" through various techniques, such as depositions and interrogatories.
▶ The deposition is a structured interview under oath that is used to discover facts and circumstances surrounding the alleged malpractice.
▶ The following persons may be deposed in a lawsuit: plaintiff, defendant, expert witness, material or fact witness, and custodian of important records.
▶ *Before* your deposition, prepare, review important documents, and meet with your attorney.
▶ Medical malpractice claims may be tried in state or federal court. The majority are tried in state courts.
▶ Expert witnesses are retained by attorneys to discuss the breaches of the standards of care (if any), causation, and extent and type of damages.
▶ Thorough and accurate documentation is the best defense in a medical malpractice claim.

Study Questions

1. List the four elements of negligence that a plaintiff's attorney must prove to successfully litigate a malpractice suit.
2. Discuss the types of damages that may be awarded to plaintiff.
3. What are the two suppositions that must be proved by the plaintiff in a malpractice suit?
4. Discuss: (a) the purpose of the prelitigation panel, and (b) the pros and cons of the prelitigation panel.
5. Outline the steps in a medical malpractice lawsuit.
6. Define basic defensive practice tips for nurses.
7. Outline and give an example of the various types of discovery methods used in malpractice litigation.

8. List and discuss defenses to a malpractice claim.
9. Define the purposes of depositions.
10. Outline recommendations on how to prepare a nurse for her deposition.
11. Discuss tips on what to do if you are testifying at trial.

► **ETHICS IN PRACTICE**

Mr. Steven S. is a 76-year-old retired scientist who lives by himself in a small apartment. He is admitted to the medical-surgical unit of the community hospital with a diagnosis of weakness, dehydration, electrolyte imbalance, and malnutrition. He has no close family, but a neighbor who accompanied Mr. S. to the hospital informed the nurse that she felt he had a preoccupation with his bowel movements and took large amounts of over-the-counter laxatives.

During the admission interview, Mr. S. was mildly disoriented to place and time but denied taking any over-the-counter medications. He was started on IV electrolyte and fluid replacement and placed on a high-calorie diet and bed rest. He was very compliant with the treatments, except that he frequently visited the bathroom for bowel movements.

Upon entering the room, one of the nurses on the evening shift noticed that Mr. S. was hurriedly returning what appeared to be a small bottle of laxative pills to his shaving kit. The nurse asked him about it, but was told: "It's none of your business—just stay out of my stuff!" by a very irate Mr. S. The nurse latter informed Mr. S.'s physician of the episode. The physician ordered the nurse to obtain the shaving kit and see if there were any laxatives in it. He reasoned that if the patient was taking large doses of laxatives and having diarrhea, all the treatments being given him would do no good.

Initially the nurse agreed with the physician, but after thinking about the situation further and remembering some basic principles of law she had been taught in school, she questioned the legality of searching a patient's belongings without permission. What should she do? What laws or ethical principles is she violating by searching this patient's belongings without permission? Does the principle of beneficence ever excuse breaking the law?

Informed Consent

ETHICAL CONSIDERATIONS

▼ The term **informed consent** has become a buzzword for the legal system in relation to the provision of today's high-tech, life-saving, and life-prolonging health care. Simply stated, informed consent is the voluntary permission that a patient or patient's legal representative gives to the health care provider to do something to or for that patient. The legal intricacies of determining informed consent have led to a number of successful civil suits against health care practitioners and institutions. The underlying ethical principles upon which informed consent is based are often lost in the legal maneuvering that surrounds these civil suits.

Informed consent is based upon two key ethical principles: autonomy and beneficence. Simply stated, *autonomy* is the right of patients to determine how much and what type of health care they desire to receive. It is directly opposed to the practice of *paternalism,* which is the general attitude that health care providers know what the best treatments are for the patient, with or without the patient's approval. From the ethical viewpoint of autonomy, informed consent becomes a process of giving the power of choice to patients by respecting their decisions and providing them with the information they need to make decisions about their own health care.

The ethical principle of *beneficence* should underlie all aspects of health care and should be an elemental part of the health provider's philosophy of health care. The principle of beneficence demands that the health care provider do good for patients (and avoid harming them). When the patient's personal values and beliefs are involved in the decision-making process, better decisions about health care are made. A secondary "good" that arises from informed consent is that the patient is more likely to cooperate with the treatment plan, communicate better with the health care providers, and, if possible, recover more quickly. If recovery is not possible, then perhaps the patient is allowed to die with some level of dignity.

OBJECTIVES

Upon completing this chapter, the reader will be able to:

1 Define and explain the basic elements of *informed consent.*
2 Define *capacity* as it relates to a patient's right to accept or refuse medical treatment.
3 In relation to informed consent, explain the difference between (a) an objective standard and (b) a subjective standard.
4 Describe situations in which consent to treat would be implied.
5 State situations that are exceptions to the duty to disclose risks of treatment.
6 Discuss the basic standards relied upon by courts for determining what information must be disclosed to the patient in order to obtain informed consent to treatment.
7 Describe the duty imposed upon health care facilities by the 1990 Patient Self-Determination Act.
8 Define *advance directive* and explain types of advance directives.
9 Explain the prerequisites for a "Do Not Resuscitate" or "No Code" order.

INTRODUCTION

To be legally effective, consent to treatment must be what the law considers "informed consent." This means that the physician or health care practitioner has given the patient enough information regarding the risks and benefits of the proposed treatment and its alternatives for the patient to make an intelligent or "informed" decision. If the patient is not a legally competent adult, health care decisions can be made by the patient's parents, legal guardian, or, in some states, next of kin or friend. Health care decisions can also be made by a surrogate decision maker, someone the patient designated before becoming incompetent. Depending upon the law of a particular state, a minor who is mature for his or her age, married, or serving in the military may be considered emancipated and consent to or refuse treatment.

It is generally accepted that a competent adult has the right to consent to or refuse any medical or surgical treatment. However, this "right" is not absolute; courts have not allowed patients in certain cases involving minor children, mental illness, and substance abuse to refuse life-saving treatments. For example, the court authorized a hospital and its medical staff to provide all reasonable medical care, including blood transfusions, to save the life of an 8-year-old child, even though such treatment violated the parents' religious beliefs.[1]

This chapter discusses the law of informed consent generally. The court decisions and statutes cited in this chapter are used as examples to illustrate specific points of law. The law, including the law of informed consent, varies from state to state. Therefore, it is necessary to consult each state's statute for specific information of a particular state's law. Most state legislatures have enacted specific statutes dealing with the issue of informed consent. Generally they state that if the language of the consent form signed by the patient meets the requirements in the statute, there is a legal presumption that the patient gave informed consent.

Along with state case law and statutory law, health care providers should also comply with the rules of the appropriate regulatory and accrediting agencies. For example, in the *Accreditation Manual for Hospitals,* the Joint Commission on Accreditation of Health Care Organizations (JCAHO) has issued the following accreditation standards for hospitals and other health care facilities:

> The patient has the right to reasonable informed participation in decisions involving his health care. To the degree possible, this should be based on a clear, concise explanation of his condition and of all proposed technical procedures, including the possibilities of any risk of mortality or serious side effects, problems related to recuperation, and probability of success. The patient should not be subjected to any procedure without his voluntary, competent, and understanding consent or that of his legally authorized representative. Where medically significant alternatives for care or treatment exist, the patient shall be so informed.
>
> The patient has the right to know who is responsible for authorizing and performing the procedures or treatment. The patient shall be informed if the hospital proposes to engage in or perform human experimentation or other research/educational projects affecting his care or treatment, and the patient has the right to refuse to participate in any such activity.[2]

TREATMENT WITHOUT CONSENT

Treatment or attempts to treat without such consent may result in a lawsuit in which the *plaintiff* (the person filing the lawsuit) claims that the *defendant* (the physician or health care practitioner) is liable either for (1) assault and/or battery or (2) negligent failure to obtain informed consent. If the defendant is found to be liable, he or she will have to pay money ("damages") to the plaintiff in an amount determined by the judge or jury. To prove that the defendant is liable, the plaintiff must present evidence in court to a judge or jury. Such evidence may be the testimony of "lay" or "material" witnesses who can testify regarding the facts of the case or "expert" witnesses who are professionals in the same field as the defendant. In a case against a nurse, the expert witness should be a nurse of the same specialty who can give a professional opinion about whether the defendant failed to meet standards of care. The defendant will present lay and/or expert testimony in support of her defense.

BOX 6–1   TREATMENT WITHOUT CONSENT

Treatment or attempts to treat without consent may result in a lawsuit based on the following claims:

1. Assault and/or Battery.
2. Negligent failure to obtain informed consent.

Assault and Battery

Any unauthorized touching or threat of touching of another person may precipitate a legal action for "assault" or "battery." An **assault** is an intentional act by one person that causes another person to fear that he or she will be touched in an offensive or injurious manner—even if no touching actually takes place. If the act results in actual physical contact or touching, a **battery** has occurred. Assault and battery can occur when medical examination or treatment is provided without first obtaining the patient's informed consent. A classic example is the surgeon who has the patient's consent to amputate the left leg, but actually amputates the right leg. The plaintiff can file a lawsuit based on medical negligence plus medical assault and battery (because it is an unpermitted touching of the *right* leg since informed consent was only for surgery on the *left* leg).

The law makes an exception to the informed consent rule for medical emergencies by recognizing that, in some emergency situations, obtaining informed consent is not possible. In those situations the law "presumes" the patient would consent to treatment and he or she is treated under the doctrine of implied consent. Consent may also be implied in situations where a patient voluntarily goes to a clinic or a physician's office and accepts treatment. In the case of *O'Brien v. Cunard S.S. Co.*, the court found that, by extending her arm and not objecting to the administration of a vaccination, a woman gave her implied consent to be vaccinated.[3]

If health care providers examine patients, conduct diagnostic tests, or treat patients without first obtaining the proper consent, they can be held liable for assault or battery[4] even if the patient is not harmed by the procedure or the procedure is actually beneficial to the patient.[5] To prove that assault and battery has occurred, the patient has to convince the jury that no consent was given or that the practitioner exceeded the scope of consent given. In a recent case, a Pennsylvania court held that an action based on lack of informed consent was one for assault and battery, but noted that such a characterization was a "quirk" in the state's law and "clearly out of line" with modern cases from other jurisdictions where such an action would be for professional negligence[6] (see Chapter 9).

Negligence

Lawsuits alleging lack of consent are likely to be based upon principles of professional negligence rather than claims of assault and battery. In a professional negligence case, testimony by an expert witness is required to prove or disprove the patient's case. Such testimony focuses on what constitutes the accepted standard of care for nurses or physicians under the same or similar circumstances. The question experts are asked is: What would a reasonable health care provider with the same knowledge, experience, and expertise do under similar circumstances? In a case based on lack of informed consent, the plaintiff has to prove that the health care provider, by failing to provide the appropriate information, breached a duty, and that breach of duty caused the plaintiff (or a reasonable person in the plaintiff's position) to make a different decision than he or she would have made with more complete knowledge.[7] It would be argued that it is the breach of duty that caused the plaintiff's injury.[8] For example, one court held that a physician could be sued for a patient's death when the physician did not inform the patient of the risk of refusing a routine test such as a Pap smear.[9] In this case, the physician had a duty to inform the patient, but breached this duty and, as a result of the breach of duty, the patient died.

ELEMENTS OF INFORMED CONSENT

Consent to medical treatment is "informed" when the patient has been provided with sufficient information to make an intelligent decision to accept or reject treatment based on a full disclosure of the facts.[10] This information should be provided by the person who is responsible for performing the procedure or providing the treatment—generally the physician. The patient must be advised of the nature of his medical condition and the benefits of the proposed treatment or procedure, the risks involved in accepting the proposed treatment or procedure, and the significant available alternatives, and the consequences if he receives no treatment or procedure.

Although the "elements" of informed consent are similar from state to state, the courts differ in what the plaintiff is required to prove. For example, a Hawaiian court requires not only evidence of the basic elements of informed consent, but also evidence that the individual plaintiff would not have consented to the treatment if he or she had been provided with adequate information. This court states:

> [A] physician's negligent failure to disclose the risks of harm prior to treatment involves the following five material elements: (1) the physician owed

a duty to disclose to the patient prior to treatment the risk of the harm suffered by the patient; (2) the physician negligently performed, or failed to perform, his or her duty of disclosure; (3) the patient suffered the harm; (4) the physician's negligent performance, or nonperformance, of duty was a cause of the patient's harm in that (a) the physician's treatment was a substantial factor in bringing about the patient's harm, and (b) the patient, acting rationally and reasonably, would not have undergone the treatment had he or she been properly informed of the risk of the harm that, in fact, occurred; and (5) no other cause is a superceding cause.[11]

This court uses a "subjective" standard, that is, what *this patient* would or would not do under the circumstances. The majority of courts do not look at the decision of a particular patient involved, but at what a "reasonable" patient would do under the same or similar circumstances. This is an "objective" standard.

A Louisiana court relied upon an objective standard in a case in which the patient-plaintiff underwent a decompressive central laminectomy by an orthopedic surgeon. The patient immediately lost his bowel and bladder control and remained incontinent until his death from an unrelated cause six years later. The patient and his wife filed a medical malpractice lawsuit, alleging that the doctor was negligent in performing the surgery and in failing to adequately warn the patient of the risks involved in the surgery. The case was tried before a judge who found that the doctor failed to obtain the patient's informed consent.

The doctor appealed to a higher court. The appeals court sent the case back to the lower court for a new trial in which the plaintiff would have to prove the following essential elements of an informed consent case:

"1. the existence of a material risk unknown to the patient;
2. a failure to disclose the risk on the part of the physician;
3. that a disclosure of the risk would have led a reasonable patient in plaintiff's position to reject the medical procedure or choose a different course of treatment; and
4. injury."[12]

Although worded differently, both of the above explanations of the elements of informed consent establish that the physician has a duty to disclose certain information and that it can be shown that breaching that duty caused injury to the patient. What these courts require the plaintiff to prove, however, is very different. For example, under the subjective standard, the plaintiff must only prove that he or she would have refused the proposed treatment if properly informed. Under the objective standard, the plaintiff must prove that a hypothetical "reasonable person" in the plaintiff's position would have refused the treatment if the physician had properly explained the risks, benefits, and alternatives of the proposed treatment.

BOX 6–2   EXCEPTIONS TO DUTY TO DISCLOSE
1. Emergency 2. Waiver of right to receive information 3. Medical judgment that information would be harmful to patient 4. Obvious risk

Exceptions to Duty to Disclose

The law imposes a duty upon the physician to disclose certain risks of treatment to the patient. Exceptions to this duty to disclose include situations in which:

1. Disclosure is precluded by an emergency situation.
2. The patient has waived the right to receive the information.
3. The physician believes the information would be harmful to the patient and invokes a therapeutic privilege.
4. The risk is obvious.[13]

Exceptions are rare and vary from state to state. If the patient is not informed, the reasons must be thoroughly documented. There are two basic rules regarding the physician's duty to disclose. The traditional or majority rule requires the physician to disclose the same information that others in the medical community would reveal under the same or similar circumstances.[14]

The rule adopted by other courts is patient-oriented and focuses on what information a reasonable patient would need in order to make an informed decision.[15]

Capacity to Consent

To be effective legally, any consent to, or refusal of, medical treatment must be made by a patient who possesses the legal capacity to make his or her own health care decisions. **Capacity** is defined as the "ability to understand the nature and effects of one's acts."[16] Frequently this is a matter of interpretation for the courts, depending upon the evidence presented. Courts often favor a presumption that a person is competent unless he or she has been proved incompetent by a court.

For a patient who does not possess the legal capacity to consent, health care decisions may sometimes be made by his or her legal representative, for example, a parent, a guardian, a surrogate decision maker, or an agent appointed under a state statute that allows for surrogate health care decision makers. Most states have "durable power of attorney" statutes that allow individuals, while they are still competent, to appoint an agent to make health care decisions for them if and when they become incompetent to do so. A few states allow the next of kin or a friend to make health care decisions. As a practical matter, families of incompetent patients often consent to the patients' treatment. Such consent is not legally binding, unless the state has a law that specifically allows the spouse or next of kin to make health care decisions for incompetent persons. If an incompetent patient has no legal representative, the probate court, upon application, may appoint a guardian to make health care decisions for the patient.

Obtaining Informed Consent

The patient's consent to be treated may be *express* or *implied.* Although express consent can be oral or written, written consent is preferable because of the difficulty of proving oral consent. Implied consent may be presumed in emergency situations or inferred from the patient's actions. For example, it is expected that a person presenting at a physician's office for a physical examination consents to whatever touching is reasonably necessary to conduct the examination. Similarly, implied consent applies in an emergency situation where a surgeon encounters a complication, such as hemorrhaging, during an operation that requires additional emergency procedures to correct. On the other hand, consent is not implied for a nonemergency procedure, such as a mastectomy following a breast biopsy, if the patient has not previously consented to the second procedure.

If consent is not implied or waived, it is the responsibility of the person performing the procedure, usually the physician or surgeon, to obtain the patient's informed consent. Nurse practitioners, however, are responsible for obtaining informed consent when they perform procedures.

In most states, health care facilities that ask patients to sign informed consent forms are not held liable if the physician fails to obtain informed consent—unless the physician (or other independent practitioner) is an employee of the health care facility.[17] There are exceptions to this rule, however. Although the physician has a duty to obtain the patient's informed consent, some courts place a duty on the hospital to make sure that the physician obtained the proper consent.[18]

Ideally, the physician has the patient sign the consent-to-treatment form at the time the proposed treatment is discussed. As a practical matter, however, this does not happen. Typically, the patient is seen in the physician's office where treatment is discussed. Subsequently the patient is admitted to a hospital where a nurse asks him or her to sign a preprinted consent form stating that he or she has been throughly informed and consents to the proposed treatment.

If the doctor has not informed the patient, or refuses to answer the patient's questions, the nurse should take steps, through the chain of command, to ensure that the appropriate person has the physician fulfill his or her responsibility to obtain consent. The physician owes a legal duty to the patient and must act within the acceptable standards to give the information to the patient to meet that legal duty. This duty should not be delegated to the nurse or any other third party.

DOCUMENTING INFORMED CONSENT

Nurses who sign as witnesses are not obtaining informed consent; they are only witnessing the person signing the informed consent form. The nurse does not verify the information given to the patient and should not do so on a form unless actually present when the physician talks to the patient. The responsibility remains with the physician—provided that the nurse does not attempt to answer additional questions asked by the patient. If the patient has additional questions, the nurse should refer the questions to the treating physician. The nurse may reinforce the information provided by the physician but may not assume the physician's legal duty to inform the patient.

In the event of a lawsuit, proper documentation supports the health care practitioner's testimony regarding informed consent. Documentation includes both a written consent signed by the patient and the health care practitioner's notation of the discussion and consent in the patient's medical record. The type and amount of documentation required depends upon the law of the state in which the patient is being treated. Some states have statutes that spell out requirements for written consent forms. They are considered valid unless the patient can prove that the consent was obtained in bad faith, by fraud, or from a patient who could not understand English.

If a lawsuit is filed, a consent form that is not specific, but merely states that the elements of informed consent have been discussed with the patient, may not be sufficient to prove that the patient actually gave informed consent. If it is not clear that the patient receives the required information before consenting to treatment, additional documentation must be included in the medical record. Such documentation includes a summary of the information given to the patient, a statement dictating that all of the patient's questions were answered, and any response by the patient acknowledging his or her understanding of the information provided.

STANDARDS OF DISCLOSURE

BOX 6–3   STANDARDS OF DISCLOSURE

1. Medical community standard
2. Material risk or prudent patient standard

In deciding informed consent cases, courts have relied on two basic standards (or a combination of the two) for determining what information the physician must disclose for the patient to make an intelligent and informed decision. These two basic standards are: (1) the **medical community standard** and (2) the *material risk* or **prudent patient standard.**

Under the medical community standard, the physician's duty to inform the patient depends upon the circumstances of the case and the general practice of the medical profession in such cases. To prevail, the patient must prove, by the testimony of an expert witness, that the defendant physician did not disclose what a reasonable physician, under the same or similar circumstances, would have disclosed, and that such nondisclosure caused the patient's injury. This standard is relied upon by a majority of the states.[18]

The second standard of disclosure, the prudent patient or material risk standard, is based on the concept of patient self-determination. A Pennsylvania court explained that a prudent patient standard is one which focuses on the risks a reasonable person considers when making a decision of whether to undergo treatment. The court further noted that it is the jury, not the expert, who must decide how material the risk is and whether the probability of that type of harm is a risk a reasonable patient would consider.[19] The courts that follow this patient-oriented standard must focus on what a "prudent person in the patient's position would have decided if adequately informed of all significant perils."[20] This standard does not require the testimony of an expert witness.[21] Under the material risk standard, the court does not consider what a reasonable physician would have done, but what a reasonable patient needs to know in order to make an informed decision. This standard is based on the premise that each individual has a right to make his or her own health care decisions.

In a Wisconsin case, the patient-plaintiff became a paraplegic following an aortogram. The court rejected the medical community standard in favor of a rule that the physician had a duty to disclose significant risks so that the patient could make an intelligent and informed decision.[22]

This, of course, raises the question of the definition of a **significant or material risk.** Some courts specify that the risk must be a *known* significant risk of the treatment. One defense to a claim of failure to obtain informed consent is that the risk is either too commonly known or too remote to require disclosure.

The "material risk" issue is addressed in the case of a child who died following a lumbar puncture. The parents sued the hospital and the child's treating physician, claiming that the lumbar puncture was performed negligently and without the actual or informed consent of the mother.[23] The child, who was born with anachondroplasia and hydrocephalus, was experiencing symptoms that suggested meningitis. After several unsuccessful attempts, a lumbar puncture was performed and the child went into cardiac arrest. The court, finding no evidence that negligence caused the child's injuries, held that the physician could not be liable for failure to obtain informed consent because there was no evidence that cardiac arrest was a significant risk of a lumbar puncture. The judge in this case noted that to prevail, the parents had to prove that they would have considered the undisclosed risk significant in making their decision to consent to the lumbar puncture and that they would have chosen not to permit it.

Although other courts have agreed that the risk must be material or significant to the particular plaintiff (a subjective standard), most hold that the risk must be one that a "reasonable person" would consider material (an objective standard).

In a Louisiana case, the patient-plaintiff, who suffered from severe pelvic inflammatory disease (PID), was hospitalized and treated with intravenous antibiotics for 2 weeks. Two years later, she had an IUD inserted by the defendant physician. She subsequently delivered a baby after which the IUD was removed, not from her uterus, but from her rectum. The plaintiff's expert witness testified that, because of the patient's history of PID, the physician should have explained to the patient the purpose and possible complications of the IUD and the alternative methods of contraception. The jury, however, found that the physician was not required to advise the plaintiff of the risks involved in the insertion of an IUD. The court concluded that the duty to disclose only applies to "reasonably foreseeable material risks," and not to the remote possibility that an inserted IUD would perforate the uterus, migrate, and protrude from the rectum.[24]

Some states do not specify which standard of disclosure must be followed. Whatever the standard, it seems likely that the health care practitioner who properly informs the patient of the major risks of a procedure and the feasible alternative treatment should be protected. It would not be credible to a jury that a patient would have refused a particular procedure because of a minor risk if he or she had consented to the procedure after being informed of more serious risks.

However, additional information is required if the patient requests it. Most consent forms indicate that all of the patient's questions have been answered. Before witnessing a patient's signature on a consent form, the nurse should ask him or her if the physician has explained the treatment, the risks, and the alternatives. If not, or if the patient then asks questions, the questions should be referred to the treating physician. If the physician refuses to answer or fails to discuss the questions further with the patient, then the nurse must report the patient's inquiries through the chain of command.

THE PATIENT'S RIGHT TO SELF-DETERMINATION

The Patient's Right to Self-Determination versus the State's Interests

Although it is generally accepted that a competent patient may refuse medical or surgical treatment, there are circumstances when an interested party petitions the court to intervene and requires the patient to consent to treatment. In such cases, the courts balance certain state interests against the patient's "rights."

In a Georgia case, a pregnant patient refused a caesarean section on religious grounds. Her physician testified that because of placenta previa, there was a 99% chance that the infant would not survive a natural delivery. The court's order that the mother undergo the caesarean section was upheld by the Georgia Supreme Court on the grounds that the state's interest in protecting the potential life of an unborn child outweighed the mother's constitutional right to privacy.[25]

A more difficult question arises when the patient is incompetent to make his or her own health care decisions. The courts may also balance the incompetent patient's "rights" to refuse treatment against certain interests of the state.

A typical case is *Leach v. Akron General Medical Center.*[26] In the *Leach* case, an Ohio appeals court found that an incompetent patient has a right to forego treatment based on the right to privacy. This court balanced the patient's right to privacy and the state's interests in keeping the patient alive (the preservation of life, the protection of third parties, the maintenance of the ethical integrity of the medical profession, and the prevention of suicide), and concluded that the patient's right to privacy guaranteed by the U.S. Constitution outweighed the state's interests. The court, however, required the highest possible standard of proof for a civil case, that is, clear and convincing evidence of what the patient would have wanted if she had been competent to decide for herself.[27]

Many courts have found that the patient's right to privacy outweighs the state's interests.

In 1985, a New Jersey court decided the well-known Karen Quinlan case, the first major case on the right to refuse or discontinue treatment. The court permitted the guardian to consent to the removal of Ms. Quinlan's respirator. The court held that the constitutional right to privacy found in the Fourteenth Amendment protects an individual's right, exercised through his or her guardian, to forego or terminate life-prolonging treatment.[28]

Other courts have upheld patients' decisions to refuse medical treatment because of religious beliefs. For example, one court found that the right of an adult Jehovah's Witness to refuse blood transfusions outweighed the state's interest in preserving the life of the only witness to a murder.[29]

In 1990, the U.S. Supreme Court decided the *Cruzan* case, which involved a guardian's decision that Nancy Cruzan, an incompetent person, would want to exercise her "right to die."[30] The Supreme Court acknowledged that a competent adult has a constitutionally protected right to refuse unwanted medical treatment. However, it found that for an incompetent patient, in order to protect the state's interests, the court may require "clear and convincing" evidence of what the patient, if competent, would want. The Court did not define "clear and convincing," but it did acknowledge that a proper **Living Will,** a legal document stating what health care a patient will accept or refuse, would have satisfied this higher standard. Nancy Cruzan never executed a Living Will, but there was evidence that she once told a roommate that she would not want to be kept alive on machines. This evidence, according to the Court, was sufficient to meet the clear and convincing test and overcome the state's interests in the preservation of life, and so she was allowed to be taken off feeding tubes so that she could die.

The Patient Self-Determination Act

Many state legislatures have enacted statutes that allow competent persons to execute documents in order to exercise control over their future health care. These documents include Living Wills and Durable Powers of Attorney for Health Care and are called **advance directives.** An advance directive is a document by which a competent person (1) makes a declaration regarding future health care he or she will accept or refuse (a Living Will), (2) designates another person to make health care decisions if he or she becomes incompetent in the future (a Durable Power of Attorney for Health Care or "proxy" decision maker), or both.

In general, a Living Will must be executed with the same formality as a Last Will and Testament. A Durable Power of Attorney for Health Care (DPAHC) or Medical Durable Power of Attorney permits a competent adult (the principle) to appoint a surrogate or proxy (the attorney-in-fact) to make health care decisions in the event he or she becomes incompetent to make such decisions. The various state statutes outline the requirements for executing and revoking a DPAHC. DPAHC statutes provide that the surrogate will receive the same information as an aid to informed decision making that the principle, if competent, would be provided.

Almost every state has enacted legislation that allows individuals to execute Living Wills or DPAHC. These directives are binding on health care providers. Historically, there were problems between states that had no such legislation and states that did because some states would not accept advance directives from other states.[31] To remedy these problems, Congress passed legislation that requires hospitals and other health care facilities, including managed care organizations that receive Medicare or Medicaid funds, to advise all patients of their rights to refuse treatment and of any relevant state law dealing with advanced directives.[32] This legislation, the Patient Self-Determination Act of 1990, was sponsored by Senator Danforth, who introduced it as follows:

> Advance directives encourage people to discuss and document their views of life-sustaining treatment in advance They uphold the right of people to make their own decisions. And they enhance communication between patients, their families, and doctors, easing the burden on families and providers when it comes time to decide whether or not to pursue all possible treatment options. . .
>
> Advance directives will not solve all problems related to end-of-life decision . . . they do not take the pain away from someone we love, but they do ensure that a person's voice continues to be heard, and they do ease the burden, pain, and guilt that families often feel when making decision(s) for their dying loved one.[33]

The Incompetent Patient's Right to Self-Determination

If a patient is unconscious or otherwise unable to make health care decisions, someone else may have to make those decisions. If the patient, like Nancy Cruzan, has never discussed his or her wishes with the family and has never executed an advance directive, any assumption made by a surrogate decision maker may not be the decision the patient would have made if competent. Because of this possibility of error, the courts are very protective of the rights of incompetent patients and may, as in the *Cruzan* case, require a very high standard of proof before allowing the physician to terminate any life-sustaining treatment. In *Cruzan,* the court held that, because of the obvious and overwhelming finality of such life-and-death decisions, the state had the right to err on the side of life.[34] The U.S. Supreme Court, however, recognized that a Living Will would have been sufficient evidence of Ms. Cruzan's wishes to sustain an order removing her feeding tube.

As a practical matter, physicians face such decisions daily. Generally, they have been able to rely upon close family members to make decisions for the incompetent patient, because it is the family that usually cares about the patient and has knowledge of the patient's wishes. This does not mean that a family member has a legal right to accept or refuse treatment for an incompetent patient. In most states, only a legal guardian (or parent in the case of a minor) can make health care decisions for another— unless the patient has executed an advance directive appointing another person to make health care decisions in the event of incompetency.

However, even if a patient is conscious, there may still be a question of whether he or she is competent to consent to or refuse treatment.

A woman with cancer was admitted to a hospital under a Mental Illness/ Mental Health statute. The patient believed that she would be spiritually cured and refused treatment on religious grounds. The patient's physician requested that the court order treatment for the cancer, claiming that the patient's belief was a "delusion," which affected her ability to give informed consent. He also claimed that she was incompetent, because she was hospitalized pursuant to the mental illness statute. The court disagreed, finding that the patient was not legally incompetent and that she had a constitutional right to refuse treatment.[35]

Informed Consent and the Living Will

The concept of a Living Will is based on the doctrine of informed consent.[36] One of many criticisms of Living Wills, however, is that they cannot be based upon informed consent, because the patient cannot know what treatment options will be available many years later. The opposite argument is that, by voluntarily executing a binding directive, the individual indicates that he or she has weighed all of the factors and has chosen to remove the decision to prolong his or her life from the physician's discretion.[37] Even where there is no state law making Living Wills "legal," a Living Will is strong evidence in court of the patient's wishes if a court must make health care decisions for an incompetent patient.[38] (See an example of a Living Will declaration at the end of this chapter.)

"Do Not Resuscitate" Orders

Upon admission to a health care facility, a competent adult may also exercise control over future medical or surgical treatment by asking the physician for an order "not to resuscitate." Per the patient's decision, the physician writes "No Code" or "Do Not Resuscitate" (DNR) orders on the patient's chart. Such an order instructs the nurses and medical staff to refrain from resuscitating the patient in the event of cardiovascular or respiratory arrest. Such orders do not indicate that other treatment, to which the patient has consented, must be withheld or terminated.

Each health care facility should have its own DNR policy. These policies generally require that patients with DNR orders be terminally ill. They also should require the physician to note in the medical record that the patient's decision was made after consultation with the physician regarding his or her medical condition and prognosis. Do Not Resuscitate or No Code orders should always be written in the patient's medical record and periodically reviewed and updated.

There is very little statutory or case law that deals with DNR orders. The State of New York has enacted a DNR statute that provides for a hierarchy of surrogates who may request a DNR order for incompetent patients.[39] The spouse is first on the list and a "close friend" is last. An interesting interpretation of this statute is that the homosexual partner of an AIDS patient may act as a decision maker for an AIDS patient if there is no eligible spouse or family to be the surrogate. Also, in 1990, an Indiana court was the first court to consider the issue of whether a doctor was liable for issuing a DNR or "no code" order without the patient's informed consent.[40]

CONCLUSION

Before the era of high-tech medicine, there was little, if any, need for courts and legislatures to be concerned about an individual's right to refuse treatment. This changed dramatically as it became possible to maintain such vital functions as respiration by artificial means with ventilators and to provide nourishment via tubes and needles. Many people began to view the invasive procedures required to keep the body functioning as violations of their right to die with dignity. Initially, these matters were handled by the patient or the immediate family and physician. If the patient (or the family of an incompetent patient) wished to forego artificial life-prolonging treatment, the physician complied by not ordering the treatment. Although this continues to be the practice in most situations today, the courts and legislatures are becoming increasingly involved in these matters.

As more laws are passed giving patients the right to refuse life-sus-taining treatment and with the passage of the federal Patient Self-Deter-mination Act, health care providers are at increased risk of liability for keeping patients alive against their expressed wishes. Some advocates of the right to die have proposed that health care providers who fail to honor the patients' wishes be held liable for the patients' resulting "wrongful living." In drafting DPAHC and Living Will statutes, state legislators have recognized that some health care providers may not be able to honor the patient's desire to refuse treatment and have granted providers immunity from liability as long as the provider does not prevent the transfer of the patient to a provider who will honor his or her wishes. This reasoning also applies to DNR orders; a physician should not oppose the transfer of a terminally ill patient who desires a DNR order to another physician if that physician cannot, in good faith, write the order.

The courts and legislatures are attempting to protect not only the patient's right to self-determination, but also the rights of health care pro-viders who now have the power to keep patients "alive" by technical and artificial means. Individuals, however, must exercise their rights to make decisions in advance regarding the health care they wish to receive in the future. In their role as educators in the community, nurses are in a unique position to inform individuals of their rights and to encourage the exercise of such rights.[41]

Points to Remember

▶ In most circumstances a competent adult has the right to consent to or refuse medical treatment.

▶ To be legally effective, a patient's consent to medical or surgical treat-ment must be what the law considers "informed consent."

▶ Assault and battery can occur when medical examination or treatment is provided without first obtaining the patient's consent.

▶ Today, lawsuits alleging lack of informed consent are more likely to be based upon professional negligence principles than upon claims of assault and battery.

▶ Consent to treatment is "informed consent" when the patient has been provided with sufficient information to make an intelligent decision to accept or reject treatment that is based upon a full disclosure of the relevant facts.

▶ It is the responsibility of the health care practitioner performing the procedure, usually the physician, to obtain the patient's informed consent.

▶ Signing as a witness does not subject the nurse to liability for failure to obtain informed consent.

▸ A court may require a very high standard of proof of an incompetent patient's desires before ordering the removal of life-sustaining treatment.

▸ An advance directive is made by the individual while he or she is competent but becomes effective only if and when the individual becomes incompetent to make health care decisions.

▸ By executing a Living Will, a competent individual can instruct his or her physician regarding the type of medical treatment the individual will accept or refuse if he or she becomes unable to make health care decisions in the future.

▸ A DPAHC permits a competent adult to appoint a proxy to act on his or her behalf and to make health care decisions if the person becomes incompetent.

STUDY QUESTIONS

1. What information must be provided before the patient can give informed consent to treatment?

2. Define *capacity* as it relates to a patient's right to accept or refuse medical treatment.

3. Explain *assault and battery* in accordance with medical treatment and give an example of how it may apply to informed consent.

4. What basic elements must be proved before a physician may be found negligent for failure to obtain a patient's informed consent to medical or surgical treatment?

5. Describe two situations in which the consent to treat would be implied.

6. Describe four situations that are exceptions to the duty to disclose risks of a treatment.

7. Discuss the two basic standards relied upon by courts for determining what information must be disclosed to the patient in order to obtain informed consent to treatment.

8. Explain what is meant by (a) an objective standard and (b) a subjective standard, as each relates to what a patient must prove in a lawsuit involving informed consent.

9. What duty is imposed upon health care facilities by the Patient Self-Determination Act?

10. Define *advance directive* and give examples of the two primary kinds of advance directives and how they relate to the concept of informed consent.

REFERENCES

1. *Matter of McCauley,* 409 Mass. 134, 565 N.E.2d 411 (1991).
2. See Accreditation Manual for Hospitals, 1990, p xv.
3. *O'Brien v. Cunard S.S. Co,* 154 Mass. 272, 28 N.E. 266 (1891).
4. Some states have enacted statutes prohibiting assault and battery lawsuits against health care providers. For example, Arizona Revised Statute § 12–562 (1989) states: "No medical malpractice action brought against a health care provider shall be based upon assault and battery."
5. *See Lacey v. Laird,* 166 Ohio St. 12, 139 N.E.2d 25 (1956).
6. *Levenson v. Souser,* 384 Pa. Super. 132, 557 A.2d 1081, 1085–1086 (1989).
7. *See, e.g., Holten v. Pfingst,* 534 S.W.2d 786 (Ky. 1975), in which the court held that a negligence cause of action would accrue where there is a failure of a physician to disclose a particular risk and the nondisclosure proximately injures the patient. *See also Jones v. Howard University, Inc.,* 589 A.2d 419, 422 (D.C. App. 1991), in which the court pointed out that a breach of duty to disclose will not establish liability on the part of the physician; the unrevealed risk must actually materialize and injure the patient.
8. *See, e.g., Hidding v. Williams,* 578 So.2d 1192 (5th Cir. 1991).
9. In *Truman v. Thomas,* 27 Cal. 3d 285, 611 P.2d 902 (1980), the court held that where a patient indicates a refusal to undergo a risk-free test or treatment, a doctor must advise of all material risks of which reasonable persons would want to be informed before deciding.
10. Black's Law Dictionary, ed 5. West Publishing Co, St. Paul, Minn, 1979.
11. *Mroczkwski v. Straub Clinic & Hospital,* 6 Haw. App. 563, 732 P.2d 1255, 1257 (1987).
12. *Hidding v. Williams,* 578 So.2d 1192 (5th Cir. 1991).
13. *See, e.g., Mroczkwski v. Straub Clinic and Hospital,* 732 P.2d 1255 (Hawaii, App. 1987). *See also* Alaska Stat. § 09.55.556, which provides for less than full disclosure if a health care provider reasonably believed that a full disclosure would have a substantially adverse effect on the patient's condition.
14. *See, e.g., Dessi v. United States,* 489 F. Supp. 722, 727 (E.D.Va. 1980), applying Virginia law. The scope of a physician's duty to disclose typically is determined by the prevailing medical practice in the community, that is, what a reasonable physician in the community, of like training, would customarily disclose under the same circumstances.
15. *Small v. Gifford Memorial Hospital,* 133 Vt. 552, 349 A.2d 703 (1975). This rule and the medical community rule are discussed in greater detail in Section D, *infra.*
16. Black's Law Dictionary, ed 5. West Publishing Co, St. Paul, Minn, 1979.
17. Ohio Revised Code Ann. § 2317.54 (Supp. 1988), for example, states: "A hospital shall not be held liable for a physician's failure to obtain an informed consent from his patient prior to a surgical or medical procedure or course of procedures, unless the physician is an employee of the hospital." In *Robertson v. Menorah Memorial,* 588 S.W.2d 134 (Mo. 1979), the Missouri Supreme Court rejected the plaintiff's argument that by having the patient sign the consent form, the hospital was responsible for informing the patient of the risks and benefits of treatment. The court held that the physician alone was qualified to obtain the patient's informed consent. *Id.*
18. The following state statutes require the scope of the physician's disclosure to be governed by the professional community standard: Alabama Code, § 6-5-484; Arizona Revised Statutes, § 12-561(2), Arkansas Statutes Annotated, § 16-114-206(b)(1), (2); Delaware Code Annotated, Title 18, § 6852(a)(2); Florida Statutes Annotated, § 76.103(3)(a); Idaho Code, § 39-4304; Kentucky Revised Statutes Annotated, § 304.40-320; Maine Revised Statutes, Title 24 § 2905; Nebraska Revised Statutes, § 44-2816; Nevada Revised Statutes, § 41A.100; New Hampshire Revised Statutes Annotated § 507-E:2.II.(a); New York Public Health Law, § 2805-d; North Carolina General Statutes, § 90-21.13(a)(1); Tennessee Code Annotated, § 29-26-118; and Vermont Statutes Annotated, Title 12, § 1909(a)(1). (This list is, of course, subject to change as more states enact such legislation.)

19. *Clemons v. Tranovich,* 589 A.2d 260, 262 (Pa. 1991) (citing *Jozsa v. Hottenstein,* 364 Pa. Super. 469, 528 A.2d 606, 608 (1987).

20. *Cobbs v. Grant,* 104 Cal. Rptr. 505, 515, 516, 502 P.2d 1, 11-12 (1972).

21. At least five states have enacted statutes which place emphasis on the information needs of the patient and do not, therefore, require the testimony of an expert witness. These states are Iowa, North Dakota, Pennsylvania, Texas, and Washington. Other state legislatures have passed informed consent laws but have not specified the required standard of disclosure.

22. *Scaria v. St. Paul Fire & Marine Insurance Co.,* 68 Wisc. 2d 1, 227 N.W.2d 647 (1975).

23. *Plutshack v. Univ. of Minn. Hospital,* 316 N.W.2d 1, 3 (Minn. 1982).

24. *Wright v. Hirsch,* 572 So. 2d 783, 789–791 (La. App. 4th Cir. 1990).

25. *Jefferson v. Griffith, Spalding County Hospital Authority,* 247 Ga. 86, 274 S.E.2d 457 (Ga. 1981). *See also Norwood Hospital v. Munoz,* 564 N.E.2d 1017 (Mass. 1991). (The state's highest court reversed a lower court's order that a mother consent to a blood transfusion to save her own life in order to prevent her abandonment of a dependent child on the ground that the father had the financial resources to care for the child.)

26. *Leach v. Akron General Medical Center,* 13 Ohio App. 3d 393, 469 N.E.2d 1047 (Summit Co. 1984).

27. *Leach v. Akron General Medical Center,* 13 Ohio App. 3d 393, 469 N.E.2d 1047 (1984).

28. *In re: Quinlan,* 355 A.2d 647 (N.J. 1976).

29. *In re: Brown,* 478 So. 2d 1033 (Miss. 1985).

30. *Cruzan v. Director, Missouri Department of Health,* 110 S. Ct. 2841 (1990). In *Cruzan,* the Court did not distinguish between treatment with artificially administered food and water and other life-sustaining measures such as respirators. Some state laws make such distinctions. In the wake of the *Cruzan* decision, these laws may be challenged in the courts and found unconstitutional.

31. Because every state statute is different and subject to be changed, it is important for the nurse to become familiar with the specific law of the state in which he or she practices.

32. Omnibus Budget Reconciliation Act of 1990. This act has been called the Medical Miranda Act because, like the "Miranda" rule, which requires police officers to read a list of "rights" to persons arrested, it requires health care providers to inform patients of their "rights" to accept or reject treatment.

33. 135 Cong. Record at 513567 (daily ed., Oct. 17, 1989).

34. *Cruzan v. Director, Missouri Department of Health,* 110 S. Ct. 2841 (1990).

35. *In re: Milton,* 29 Ohio St. 3rd 20, 505 N.E.2d 255 (1987).

36. "The essence of the Living Will is informed consent of the person to the status of irreversibility of dying or living maimed." Kutner, The Living Will—Coping with the Historical Event of Death. 17 Baylor Law Review 17:29, 1975.

37. Note, Statutory Recognition of the Right to Die: The California Natural Death Act. 57 Boston University Law Review Rev. 57:148, 167, 1988.

38. *See, e.g., Cruzan v. Director, Missouri Department of Health,* 110 S. Ct. 2841 (1990).

39. New York's *Health Care Agents and Proxies Statute.*

40. *Payne v. Marion General Hospital,* 549 N.E.2d 1043 (Ind. App. 2 Dist. 1990).

41. Such education should take place in the community, however, as many state statutes prohibit hospital employees from involvement with the execution of advance directives by hospitalized patients.

▶ **ETHICS IN PRACTICE**

Mr. S., 72 years old, was found at home by neighbors, unconscious, with multiple ecchymotic areas on his body and a fractured wrist. Because he lived alone, had no known relatives, and was unresponsive when he was admitted to the hospital, the history of the present illness was not obtained. Initially, it was thought that he had been beaten by an intruder in his home.

He was admitted to the ICU and connected to a cardiac monitor. After several hours of monitoring, he began to have transient episodes of complete heart block with ventricular asystole. A diagnosis of Stokes-Adams syndrome was made. This diagnosis would account for his current injuries. Mr. S. also became more responsive, although he experienced episodes of disorientation.

The cardiologist was contacted by Mr. S.'s primary physician, and plans were made to insert a permanent pacemaker, a standard treatment for this condition. The cardiologist talked to Mr. S. briefly about the procedure and then told the nurse caring for the patient to have Mr. S. sign a surgical consent. The nurse brought the consent to the room and asked Mr. S. a few questions about what the physician had told him and his understanding of the pacemaker insertion procedure. Mr. S. seemed to have no understanding at all of the underlying disease process, the procedure, or the requirement for an informed consent.

The nurse proceeded to present some simple information to the patient about the procedure, its risks, and its benefits. After hearing this information, Mr. S. stated that he did "not want that thing inside of him" and refused to sign the consent form.

The nurse called the cardiologist later that evening and told him about what she had told Mr. S. and his refusal to sign the consent form. The cardiologist was furious, accused the nurse of undermining his authority, and demanded that she "get that consent signed" no matter what it took. He insisted that the patient was still somewhat disoriented and that the nurse's teaching had only confused him more.

What are the ethical issues involved in this case study? Was the nurse "wrong" in teaching this patient? What should the nurse do at this point?

Living Will Declaration

INSTRUCTIONS
Consult this column for guidance.

To My Family, Doctors, and All Those Concerned with My Care

I, _____, being of sound
mind, make this statement as a directive to be followed if I become unable to
participate in decisions regarding my medical care.

This declaration sets forth your directions regarding medical treatment.

If I should be in an incurable or irreversible mental or physical condition with
no reasonable expectation of recovery, I direct my attending physician to with-
hold or withdraw treatment that merely prolongs my dying. I further direct that
treatment be limited to measures to keep me comfortable and to relieve pain.

*You have the right to refuse treat-
ment you do not want, and you
may request the care you do want.*

These directions express my legal right to refuse treatment. Therefore I expect
my family, doctors, and everyone concerned with my care to regard themselves
as legally and morally bound to act in accord with my wishes, and in so doing to
be free of any legal liability for having followed my directions.

*You may list specific treatment
you do not want. For example:*

   Cardiac resuscitation
   Mechanical respiration
   Artificial feeding/fluids by tube

*Otherwise, your general statement,
top right, will stand for your wishes.*

I especially do not want: _____

_____

_____

_____

_____

_____

*You may want to add instructions
or care you do want—for example,
pain medication; or that you prefer
to die at home if possible.*

Other instructions/comments: _____

_____

_____

Proxy Designation Clause: Should I become unable to communicate my instructions as stated above, I designate the following person to act in my behalf:

Name _____

*If you want, you can name
someone to see that your wishes
are carried out, but you do not
have to do this.*

Address_____

If the person I have named above is unable to act on my behalf, I authorize
the following person to do so:

Name _____

Address_____

This Living Will Declaration expresses my personal treatment preferences. The
fact that I may have also executed a document in the form recommended by
state law should not be construed to limit or contradict this Living Will Declaration, which is an expression of my common-law and constitutional rights.

Signed: _____ Date: _____

*Sign and date here in the
presence of two adult witnesses,
who should also sign.*

Witness: _____ Witness: _____

Address: _____ Address: _____

*Keep the signed original with your personal papers at home. Give signed
copies to doctors, family, and proxy. Review your Declaration from time to
time; initial and date it to show it still expresses your intent.*

CHAPTER

Common Areas of Negligence and Liability

ETHICAL CONSIDERATIONS

▼ During the course of an average work day, the typical floor nurse carries out numerous treatments, passes a larger number of medications, performs frequent physical assessments, and makes multiple decisions that affect the health and well-being of patients. These nurses rarely have the time to fully investigate and consider all the ethical and legal implications of their actions. They often make critical decisions about patient care during high-pressure situations that force them to act quickly. Sometimes nurses make mistakes.

Fortunately, only a small percentage of the mistakes made by nurses actually produce injury to patients. Of this small number of injured patients, an even smaller percentage go on to seek compensation for damages through legal action. Nevertheless, the numbers of lawsuits filed against nurses continue to increase. Many of these suits are well publicized in the news media and give the impression that every action a nurse takes can leave him or her open to a lawsuit. This is a false impression.

The best defense a nurse can have against being sued by patients is to remain competent in his or her skills and knowledge, and to practice nursing at the highest standards of care. Remaining competent and knowledgeable about nursing skills, techniques, treatments, assessments, and medications is not only a legal imperative but is also one of the key requirements for ethical nursing practice. Nurses have the minimal ethical obligation or duty of nonmaleficence, that is, doing no harm to patients. If nothing else, remaining competent in one's skills and knowledge helps prevent injury to patients.

Another important factor in preventing lawsuits is to establish a friendly, trusting relationship with the patient and his or her family. As nursing has sought more independence and status as a profession, there has been an unfortunate movement toward less personalized care. Most patients and their families have an inherent positive attitude toward nurses and see nurses as the lone individuals in the often impersonalized institutional atmosphere who personally care about them.

Nurses teach, counsel, and provide comfort and understanding to patients and families in stressful situations. A little extra time spent talking with a patient, allowing him or her to express anger, fear, or anxiety, or even "bending" the rules to accommodate visitors, often pays off in big dividends later on. The reality is that if a patient truly likes the nurse and feels that the nurse has the patient's best interests in mind, he or she will be less likely to sue the nurse if the nurse should make a mistake.

OBJECTIVES

Upon completing this chapter, the reader will be able to:

1 Recognize common areas of nursing negligence and liability.
2 Recognize common deviations from the nursing standard of care.
3 Identify areas in which nursing risk management can reduce patient injury and resulting exposure to nursing liability.
4 Identify appropriate measures to minimize risks and avoid liability

INTRODUCTION

The focus of this chapter is common areas of nursing negligence and liability. The chapter provides examples of common areas of nursing practice and situations where nurses were held liable or responsible for their negligence in patient care delivery.

Nursing negligence is conduct that is unreasonable under the circumstances or conduct that fails to meet the appropriate standard of care as discussed in Chapter 4.

Liability means legal responsibility; a nurse is legally responsible for actions that fail to meet the standard of care or for failing to act and thereby causing harm. For example, when a nurse gives the wrong medication to a patient and the patient suffers harm, the nurse may be liable for negligent administration of the drug.

Many of the cases in nursing negligence also involve other parties. For example, a patient may argue that his or her injury is the result of negligence on the part of a nurse and a doctor, hospital, or other employer; any combination of defendants may be found responsible for the injury and liable for a deviation from the standard of care.

RECURRING CAUSES OF LIABILITY

Nursing negligence cases are found in legal reports, legal journals, or insurance company publications. Northrop[1] reviewed 33 cases reported in 1 year by plaintiffs' attorneys alleging nursing malpractice. These types of nursing actions fell into the following categories: (1) treatment, (2) communication, (3) medication, and (4) monitoring, observing, and supervising.

Box 7–1   NURSING NEGLIGENCE CASES

Treatment
1. Enema to a preoperative patient with appendicitis which resulted in ruptured bowel and appendicitis
2. Improperly used equipment resulting in air embolisms
3. Failure to administer the correct oxygen level
4. Failure to attach a fetal monitor as ordered
5. Burns to infant from formula heated in a microwave
6. Failure to attend patient having asthma attack resulting in injuries, such as brain damage

Communication
1. Failure to notify physician of changes in signs and symptoms
2. Failure to chart vital signs for hours in a labor room
3. Failure to advise physician of jaundice
4. Failure to notify physician of circulatory compromise in a casted leg

Medication
1. Wrong medication given upon discharge (topical eye anesthetic instead of artificial tears)
2. Failure to give diazepam (Valium) as ordered
3. Improper administration of potassium chloride

Monitoring/Observing/Supervising
1. Failure to recognize dehydration and electrolyte imbalance
2. Failure to monitor intravenous therapy
3. Failure to monitor fetal heart rate
4. Negligent supervision of psychiatric patient who attempted suicide
5. Negligent assignment and supervision of a student nurse who did not take blood pressure for 6 hours

Another study ranked the top 10 most common allegations in nursing malpractice claims in one insurance program over a period of 6 years.[2] The top 10 allegations found were:

1. Patient falls
2. Failure to monitor
3. Failure to ensure patient safety
4. Improper performance of treatment
5. Failure to respond to patient
6. Medication error
7. Wrong dosage administered
8. Failure to follow hospital procedure
9. Improper technique
10. Failure to supervise treatment

Nurses can best avoid liability for negligence by giving safe, high-quality nursing care. It is also helpful to be aware of potential problem areas, identifying the risk areas in individual practice, and taking measures to minimize exposure to those risks. Such measures include staying current in your field, establishing a good relationship with your patients, and following approved procedures.

In the following sections, a variety of common types of patient incidents are reviewed, and a sample of typical lawsuits related to that type of injury is discussed. These are not listed in any particular order, but they are fairly representative of the types of lawsuits staff nurses in a hospital might be exposed to during their practice.

PATIENT FALLS

Falls are common among the elderly. The most important lawsuit preventative measures are assessing for fall potential and implementing measures to prevent falls. There must be documentation that the patient was instructed to remain in bed or a family member was told and voiced understanding, that the side rails are up, and that the call light is at the bedside. It is difficult to defend a claim if there has not been frequent documentation of the patient.

If a "fall warning" mechanical device or alarm is used, record its use on the chart. This gives the appearance to a judge or jury that the nurse is aware of the potential problem and attempted to prevent any injuries and provide a safe environment for the elderly patient.

If a patient falls, information on the chart and in an incident report must include an evaluation of the patient's physical and mental condition (including the integumentary, respiratory, cardiovascular, musculoskeletal, and neurological systems). Most cases are lost because of the lack of documentation regarding the circumstances prior to the fall rather than after the incident.

Patients in hospitals and nursing homes may be medicated, sedated, disoriented, or restricted by a cast or walker. They may not be expecting sudden dizziness upon rising from a recumbent position. They may be confused by unfamiliar surroundings. Particular problems arise with elderly and senile patients. Injuries often occur when a patient slips on a wet floor or falls trying to climb over a side rail. Many patients fall when they are trying to walk without needed assistance or getting up from a wheelchair that has not been locked. The nurse has a duty to assess the situation and then provide adequate assistance, supervision, or restraint to assure patient safety; failure to do so may result in liability.

RESTRAINTS

Physical restraints can cause skin breakdown, impaired respiratory status, strangulation, and death. Chemical restraints may increase drowsiness, decrease coherence and judgment, and cause confusion in the elderly. If a patient must be restrained, it is important to chart the following items:

1. Ineffective alternatives that are used prior to restraints.
2. Reason for restraints. Describe the patient's specific behavior and the type of restraint used.
3. The time and date when restraints are applied.
4. The times when the restraints and patient are monitored.
5. Patient's response to restraints.
6. How hospital policy and procedures are followed with regard to how often a patient in restraints must be checked and released from restraints. Also, the care to be given the patient when out of restraints.
7. For a patient check: skin integrity; circulation; respiratory status; patient's verbal response; reasons, based on patient behavior, for continued restraints; and physician's orders.

Most institutions, hospitals, clinics, and nursing homes have policies and procedures addressing restraints and other patient safety measures that nurses may require to protect patients from falls. It is important to know and follow these guidelines for assessing patients to prevent injuries.

One Massachusetts case involved an elderly man who fell out of bed following eye surgery.[3] The nurse's notes indicated that the patient returned from surgery "very sleepy" but did not note anything about side rails or instructions to the patient regarding ambulation. In the early morning of the first postoperative day, the patient was found on the floor, disoriented, with a fractured wrist. The patient's family alleged that they had requested that the patient be restrained for his own protection because he "seemed so disoriented" after surgery. This case resulted in a payment to the patient on behalf of the hospital and nurses involved.

In a recent Nebraska case,[4] a patient sued a hospital and others for injuries she sustained when she fell from a hospital cart while in the emergency room. The patient was admitted to the emergency room semiconscious and unstable. She was placed on a cart with the side rails raised but was not strapped in or otherwise restrained. The physician testified that after he examined the patient, he requested that someone remain with her at all times, but he did not recall to whom he gave that order. The nurse attending the patient was called from the room by the charge nurse on another task. The charge nurse asked the patient's father to remain in the room with her. However, the father left, and, while attempting to climb off the end, the patient fell from the cart and suffered a severe blow to her face and temporomandibular joint. The patient alleged negligent failure to restrain and negligent failure to provide attendants or supervision.

At trial, the defendants were granted a summary judgment in their favor due to the absence of expert testimony from the plaintiff on the standard of care. The appeals court reversed in part and remanded (returned the case to the lower court) for further proceedings against the hospital on the question of adequate supervision.

An Alabama case[5] addressed whether a nurse was negligent in spilling or failing to warn a patient about spilled water. A 71-year-old patient in a psychiatric ward complained of sore and swollen feet following a day trip. She was given a bucket of warm water to soak her feet in while sitting in the recreation room. Afterward, the nurse carried the bucket of water to the patient's room. The patient testified that the nurse pushed the door open with the bucket. As the patient stepped from the carpeted hall to the tile floor, she slipped, fell, and broke her right arm. At the close of the plaintiff's case, a directed verdict was granted to the defendants. On appeal, the decision was reversed and the case remanded for resolution of the issue in dispute as to whether the nurse was negligent in spilling the water or failing to warn the patient about spilled water. The final outcome of the case is not reported.

A New Hampshire case[6] illustrates how charting practices can complicate the question of liability for a fall. A 36-year-old patient underwent brain surgery. Three days postoperatively he pressed his call light for assistance to the bathroom. When no one responded, he got out of bed and fell, breaking his hip. The nurse, who had heard a "thump," wrote in the clinical record: "Found pt. (patient) on floor—Apparently crawled out of bed—trying to get to BR (bathroom)—had called for help but not a quick enough response." This speculation was damaging for the nurse. Further problems for her defense arose when the patient's mother testified that the nurse admitted that she had heard the patient but could not respond because the hospital was shorthanded. The court affirmed a verdict against the hospital.

There is no absolute liability for falls that occur in hospitals. There must be proof that the nurse had reason to foresee that a patient could be harmed by falling before the duty to protect the patient arises. This is illustrated in a New York case[7] in which a plaintiff was denied recovery after a fall in the hospital. The patient was recovering from surgery on his leg. On the ninth postoperative day he fell from the bed and suffered serious injuries. The nurses testified that they had no reason to foresee this fall and that the patient was alert and oriented. The physician testified that the patient's condition did not warrant the use of side rails. The court denied recovery to the patient.

MEDICATION ERRORS

Errors in the administration of medications are another common source of liability for nurses. Examples of negligence in medication administration are plentiful. Frequent errors include administration of the wrong drug; administration of a drug to the wrong patient; administration of the wrong dose or by the wrong route; improper injection technique; or administration of a drug that the nurse knows is contraindicated. The standards of nursing care require that nurses understand the medications they administer and use their judgment in following medication orders. When a physician orders a medication for a particular patient, the dose, route, frequency, and other parameters are specified. Failure to meet any one of these specifications may cause an injury to the patient and result in liability for the nurse.

A frequent error involves the administration of the wrong drug. An older case illustrates this situation.[8] A hospital operating room nurse inadvertently supplied formalin instead of the Novocain requested by the surgeon who was preparing to anesthetize the patient. Several drops were injected before the error was discovered. The patient suffered great pain and required excision of an area of tissue. In affirming a judgment against the nurse, the court noted that there was no question that the nurse was negligent. In fact, the nurse accounted for her mistake by frankly admitting that she took no pains to read the label on the formalin bottle before pouring.

Nursing professionals are constantly reminded of the importance of knowing the reason a drug is administered and how treatments are to be administered. In the *Penaloza*[9] case, a nurse mistakenly administered a potassium permanganate pill to the patient orally when it was meant for external use only. The patient was receiving daily baths in water in which potassium permanganate had been dissolved for treatment of a rash. The labeled container of potassium permanganate pills was kept in the patient's medication box. One evening the supervisor made a change of nursing personnel on the unit, and the nurse giving medications administered all of the pills in the patient's box orally. She testified that the medication was clearly labeled and that she knew that it should not be administered internally. The court affirmed a judgment in favor of the hospital, noting that the hospital was not negligent in assigning the nurse to give medications. This nurse was licensed and had 3 years of continuous competent service. The suit did not individually name the nurse as a defendant.

In a North Carolina case,[10] a patient alleged negligent injection technique by a nurse. The patient testified that she was given an intramuscular injection of Demerol and Vistaril approximately 3 to 4 inches above her knee and subsequently suffered nerve injuries. An expert nurse witness testified that the location in question would not be in accordance with the standard of care among members of the nursing profession in the community and in similar communities. A physician testified that the injection could have caused the nerve damage alleged by the patient. The court ordered a new trial on the issue of nursing malpractice.

In another case, the patient alleged that he had a psychotic reaction to preoperative medication.[11] The court ruled in favor of the defendant nurses. This case shows how important accurate documentation of medications can be in preventing liability exposure. The patient alleged that he received a double dose of his preoperative medication because the medications were noted twice on his "PRN and One Time Medication Records." The evidence showed that he, in fact, received only one dose of medication despite the double notation. Two student nurses were both training on the ward where Mr. Biggs was hospitalized. One of the student nurses had previously administered injections of preoperative medications. However, the other student nurse had no experience in this skill, and the nursing supervisor suggested that she administer the preoperative medication to Mr. Biggs even though he was not her assigned patient. The student nurses testified that they prepared the injection together, and the inexperienced nurse gave it. Both recorded the medication. Fortunately, the student who administered the injection remembered this incident clearly because it was her first preoperative injection. Also, it was clearly documented in the written nurses' notes that the injection was given by the student nurse with no injection experience.

BURNS

Patient burns are another common source of nursing liability. Burns can be caused by heating pads, hot bath and shower water, hot water treatments including enemas and sitz baths, electrocautery equipment, heat lamps, and warmer beds. Chemical burns can occur from operative prep solutions. Cigarette-related burns are common. Nurses must be particularly alert to the risk of burns when the patient has decreased sensitivity to heat or is unable to communicate discomfort. Children, the elderly, and patients who are sedated or anesthetized are frequently victims of burns.

In an Oklahoma case[12] the court held the hospital responsible when two nurses, who were hospital employees, placed an unshielded lamp globe directly on the naked flesh of an unconscious patient and covered it with a towel while a physician was involved in emergency treatment of the patient. Another case involved a patient undergoing a breast biopsy and removal of a lesion from her arm.[13] Tincture of Zephiran disinfectant was applied to the patient, and fumes from the disinfectant ignited on contact with a heated needle. The patient suffered second-degree burns over a 4-inch area of arm, resulting in permanent scarring. The nurse involved was not sued; however, on appeal the issue of nursing negligence was raised, and the court noted that the patient could have sued the hospital and nurse as co-defendants in addition to the doctor because of the nurse's actions.

A 3-month-old child suffered second- and third-degree burns on his buttocks while undergoing surgery.[14] The infant was placed on a heating pad to keep him warm during a hernia repair. At the request of the anesthesiologist, the circulating nurse placed the pad in the operating room. Nothing unusual was noted after surgery. When the parents got home, they discovered blisters draining bloody fluid on the infant's buttocks. The child required skin grafting. The defendants admitted liability and, prior to trial, sought to exclude from evidence the warnings on the heating pad that read, in part: "Burns will result from improper use. Never use pad without cover in place. . . . Caution do not use on an infant, invalid, or a sleeping or unconscious person."

Finally, a patient was burned when he was unable to smoke his pipe safely.[15] The patient, a paraplegic, was given his pipe. While the nurse was out of the room, he dropped the pipe and set the bed on fire. The court wrote that the nurse had a duty to ensure the safety of patients, especially protecting them from known hazards such as fire.

EQUIPMENT INJURIES

Another patient safety concern for nurses involves the equipment used in patient care. The nurse's duty to exercise reasonable care includes a duty to select, maintain, and use equipment properly. This can pose quite a challenge in today's highly technological health care environment. The patient is often surrounded by complex and confusing monitors and other machines that require familiarity on the nurse's part. Most hospitals and other health care organizations have policies addressing the need for orientation to new equipment and the procedures for identifying items in need of repair or maintenance. Anyone who is expected to use new or modified equipment should be provided with an adequate orientation. Nurses faced with an unfamiliar device to be used in patient care have a duty to seek the necessary orientation and training.

Many equipment injuries result not from unfamiliarity with the equipment, but from haste, carelessness, or outright misuse. Nurses should never make their own modifications to patient equipment, unless after careful review of the intended and safe uses of the equipment, such modifications have been recommended by the manufacturer or by the institution. Sometimes patient injuries are the result of poorly designed or improperly manufactured devices. In these situations, it is especially important for the nurse to use the equipment in the way in which it is meant to be used.

In the *Martin*[16] case, the patient was a paraplegic with a gunshot wound to his neck. He was in a special bed that enabled immobilized patients to be rotated to a vertical position. The nurse responsible for checking the position of an essential bolt failed to do so, and as she rotated the bed, the patient fell. A jury awarded $350,000 in damages to the patient. The case was remanded on appeal for a new trial on damages because there was a dispute in the testimony regarding which of the injuries were actually the result of the fall.

A Kentucky case[17] involved a postoperative patient on a heart monitor. A recovery room nurse observed that the patient was not breathing and was turning blue. The heart monitor showed no heart beat, but the alarm had not sounded because either it had not been turned on or its volume had been set too low to be audible. The patient was resuscitated, but remained comatose. A malpractice suit naming numerous defendants was brought, and a jury found in favor of all the defendants. On appeal, the court noted that at the time the patient suffered cardiopulmonary arrest, the heart monitor alarms were either disconnected or inaudible, and evidence was introduced that this was a deviation from the accepted nursing care standards. The nurses testified that the alarms were unreliable and not necessary because the patients were constantly watched in the recovery room. The case was remanded to the trial court for a new trial.

In another case a premature infant died 1 week after receiving an excessive amount of hyperalimentation fluid in a short time because of an incorrectly set intravenous infusion pump.[18] A nurse who did not have primary responsibility for the infant but who was assigned to the unit, made an IV adjustment that resulted in the IV fluid being pumped directly into the infant, bypassing the infusion pump. The infant received 300 mL of solution over 30 minutes, resulting in a severe fluid overload. The case was settled without trial.

RETAINED FOREIGN OBJECTS

Retained foreign objects are a problem primarily for operating room nurses and others who are involved in invasive procedures where drains, instruments, sponges, or monitoring devices are inserted into the patient. Hospitals generally have very specific instrument and sponge count policies and procedures. Most cases in which a patient alleges that a foreign object was retained will involve extensive examination of the hospital's count policy and the nurse's compliance with that policy.

A Washington, DC, case[19] involved the failure of a surgeon to remove a laparotomy pad before closing the patient's incision. The patient had undergone surgery for intestinal cancer, and according to the records, over 400 items including instruments, needles, sponges, and lap pads were accounted for using the standard procedure prescribed by the hospital. The nurses testified that they had meticulously conformed to all of the procedures set forth in the hospital policy manual. Although the hospital settled out of court during the trial, the jury found no negligence on the part of the nurses or the physician. The verdict was affirmed on appeal.

Another example is the *Truhitte*[20] case in which a surgeon failed to remove a large surgical sponge (a pad used to soak up blood during surgery) from the patient's abdomen after a hysterectomy. The jury returned a verdict finding the hospital 55% negligent and the physician 45% negligent. The jury also specifically found that the operating room nurses were the agents of the hospital and not of the doctor. The nurses testified that the particular sponges in question could have been omitted from their handwritten list of sponges prepared at the initial count because they were packaged separately from the usual linen pack used for gynecological surgery. On appeal, the court found that the jury could reasonably infer from the evidence that the initial inventory of sponges was performed negligently or that the procedure for counting sponges was below the standard of care required of the hospital. The court ordered a new trial unless the doctor agreed to a $125,000 damage award apportioned between the defendants.

FAILURE TO MONITOR ADEQUATELY

While many lawsuits involve a specific act by a nurse, such as administering an incorrect medication, a failure to act can also result in allegations of nursing negligence. For example, a nurse does not have a duty to continuously watch or provide electronic monitoring of a patient unless some special need makes such observation necessary. Such a circumstance typically arises in clinical areas where the patient's condition changes rapidly, for example, in the postanesthesia recovery unit, the intensive care unit, or the labor and delivery unit. The nurse also has a duty to monitor closely those patients who have known self-destructive tendencies, or those situations where a severe drug reaction is possible.

A typical example is the *Gillis*[21] case, in which a patient alleged that the late application of a fetal heart monitor and resulting delay in diagnosis of fetal distress caused severe neurological problems in her infant. The mother testified that she came to the hospital in labor at 7:30 P.M. and was left unattended in her room until the fetal monitor was applied at 10:30 P.M. She denied that any examinations, procedures, or visits from physicians or nurses occurred during that time. When the fetal monitor was applied, fetal distress was noted, and after attempts to relieve the fetal distress by the usual measures, a caesarean section was performed.

The nurse's notes and testimony differed sharply from the mother's testimony. The records and testimony indicated several examinations by physicians and nurses and the administration of an enema. The nurses noted that the patient was assisted to the bathroom to expel the enema. When she returned to her bed, the nurses had their first opportunity to apply the fetal monitor, which had been ordered 40 minutes earlier. The court found that the failure to monitor during this period was not outside the standard of care and, since there was no breach of duty, dismissed the plaintiff's claim. This case is an example of how accurate, detailed nursing notes can help in the event of a lawsuit. Although the nurses involved in this case may not have remembered the details of this particular evening, their notes indicated their assessments and interventions and the patient's responses in sufficient detail that they were able to convince the court of the patient's inaccurate recollection of the events that transpired. The court noted:

> Too many documents show that Mrs. Gillis did receive attention . . . [T]hese documents were not falsified. True, some portions of the documents are ambiguous, and the brevity of some remarks does not help matters, but one must remember that these documents were not created for the primary purpose of detailing all relevant events for a lawsuit almost eight years later. They are, nevertheless, strong evidence of the unreliability of Mrs. Gillis' claim.[22]

FAILURE TO TAKE APPROPRIATE NURSING ACTION

As the profession of nursing has developed over the years, it has become widely recognized that nurses have a much higher duty to patients than to merely follow physician orders. The nurse is expected to exercise good nursing judgment and to intervene on the patient's behalf when a physician's order seems inappropriate, or where a physician does not respond. Nurses are also expected to recognize patient responses that are unusual and to report such responses to the physician. There are many case examples of situations where a nurse's actions are inappropriate, resulting in allegations of nursing negligence.

Some cases involve simply failing to recognize that a patient's needs are beyond the nurse's training or expertise; others involve acts of nursing incompetence that appear to be almost intentional mistreatment of the patient.

For example,[23] a plaintiff alleged that the nurse came into her husband's room and began to pour a tube feeding rapidly into his nasogastric tube, without checking the placement of the tube. The plaintiff claimed that the nurse, who was in a hurry to go home, continued the tube feeding even though fluid was coming out of his mouth and nose, and he was gagging and in respiratory distress. Despite the patient's distress, the nurse left. An orderly came in some time later and sought assistance for the patient who was now unresponsive. The patient died a short time later. The lawsuit against the hospital was dismissed because the plaintiff failed to file within the time required by the statue of limitation.

In a Washington, DC, case,[24] a patient, who had recently been seen by a physician for possible cardiac problems, called a health plan "advice nurse" to report that he had experienced vomiting, weakness, heavy sweating, and exhaustion after mowing his lawn. The nurse allegedly responded that he should "sweat it out." The patient died a short time later in an ambulance en route to a hospital. The health plan was held liable for the negligence involved in this case.

An older case illustrates the nurse's duty to recognize the limits of nursing interventions when a patient is not responding to a treatment.[25] An occupational health nurse failed to refer a patient for medical treatment even though a wound she had treated had not healed over a period of 10 months. The patient eventually discovered that the lesion was cancerous and had to have an extensive resection of the area done. The nurse was found liable. She had testified that she was aware of the warning signs of cancer, yet she continued to treat the wound in spite of its failure to heal as expected. The court noted that the nurse should know whether a condition is within her authority or whether it should be referred to a physician.

Another case[26] involved a patient who was discharged from the hospital, according to the physician's orders. Although the nurses knew that the patient had a fever, they neglected to inform the physician before the patient was discharged. The patient was readmitted 3 days later with sepsis, and died of multiple organ failure. It was argued that, by failing to confer with the physician and prevent the discharge of a patient who they knew was to be released, the nurses did not fulfill their advocacy role. The case was remanded for a trial on this and other issues.

COMMUNICATION PROBLEMS

Communication of patient care information among members of the health care team is a major area of concern to every hospital, clinic, physician's office, or other health care delivery site. Much time is spent devising and refining documentation systems and forms for patient records. It is important to have thorough and accurate communication and to preserve information learned about patients from interviews, examinations, laboratory studies, phone calls, literature searches, consultations, and conversations with other health care providers. Failures in communication can have serious consequences for a patient and can result in liability for nurses.

A hospital[27] was found liable in a case where alleged failure to diagnose Rocky Mountain spotted fever in two children resulted in the death of one child. The two children were brought to the emergency room with a rash and high fevers. The mother told the nurse that she had removed two ticks from one of the children. The physician was not told about the ticks. In the absence of this history, measles were diagnosed. The younger child died 4 days later of Rocky Mountain spotted fever. The older child was subsequently treated and cured, but sustained a limp that resolved within 6 months.

Undisputed evidence that the nurse knew that ticks had been removed from one of the boys was presented. A medical expert testified that:

> It is incumbent upon an emergency room staff . . . to record significant medical data. I feel that the knowledge by a nurse that ticks were removed from a patient in the spring . . . represents significant data. If this were not passed on I would consider that a failure to apply an adequate level of conformance as to standards. . . .[28]

The court wrote that there was ample evidence that the failure of the nurse to communicate this element of the patient's history to the attending physician was a serious violation of her duties as a nurse. Further, there was evidence that this failure to communicate was a contributing proximate cause of the injuries suffered by the children.

In a Maine case,[29] a patient died from an infection that resulted from a 6-hour delay in surgery after a nurse failed to tell the physician that the patient had the signs and symptoms of an esophageal tear. The patient underwent surgery to remove a foreign object lodged in his esophagus. About an hour after surgery, the patient's wife reported to the recovery room nurse that her husband was wheezing and in pain. Although the symptoms indicated a possible tear in the esophagus, the nurse failed to inform the surgeon. Six hours later, the surgeon was finally advised of the patient's distress, and corrective surgery was performed. Unfortunately, the patient's condition worsened because of an infection transmitted from the intestinal tract during the 6 hours before the tear was repaired. The patient died, and his wife brought a malpractice action against the hospital, alleging negligence through the actions of the nursing staff. After a jury trial, judgment for over $1 million was entered for the plaintiff. On appeal, the court wrote that the failure of the hospital staff to promptly notify the surgeon was a departure from the standard of care, but ordered a new trial unless the plaintiff agreed to accept a damage award of $370,000.

Communication is important; however, it is not necessary, and would in fact be impossible, for a nurse to notify the physician of every single thing that a patient relates. The nurse must exercise good judgment and must advise the physician promptly of significant history, symptoms, reactions, and other observations that the physician relies upon the nurse to make.

In a North Carolina case,[30] no liability was found in a situation where the patient alleged that the nurses failed to communicate information to the patient's doctor. The patient had received eight electroconvulsive treatments for depression and migraine headaches. He testified that after each treatment he complained to the nurses that he had pain and soreness in his hips and legs. He alleged that the nurses not only failed to document his complaints but also failed to ensure that the physician was aware of his pain. A summary judgment for the hospital and physician was upheld because the plaintiff had stated at a deposition that he had also complained directly to the physician. The physician testified that the patient's treatment would not have been any different had the nurses relayed information to him that the patient had already stated to him directly.

FAILURE TO CONFIRM ACCURACY OF PHYSICIAN'S ORDERS

Nurses are not protected from liability simply because they followed a physician's order. Nurses are expected to use good nursing judgment and to be familiar with medications, procedures, and anticipated responses to treatments, and to be able to recognize an unusual medication or treatment that might be ordered for a patient. When the nurse is unfamiliar with a medication, or uncomfortable with any order, the prudent nurse is expected to investigate further. He or she may consult a textbook, formulary, or pharmacist to check dose ranges for medications, or call the supervisor or head nurse to ask about a procedure.

It is also important that the nurse confirm any order that cannot be understood. Whether the problem is illegible handwriting or an unclear or incomplete order, the standard of care generally requires that the nurse must not carry out any order that is not clearly understood.

CONCLUSION

Allegations of nursing negligence can arise from almost any act or omission by a nurse that results in injury to a patient. This chapter has reviewed some of the commonly recurring areas of nursing negligence and liability. These cases illustrate the importance of several basic guidelines for protecting yourself from liability exposure that are present as repeating themes throughout the cases reviewed.

Points to Remember

▶ Be familiar with applicable policies and procedures.

▶ Do not deviate from approved policies and procedures.

▶ Assess patients carefully for foreseeable risks, such as falls and burns.

▶ Document accurately, timely, and concisely.

▶ Concentrate on what you are doing when preparing or administering medications. Remember that many medication errors can be avoided by using care in reading orders, labels, and patient identification tags.

▶ Be sure you are familiar with the proper uses of equipment before using any machine in patient care.

▶ Never continue to use equipment that is malfunctioning, and never modify equipment yourself.

▶ Carefully assess patients for monitoring needs.

▶ Use good nursing judgment when deciding when to notify the physician of patient status.

▶ Know the limits of your training, expertise, and license, and do not practice beyond those limits.

▶ Do not carry out an order that you do not understand, or that is clearly inappropriate.

▶ Remember that excellent communication between health care providers will help all in meeting the patient's needs.

▶ Keep up with current trends in your area of specialty. Your practice will be compared to the standard of care expected from nurses with a similar background and education.

Study Questions

1. Identify two common areas of nursing liability, and give an example of a deviation from the standard of care for each.

2. Identify two types of patients who are at a high risk of falling, and discuss nursing interventions that are appropriate to minimize those risks.

3. If a patient falls and is injured, discuss the liability issues involving the nurse who is assigned to that patient.

4. If a physician writes an order for a medication and mistakenly orders a dangerously high and very unusual dose, is the nurse automatically protected legally? Discuss.

5. Many types of equipment are used in patient care today. Discuss the types of injuries that can result from not knowing how to use the following types of equipment:
   a. Heating pad
   b. Heart monitors
   c. IV infusion pumps
   d. Electric beds

6. Operating Room instrument and sponge count policies are very important evidence in a trial involving retained foreign objects. Discuss how such a policy can help in the defense of a nurse.

7. If a suicidal patient is ordered to have "10-minute checks" and the nurse does in fact check that patient every 10 minutes, is it necessary that each check be documented? Why or why not?

8. A cardiac patient complained to the nurse that he had chest pain and shortness of breath. The nurse, who was on her way to lunch, decided to wait until she got back before calling the patient's physician. She gave the patient the medications that were ordered for him in the event he should get chest pains. She did not tell the nurse who was covering her patients during lunch. Half an hour later, when she returned from lunch, the nurse had forgotten about the patient's complaints. Later that day, the patient was found to have suffered a massive heart attack. Discuss any possible deviations from the standard of nursing care and ethical issues in this scenario.

9. If a nurse administers a medication and the patient suffers an allergic reaction, can the nurse be found negligent? Discuss.

10. Discuss the common types of nursing negligence reported in nursing journals and newspapers.

REFERENCES

1. Northrop, CE: Nursing actions in litigation. QRB 13(10):343–348, 1987.
2. McDonough, WJ, and Rioux, M: Increasing number of nurses named as sole defendants in malpractice suits. Forum Jan–Feb:4, 1989.
3. Martin, PB: Closed claims abstract. The Risk Management Foundation Forum Jan–Feb:5, 1988.
4. *Reifschneider v. Nebraska Methodist Hospital,* 387 N.W.2d 486 (Neb. 1986).
5. *Ashcraft v. Mobile Infirmary Medical Center,* 570 So.2d 593 (Ala. 1990).
6. *Brookover v. Mary Hitchcock Memorial Hospital,* 893 F.2d 411 (N.H. 1990).
7. *Mossman v. Albany Medical Center Hospital,* 311 N.Y.S.2d 131 (N.Y. 1970).
8. *Hallinan v. Prindle,* 62 P.2d 1075 (Cal. App. 1936).
9. *Penaloza v. Baptist Memorial Hospital,* 304 S.W.2d 203 (Tex. App. 1957).
10. *Holbrooks v. Duke University, Inc.,* 305 S.E.2d 69 (N.C. App. 1983).
11. *Biggs v. U.S.,* 655 F. Supp. 1093 (W.D. La. 1987).

12. *Flower Hospital v. Hart*, 62 P.2d 1248 (Ok. S.Ct. 1936).
13. *Nichter v. Edmiston*, 407 P.2d 721 (Nev. 1965).
14. *Smelko v. Brinton*, 740 P.2d 591 (Kan. 1987).
15. *Bowers v. Olch*, 260 P2d. 977 (Cal. 1953).
16. *University Community Hospital v. Martin*, 328 So.2d 858 (Fla. App. 1976).
17. *Davenport v. Ephraim McDowell Hospital*, 769 S.W. 2d 56 (Ky. 1988).
18. Martin, PB: Closed claim abstract The Risk Management Foundation Forum. Jan–Feb:15, 1989.
19. *Tams v. Kotz*, 530 A.2d 1217 (D.C. Ap. 1987).
20. *Truhitte v. French Hospital*, 180 Cal. Rptr. 152 (Cal. App. 1982).
21. *Gillis v. U.S.*, 722 F. Supp. 713 (M.D. Fla. 1989).
22. *Id.* at 715.
23. *Austin v. Conway Hospital*, 356 S.E.2d 153 (S.C. 1987).
24. *Schleier v. Kaiser Foundation Health Plan*, 876 F.2d 174 (D.C. App. 1989).
25. *Cooper v. National Motor Bearing Co.*, 288 P.2d 581 (1955 Cal. App.).
26. *Koeniguer v. Eckrich*, 422 N.W. 2d 600 (S.D. 1988).
27. *Ramsey v. Physician's Memorial Hospital, Inc.*, 373 A2d 26 (Md. App. 1977).
28. *Id.* at 30.
29. *Phillips v. Eastern Maine Medical Center*, 565 A2d 306 (Me. 1989).
30. *Myers v. Barringer*, 398 S.E. 2d 615 (N.C. App. 1990).

▶ ETHICS IN PRACTICE

Sarah T. and Beth W. were two RNs who worked the 3 to 11 P.M. shift on a busy surgical unit. Over the past 3 weeks, they had run a high census, had received a large number of seriously ill postoperative patients, and had been under a great deal of pressure to work overtime.

A particularly tenacious respiratory virus had been affecting several other members of the staff, causing many "call-ins." One afternoon during shift report, both Beth and Sarah realized that they were showing the initial symptoms of this respiratory virus. Because three very critical postoperative patients were to be admitted to the surgical unit during their shift, Beth and Sarah took some over-the-counter cold medications so that they could remain at work and not contribute to the shortage of nursing staff that already existed. They realized they probably should be at home and wondered if they might be causing more harm to the patients by communicating their illnesses to individuals who were highly susceptible to infections. They also recognized that the cold medications contained antihistamines that might affect their nursing judgments and performance of complicated skills.

What is the ethical dilemma in this situation? Did the nurses make the right decision in staying at work? What ethical principles are involved in making this type of decision? Could an "I was sick and taking medication" defense be used if either of them had made a serious mistake in patient care? What if a patient became ill with the viral infection the nurses had?

Intentional Torts

ETHICAL CONSIDERATIONS

▼ Nursing in general, and nurses in particular, are most commonly viewed by the public as the one group of health care providers whose primary goal is to understand, provide comfort, and help patients under their care. The public realizes that nurses are human, cannot know everything, and can sometimes make mistakes. The vast majority of lawsuits brought against nurses involve acts of omission, or negligence, and are, by definition, unintentional torts. Very few lawsuits brought against nurses fall into the category of intentional torts, that is, torts that require an act of intentional wrongdoing against a patient. Nurses are simply not viewed as individuals who would intentionally inflict injury upon or bring harm to a patient.

The ethical concept of **nonmaleficence**—the obligation to ''do no harm'' to a patient—is the underlying principle involved in the legal issue of intentional torts. If the principle of nonmaleficence were never violated, then no harm would ever come to patients, and there would be no grounds for lawsuits based on intentional torts.

Unfortunately, in the real world of health care, problems begin to arise when this principle is applied to actual health care situations. The principle of nonmaleficence presumes that there is a more-or-less unchanging set of criteria for determining what constitutes harm to a patient. Realistically, the term ''harm'' has a range of degrees and multiple meanings. For example, if nurses were to *never* harm their patients, they would never be able to start IVs, place nasogastric tubes, insert urinary catheters, or perform the numerous other procedures often necessary to help cure patients or even keep them alive.

Similarly, the principle of nonmaleficence has a tendency to conflict with other important ethical principles. Ethical principles such as patient autonomy, the nurse's obligation to truthfulness, and even beneficence can create situations where the nurse has to make a decision about which principle outweighs another

> ethically. It is at this point in the decision-making process that a nurse can become vulnerable to the legal system and intentional torts. Yet nurses are faced with these types of decisions on a daily basis. Often not making the decision can produce worse effects than making an informed, thoughtful decision and accepting the consequences.

OBJECTIVES

Upon completing this chapter, the reader will be able to:

1   Describe the concept of intentional torts and distinguish intentional tortious conduct from negligent conduct.
2   Discuss the elements of the intentional torts of defamation, invasion of privacy, assault, battery, false imprisonment, trespass to land, and intentional infliction of emotional distress, including the rights protected by each.
3   Give examples of each of the intentional torts described in the chapter.
4   Describe the defenses available to allegations of defamation.
5   Describe the four types of invasion of privacy and the media's right to patient information.
6   Discuss the differences between assault, battery, and false imprisonment.
7   Discuss a health facility's right to eject a patient or visitor from the premises.
8   Discuss the concept of intentional infliction of emotional distress.

INTRODUCTION

Intentional torts refer to willful or intentional acts that violate another person's rights or property. Intentional torts that can involve nurses include assault, battery, and false imprisonment. Some intentional torts such as assault and battery may also violate criminal laws, in which case defendants can be held liable for both civil damages and criminal violations.

BACKGROUND

The Nature of Intentional Torts

Legal scholars have struggled for years to define the term "tort" satisfactorily but have merely succeeded in achieving language so broad that it includes too much or so narrow that it leaves out some torts themselves.[1] It can be said that a tort is a wrong and that a tortious act is a wrongful act.

The law of torts has come to include many civil (as opposed to criminal) wrongs that have little in common except the principle that injuries are to be compensated and antisocial behavior is to be discouraged. Examples of torts include *assault, battery, trespass, false imprisonment, intentional infliction of emotional distress,* and *negligence.*

The concept of torts evolved from the fundamental principle that every person is bound to abstain from injuring the person or property of another or from infringing upon that other person's rights.[2] A distinguishing feature of tort law is that the duty to abstain from harming another is independent of any obligation created by a contract. The same act may constitute both a crime and a tort. However, a **crime** is an offense against the public that is prosecuted by the state, while a **tort** is a private injury that may be pursued in civil court by the injured party. Tort law focuses on compensating individuals for injuries they sustained because of the conduct of another.

For purposes of this discussion, torts may be divided into two clas-

---

Box 8–1   DIFFERENCES BETWEEN NEGLIGENCE AND INTENTIONAL TORTS

There are several distinct differences between intentional and nonintentional (negligence) torts. These can be characterized as differences in *intent, injury, duty,* and *consent.*

1. **Intent.** While negligence can occur without any intent to act, the person charged with an intentional tort must have intended to interfere with another person's rights, although not necessarily with a hostile motive. For example, a patient who did not consent to a surgical procedure may bring a legal action for battery, based on unauthorized touching, even if the surgical procedure was necessary and correctly done.

2. **Proof of damages.** Because intentional torts interfere with a person's rights, the plaintiffs do not have to prove that any actual injury occurred. The harm is the actual invasion of a privacy right, rather than a specific injury as required in negligence cases.

3. **Duty or standards of care.** Duty or standards of care are only relevant in negligence actions, not intentional torts. Also, expert witnesses are not needed to prove intentional torts but are usually required to establish standards of care in malpractice cases.

4. **Consent.** Consent is always a defense in intentional torts but not necessarily in negligence. For example, although patients may consent to a surgical procedure, they may still sue for negligence if injury occurs, but no legal action for battery can arise since battery is *unconsented* touching.

sifications: those arising from **intentional conduct** and those arising from *negligent conduct.* The principles of negligence and professional malpractice are discussed in Chapter 1. This chapter focuses on the legal implications of intentional tortious conduct by both health care providers and patients.

The distinction between negligent and intentional acts is also significant since most Good Samaritan statutes[3] do not protect the nurse from liability for harm caused by intentional tortious conduct.

Intent, Motive, and Damages as Elements of Intentional Torts

The concept of intent serves to distinguish intentional tortious acts from negligent tortious acts. **Intent** does not mean that the act is done intentionally; rather, it means that either the person acted for the purpose of causing an injury (or an invasion of a right) or that the person knows or is reasonably certain that an injury or invasion will result from the act. An example follows:

If a nurse picks up the wrong syringe during an emergency situation and administers epinephrine instead of aminophylline, causing cardiac arrest, there is no evidence that the nurse intended to cause the cardiac arrest. This would be an example of negligence, not the intentional tort of battery.

The motive or purpose behind an intentional act can play an important role in determining tort liability. For example, a motive like self-defense may justify an action that otherwise would be considered an intentional tort. On the other hand, an improper motive, such as the desire to harm the person, may support an additional jury award of **punitive damages,** that is, damages intended to punish the person committing the tort, in addition to the compensatory damages that are awarded for the injuries suffered by the victim.

To recover monetary damages from the person committing the tort, the victim must show injuries and damages resulting from the tortious actions. A wrong without any injury cannot be the basis of a lawsuit. However, in circumstances where there is a wrongful invasion of a clear legal right, the law presumes damage sufficient to support the lawsuit. In such a case, the damages recoverable may be nominal.

DEFAMATION

Defamation is defined as an oral or written communication that is false to a third party and that tends to *injure his or her reputation,* that is, diminish the esteem, respect, goodwill, or confidence in which the person is held, or cause adverse, derogatory, or unpleasant feelings or opinions against him or her.[4] Traditionally, **libel** is defamation in written form, while **slander** is oral defamation. Because of the nature of written documents, the libelled individual does not have to prove any actual damages in order to prevail. Certain types of slander, such as imputation of a crime or a sexually transmitted disease, also do not require proof of actual damages.

In *Schessler v. Keck*,[4a] an unmarried woman cook had a false-positive reaction to a syphilis blood test, although she had never had the disease. During treatments by a physician, a nurse had access to the medical record and was told about the false-positive condition. In spite of this information, the nurse told various friends that the physician was treating the woman for syphilis, resulting in economic losses to the woman's cooking and catering business. In the suit that followed, the appeals court found that the plaintiff had a cause of action for slander.

Frequently, defamatory remarks are made in the context of a joke. If a reasonable person understands the statement to be a joke, it is not actionable. In situations where words have an ambiguous meaning, or seem innocent, it must be proved that they contain an "innuendo" or meaning that makes them defamatory.[5]

Any living person may be defamed; however, a lawsuit may not be based upon the defamation of another. There are no grounds for a lawsuit for the defamation of a deceased person, unless the defamation is against those who are still living. Also a parent cannot sue for defamation of a child.

It is also possible to defame a corporation or other legal entity, such as a partnership or an unincorporated association, if the statements prejudice the public against the entity or injure its business reputation.

The defamatory material must be *published* or communicated to some third person who understands the defamatory meaning and recognizes that it applies to the defamed individual. A statement made only to the defamed person is not considered a publication. The publication may be oral, printed, or written, or conveyed by means of a picture, statement, or even gestures.

Publication may occur unintentionally, such as sending a defamatory personal letter knowing that the addressee is frequently absent and that others may read his or her mail. No publication occurs if the letter is stolen or opened despite the "personal" mark on the envelope and letter.

Repetition of defamatory publications is itself defamation. The person who repeats the defamation is himself or herself liable for the injury it causes to the defamed person's reputation even if he or she states the source of the information or indicates that it is only a rumor. The person who initially published the defamatory remarks may be liable for the repetition of them if the person had reason to expect that the remarks would be repeated. An example would be if nurse A tells the supervisor that she "heard" that nurse B is HIV positive and a cocaine abuser, when in fact this is not true.

Defenses

Truth

Truth is considered an absolute defense to assertions of civil liability for defamation. However, in some states, this defense is only available if the publication was made with the proper motive, that is, not intended to harm the subject of the remarks. Out of a strong regard for reputations, the law presumes that all defamation is false and the actor has the burden of proving its truth.

A person may not avoid liability by proving that the defamatory inference is true in part, nor can the proof of a single incident be a defense when the accusation alleged multiple acts of misconduct. If the accusations address specific misconduct, other acts of misconduct cannot be used to prove the truth of the accusations.

If a nurse is accused of stealing drugs, the fact that the same nurse was also caught stealing a patient's watch is no defense to the defamatory statements.

Information contained in medical records may on occasion be inaccurate and may adversely affect the patient's reputation. Allowing an unauthorized person access to records may precipitate an action alleging defamation. However, since truth is a defense to defamation allegations, the patient has to prove that the medical records were inaccurate in order to prevail.

Absolute Privilege

The law recognizes that publications made in certain legislative, judicial, and administrative proceedings are absolutely privileged and do not give rise to an action for defamation. For example, release of medical record information pursuant to a subpoena or court order is not actionable even if the medical records contained false and defamatory information.

In *Mickens v. Davis*,[6] the physician's written report stating that the plaintiff was suffering from a sexually transmitted disease (syphilis) was prepared in response to a court order entered in worker's compensation proceedings. The report was determined to be privileged.

Also, testimony given in open court or during the course of official proceedings before legislative bodies, even if defamatory, is protected by the absolute privilege.

Qualified Privilege

A **qualified privilege** is an exemption from liability for defamatory statements that are made in *good faith,* and without malice, concerning subjects in which the person has an interest or a duty to communicate to another with a corresponding interest or responsibility. A qualified privilege will not apply if the person does not believe the statement to be true or has no reasonable grounds for believing it to be true. Most states have laws that specify when a qualified privilege applies.

Medical records may contain inaccurate information that, if published, could adversely affect a person's reputation. Release of information concerning the medical condition or medical record of a patient must always be approached cautiously and must only occur in compliance with applicable state and federal laws. (For example, California state law proscribes the very limited circumstances under which information may be disclosed without the patient's written consent and to whom such disclosures may be made.) When a specific state law addresses the release of medical record information, the qualified privilege described above provides no protection if the disclosure is made in violation of the law.

The most common example of a qualified privilege occurs in employment situations:

> If a prospective employer asks a former employer about a job applicant and the prior employer divulges information about the applicant's work history, it is clear that both the potential employer and the prior employer have a legitimate interest in the exchange of information. If the information given is reasonably believed to be true, the disclosure would likely be protected by a qualified privilege.

When considering whether to disclose information, it is usually wiser to wait for a legitimate inquiry than to volunteer information.

When the speaker is protecting his or her reputation, legitimate interests, or the interest of another (providing information about a former employee who is applying for a job), the speaker is entitled to the protection of the qualified privilege. However, if a totally disinterested person requests information, the qualified privilege never applies and the speaker may be subject to allegations of defamation.

In *Bolling v. Baker,*[7] a nurse recovered $65,000. Her suit alleged defamation because, immediately after firing her, the doctor told his five office employees at a staff meeting that he could not work with her because she was a liar, not trustworthy, and not loyal to his practice.

Another context in which a qualified privilege may arise is medical staff peer review matters.

In *Murphy v. Herfort*,[8] a hospital official used qualified privilege as a defense against defamation claims by an anesthesiologist whose staff privileges had been suspended. The court ruled that statements made by the hospital official to colleagues about matters of concern to the hospital fell under the principle of qualified privilege. Although such privilege is not absolute, the anesthesiologist was not able to show that the hospital official had doubted the truth of any of his statements or that he had been motivated by a desire to injure the anesthesiologist.

Consent

If the defamed person gives consent to the publication of the defamatory material, then the person cannot later complain that it damaged his or her reputation. However, the scope of this consent may be limited, and consent to one form of publication does not imply consent to publish the defamation in a different manner. For example, permission to disclose information to a patient's spouse does not imply permission to disclose the information to the patient's employer.

Duty to Disclose Imposed by Law

When the nurse has a duty imposed by law to disclose confidential information about a patient and the disclosure is made in compliance with such law, the nurse is protected from liability. For example, under the California Penal Code section 11166, nurses are obligated to report known or suspected incidents of child abuse; the law further provides that nurses shall be immune from lawsuits when they make such a report.

There may be other circumstances in which reporting a patient's condition is mandated by state law, such as the diagnosis of certain communicable diseases. Whenever such reports are required and the report is made with the good faith belief that it is true, the patient should be precluded from bringing a lawsuit against the reporting individual.

INVASION OF PRIVACY

Another intentional tort, **invasion of privacy**, violates a person's right to be left alone and not be subjected to unreasonable interference with his or her personal life. In contrast to a defamation action, in an action for invasion of privacy, the plaintiff does not have to prove any actual damage or show false information. The plaintiff must show that:

1. The privacy right has been violated.
2. The public disclosure has occurred.
3. A reasonable person would object to the intrusion.

Examples of invasion of privacy in medical settings include using a patient's name or picture without consent in commercials or other publications or revealing names of persons in mental hospitals or drug rehabilitation centers.

The tort of invasion of privacy is fundamentally different from the tort of defamation. *Defamation* causes an injury to the character or reputation, whereas *invasion of privacy* injures the feelings without regard to any effect on the property, business interest, or standing of the individual in the community.[9] The right to privacy concerns one's peace of mind, the right to be left alone without being subjected to unwarranted or undesired publicity. The right to privacy is personal; it applies to the individual and does not extend to family members or businesses. Invasion of privacy is divided into four types of invasion:

1. Intrusion upon the seclusion or private concerns of another
2. Public disclosure of private facts
3. Publicity that places the person in a false light in the public eye
4. Appropriation of a person's name or likeness

Intrusion upon the Seclusion or Private Concerns of Another

Intrusion upon the seclusion or private concerns of another consists of intentional interference with another's interest in solitude or seclusion, regarding his or her person or private affairs. Eavesdropping upon private conversations, peering into windows, making unwanted telephone calls, illegally searching shopping bags, or invading a person's home are examples. Listening in on hospital telephone calls or searching through a patient's belongings without authorization may also be considered an invasion of the patient's privacy.

In addition, filming or otherwise documenting medical activities without the patient's permission may also be considered an invasion of privacy if it is done for purposes other than treatment of the patient.

In *Miller v. National Broadcasting Co.,*[10] an NBC news field producer was preparing a minidocumentary on fire department paramedics and their work. While filming Los Angeles fire department paramedics on their emergency calls, he entered the plaintiff's house and filmed the paramedics attempting to save the plaintiff's husband, who had suffered a heart attack. The film was broadcast on NBC's nightly news program. Although the plaintiff was present during the incident, no attempt was made to obtain her consent for the intrusion. The court ruled that reasonable people could regard the NBC camera crew's intrusion into the bedroom at a time of vulnerability and confusion as "highly offensive" conduct and a violation of the wife's right to privacy

Courts have found a right to privacy in bodily integrity regarding medical treatment and self-determination.[11] This reasoning has been used in a number of different cases: the courts have found a privacy interest inherent in the decision to forego or to remove life-sustaining treatment, because it is integral to the analysis of the issue of court-ordered medical treatment for competent adult patients. The right to privacy is also central in the debate on such issues as abortion and involuntary treatment of pregnant women to protect the well-being of the fetus.[12]

Public disclosure of private facts

Highly objectionable publicity of private information about a patient may be an invasion of privacy. (If the information is false, it may also give rise to a cause of action for defamation.) In some jurisdictions, the public must not have a legitimate interest in having the information available.[13] A notorious case of public disclosure of private facts is *Bazemore v. Savannah Hospital.*[14]

In this case, parents brought an action against a newspaper, its photographer, and the hospital for unauthorized publication of pictures of their malformed child who had been born with a heart outside of his body. The hospital had permitted a newspaper to photograph and publish pictures of the child's nude body without the permission or even knowledge of the parents. The Georgia Supreme Court ruled that the hospital had a duty to protect the child from "an invasion of an unauthorized person or persons, whereby its monstrosity and nude condition would likely be exposed to any persons, and particularly to the general public."[15]

In another case, the plaintiff was treated in the hospital for an alcohol-related illness. On admission, she had been assured of privacy by the hospital and its employees. Later, a physician sent a health insurance claim form with the medical diagnosis of "Acute and Chronic Alcoholism Detoxification" to the office of the plaintiff's employer. The employee who opened the mail was not authorized to receive insurance payment forms. The plaintiff alleged that the incident caused severe humiliation, embarrassment, and stress. The court held that the physician could be liable for violating the plaintiff's right to privacy by publishing personal information without the plaintiff's permission.[16]

Information of any kind and in any form pertaining to patients must be protected from improper disclosure. This includes medical records, diagnostic films, photographs, recordings, or tracings. The patient's written permission must be obtained prior to the disclosure of patient-identifiable data or information, unless allowed by state or federal law.

Publicity That Places the Person in a False Light in the Public Eye

Another aspect of invasion of privacy that comes up only rarely in the health care setting involves publicity that places a person in a false light in the public eye, such as the unauthorized use of a person's name on a petition or as a candidate for office, or the use of a person's picture to illustrate a book or an article implying a connection that does not exist. Although public interest may justify the use of an appropriate and pertinent illustration (such as using the victim's picture to accompany a news story), when the person has no relation to the story, use of his or her image is considered an invasion of privacy.

Appropriation of a Person's Name or Likeness

The use of a person's photograph or image without consent for commercial purposes, such as advertising, is a well-recognized basis for liability based on invasion of privacy.

Invasion of privacy occurred when a plastic surgeon used several "before" and "after" photographs of his patient's cosmetic surgery without her consent at a department store presentation and on a television program promoting the presentation.[17]

In another case, the patient had given her physician permission to film her caesarean section on the understanding that the film would be exhibited to medical societies and used to further medical science. The pictures were actually included in a motion picture entitled "Birth" that was shown in commercial theaters. The patient was allowed to sue both the physician and the camera operator for invasion of her privacy.[18]

Release of Information to the News Media

Inquiries about patients by news media present serious concerns regarding invasion of the patient's privacy. Since the right to privacy does not prohibit publication of information that is of public or general interest, the hospital may release limited information about a patient's condition in certain circumstances. Release of factual information such as births and patient admissions and discharges ordinarily does not violate a patient's privacy rights.

There is no legal obligation to disclose information of any kind about a patient to news media. Each facility should have a written policy that describes who will respond to media inquiry and what information may be released. This policy should comply with state and federal law. For example, California law[19] permits a health care provider to disclose the patient's name, address, age, and sex; a general description of the reason for treatment (whether an injury, burn, poisoning, or some unrelated condition); the general nature of the injury, burn, poisoning, or other condition; the general condition of the patient; and any information that is not medical information. However, this provision of law is ineffective if the patient specifically requests that the information not be released.

If the patient is receiving treatment for drug or alcohol abuse, the federal regulations set forth in the "Confidentiality of Alcohol and Drug Abuse Patient Records," 42 Code of Federal Regulations, Chapter 1, Subchapter A, Part 2, provide special rules regarding the disclosure of information about the patient. The regulations apply to any federally assisted program that provides alcohol or drug abuse diagnosis, treatment, or referral for treatment. No information may be disclosed about the patient, including the fact that the person is or was a patient in the facility, without either the patient's written consent or a court order. (This prohibition even applies to subpoenas for the medical records of the patient.)

There is often considerable interest in the medical treatment of a public figure. If the personality and affairs of an individual have already become public, the press has the right to inform the public about legitimate matters of public interest. To some extent that person has lost the right to keep his or her affairs private. This may continue to be true long after the person has ceased to be a celebrity. However, after some time, the individual may have the right to sue for invasion of privacy.

On occasion, private individuals may become caught up in publicity as a result of circumstances such as accidents or crimes, which make their condition of interest to the public. This involvement also causes a loss of some of their right of privacy. Publicity surrounding victims of crimes, suicides, accidents, and rare diseases does not usually give rise to liability for invasion of privacy. However, some courts have ruled that the right of privacy should include the right to obtain medical treatment without the publication of this information to the news media.

In one case, *Barber v. Time, Inc.,*[20] a patient was permitted to sue for the publication of her name and picture in a story concerning an eating disorder. Because the use of the patient's name and photograph were not considered necessary to the story, the invasion of privacy could not be justified as newsworthy.

ASSAULT AND BATTERY

Battery

Assault and battery, terms that are often used together, are distinctly different legal actions, as discussed in Chapter 6. *Battery* is the invasion of a person's privacy by unpermitted touching. The most common example of battery in the hospital setting occurs when surgical procedures are performed without patient consent.

The following case illustrates how a nurse can be held liable for battery against patients:

In a nursing home, a quadriplegic patient with an external catheter also had a p.r.n. ("as needed") order for an indwelling catheter. When the nurse inserted the indwelling catheter, the patient objected but was told to "shut up." After requests from the patient and family, the catheter was removed but subsequently reinserted. The patient begged that it not be put in because of past complications and pain, but his objections were ignored. Finally, a nurse jerked the catheter out, causing injury. The family sued for damages. The Louisiana Supreme Court found that "a nurse commits a battery upon a patient when she performs an invasive procedure like the insertion of an indwelling catheter over the objections of the patient." The patient recovered $25,000 for pain and suffering.[21]

Assault

Unlike the touching element in battery, *assault* is the fear of being touched, or a threatened battery. To bring a suit claiming assault, the plaintiff must feel fear or apprehension of an immediate harmful or threatening contact. The harm is not the actual contact (which would then give rise to a battery charge), but the mental fear caused by the threatened contact. However, most suits in which an assault has occurred also include a charge of battery.

In *Baca v. Velez*,[22] an operating room nurse in a New Mexico hospital had a disagreement with an orthopedic surgeon, during which the nurse alleged that the doctor jabbed her in the back with the sharp end of a bone chisel. Subsequently, she brought suit against the doctor for assault and battery. The appeals court found no evidence of conduct that would substantiate an assault charge, even though the physician could be found to have committed a battery on the nurse. The court explained that all batteries do not include an assault. For there to be an assault, there must have been an "act, threat or menacing conduct that causes another person to reasonably believe that he is in danger of receiving an immediate battery." Since the injury occurred to the nurse's back, the court found that there was no evidence to prove that she feared for her safety *before* the "touching" with the bone chisel took place.

When force is used to restrain a person, the person exerting the force may be liable for both false imprisonment and assault and battery. However, treatment administered to a person who has been improperly detained in the hospital will not always constitute assault or battery. If the treatment itself is proper, it does not become unlawful merely because it was given while a person is improperly detained.

CONSENT AND ASSAULT AND BATTERY

The goal of the torts of assault and battery in the medical context is to protect the sanctity of the human body. As stated by the eminent jurist Justice Cardozo:

> Every human being of adult years and sound mind has a right to determine what shall be done with his own body, and a surgeon who performs an operation without his patient's consent commits an assault for which he is liable in damages.[23]

Any kind of medical, surgical, or nursing procedure that is performed without the patient's consent is considered a battery. A claim of battery may be brought against a physician, or other health professional assisting the physician, such as a nurse or technician, who performs a medical procedure on the patient, however slight the physical contact may be, without the patient's consent. A battery may also occur if the health care provider exceeds the scope of the consent or performs a different procedure than that for which consent was obtained.

With the evolution of informed consent principles and the inquiry that many courts now make into the adequacy and quality of the physician's disclosure of information, patients are now alleging medical negligence as well as the intentional torts of assault and battery. The distinction between allegations of liability for negligence and liability for an intentional tort can be of considerable procedural importance in a lawsuit.

The difference between negligence and battery can be explained by considering the concept of informed consent. If the health care practitioner performs the treatment that the patient consented to, but fails to make a proper disclosure when obtaining that consent, the tort is negligence; if the procedure was different from the one the patient consented to, the tort is battery.[24]

In *Berkey v. Anderson*,[25] the patient thought he was consenting to a procedure no more complicated than the electromyograms that he had previously undergone. However, the actual procedure performed was a myelogram involving a spinal puncture. The situation was classified by the court as a battery because there was a deliberate intent to deviate from the given consent.

Failure to obtain the patient's consent in accordance with applicable legal standards may result in a charge of battery or negligence, or even unprofessional conduct, against the health care provider. The principles of informed consent are discussed at length in Chapter 6.

Medical or Surgical Treatment

Clearly, performing a surgical or medical procedure without consent constitutes a battery. In one case, an oral surgeon removed the lower teeth of his patient without reviewing the patient's charts, which indicated that the patient wanted to retain his five lower teeth. He was accused of battery.[26]

Mental Health Patients

Assertions of assault and battery can be an issue in the treatment of voluntary and involuntary psychiatric patients. As with false imprisonment allegations, the validity of these allegations depends upon the nature of the common and statutory law of the individual state where the treatment occurred.

After initial drug detoxification in the hospital, a mentally ill patient was committed to the psychiatric unit, where he was forcibly given antibiotics for treatment of life-threatening urinary failure. Although he charged assault and battery and false imprisonment, the court found that the treatment given to him was authorized by both the common and the statutory law of the state.[27]

Admission to a mental health facility alone, either voluntarily or involuntarily, is not the deciding factor when analyzing whether the patient is capable of making informed decisions about health care. Even if a person is involuntarily committed to a facility, he or she is considered to be capable of consenting to treatment unless there has been a judicial determination to the contrary. Involuntary commitment does not automatically deprive a person of the right to reasonably safe conditions of confinement, the right to freedom from unreasonable bodily restraints, or the right to refuse psychotropic or antipsychotic medications.[28] Disregard of a competent mental health patient's wishes may constitute assault and battery.

Defenses Available

An exception to the duty to adequately inform patients of the risk of treatment exists in the case of an *emergency* where the patient's wishes are not known. If the patient is unconscious or otherwise unable to give informed consent and the medical procedure is immediately necessary to protect the health or life of the patient, informed consent is not required.[29] The emergency treatment exception is discussed further in Chapter 6.

The principle of **self-defense** is also available to avoid liability for acts that would otherwise constitute assault or battery. The person claiming self defense must reasonably believe that a danger exists to himself or herself or to others and must use only the force that is reasonably necessary.

A 23-month-old child clamped her teeth on the finger of a medical student as he was treating her for a lacerated tongue. When he was unable to extricate his finger, he slapped the child on the cheek with his other hand. The court denied recovery for assault and battery, finding that the force was required and not applied in an improper manner. Although the court considered the medical student's action to be rash, it found it neither malicious nor severe and the child was not injured.[30]

FALSE IMPRISONMENT

False imprisonment is defined as the unlawful intentional confinement of another within fixed boundaries so that the confined person is conscious of the confinement or harmed by it.[31] The restraints used to confine another may be chemical, physical, or emotional, that is, intimidation. There must be a direct restraint of the person for some appreciable length of time, however short, compelling the person to stay or go somewhere against the person's will. Merely preventing a person from going to a particular place is not false imprisonment.

Detention of Patients

Many specialty treatment facilities have rules and policies that require the patient to agree to remain in the facility until discharge. Confinement of a patient against his or her will pursuant to such policies has been ruled to be false imprisonment.

In *Cook v. Highland Hospital*,[32] the patient was admitted to a private hospital for rehabilitative treatment. Upon admission, she signed an agreement obligating her to abide by the rules and regulations of the facility; she believed she would be free to leave whenever she wanted. However, when she refused to comply with the hospital authorities, she was confined for 32 days and was locked in a room despite her demand to leave. Even though the patient had agreed to abide by the hospital rules, the court said that this agreement did not justify detaining her against her will.

Detention of Vulnerable Patients

Many times, allegations of false imprisonment arise from circumstances involving particularly vulnerable patients such as the elderly, the impaired, or the mentally ill. Nurses must be especially aware of the rights of patients who may not be able to speak up and defend themselves.

Preventing a voluntary nursing home patient from leaving the premises may result in liability for false imprisonment.

In *Big Town Nursing Home, Inc. v. Newman,*[33] a 67-year-old man was kept against his will for 51 days. Three days after he was admitted by a nephew, the man attempted to leave, but was forcibly returned to the facility by employees. Following his five or six escape attempts, he was confined to a "restraint chair" and denied the use of the telephone and his own clothes. The court found that the actions of the nursing home staff were in utter disregard of the man's legal rights and that the staff acted recklessly, willfully, and maliciously in unlawfully detaining him.

In certain circumstances, confinement of intoxicated patients may be found to be appropriate to protect them from harming themselves.

In *Blackman for Blackman v. Rifkin,*[34] the plaintiff's extreme intoxication, coupled with her head trauma, warranted her retention in an emergency room to prevent further harm to herself or others. The court ruled that the hospital could assume that she would have consented to treatment if she had not been in that condition and dismissed the patient's false imprisonment claims.

The involuntary confinement of persons who are mentally ill or who are considered to be a danger to themselves or others is highly regulated by state laws. The involuntary hospitalization of a person in a mental institution in violation of the statute constitutes false imprisonment.[35] Nurses must be familiar with these laws since they can be quite specific in some states regarding the responsibilities of the hospital and health care providers. Failure to understand and comply with the applicable laws can lead to liability for false imprisonment.

In *Hapgood v. Biloxi Regional Medical Center,*[36] the patient charged that she was falsely imprisoned when the hospital failed to follow statutory commitment procedures and improperly subjected her to 10 weeks of involuntary treatment at the hospital, including 15 episodes of electroconvulsive therapy after she was diagnosed as exhibiting acute schizophrenic reaction.

TRESPASS TO LAND

Trespass to land is the unlawful interference with another's possession of land. The tort may be committed by an intentional or a negligent act.[37] Trespass to land may occur when a person intrudes onto a property, fails to leave a property, throws or places something on the land, or causes another person to enter the property.[38]

Trespass is most frequently encountered in the health care field when the patient refuses to leave upon discharge or the visitor refuses to comply with visiting policies or is asked to leave by facility personnel. Trespass may also occur in the context of protest actions (such as animal rights or antiabortion protests or labor disputes).

In *Fardig v. Municipality of Anchorage*,[39] antiabortion protesters were convicted of criminal trespass for refusing requests to cease distributing literature to patrons of a women's clinic and to leave its parking lot.

A private health care facility is considered private property, and people do not have the absolute right to remain on the premises. When a patient, family member, or visitor refuses to leave the facility, staff should attempt to reason with the person. If reasoning is unsuccessful, then it may be necessary to pursue legal remedies such as arresting the individual for trespass or obtaining a court order directing the person to leave the facility.

North Carolina law makes it a crime for a patient to trespass by refusing to leave a hospital once he or she has been discharged by the attending physician. The decision to discharge the patient must be based on the medical opinion of two physicians. A patient found guilty of criminal trespass may be fined or imprisoned.

During labor disputes, only peaceful, lawful strike and picketing activities are permitted. While the federal National Labor Relations Act provisions govern most aspects of strikes and picketing activities, state criminal statutes regulating strike violence and trespass may be enforced to maintain order.

INTENTIONAL INFLICTION OF EMOTIONAL DISTRESS

Intentional infliction of emotional distress is the intentional invasion of a person's peace of mind. The conduct must be outrageous and beyond all bounds of decency. Ordinary rude or insulting behavior is not enough. For an example of outrageous behavior, consider this recent case:

A chronic schizophrenic patient of low intelligence gave birth to an autistic child while she was under a doctor's care residing in a convalescent hospital. She alleged that while she resided in the hospital, the doctor knew she was of childbearing age, had been sexually active, and was in an environment where sexual relations frequently occurred. The plaintiff further alleged that the doctor failed to prescribe birth control pills, even though he knew she had requested them, and failed to examine her when she began exhibiting symptoms of pregnancy. Upon later determining that she was pregnant, he did not counsel her that her mental condition was genetically linked and could be passed to a child, nor did he discuss abortion or inform the patient that the stress of having a child frequently exacerbates the mental problems of schizophrenics. The doctor also did not take the patient off the strong psychotropic medications or inform her that these drugs were contraindicated for pregnancy and could seriously harm the fetus. The jury found that this evidence was proof of medical negligence and intentional infliction of emotional distress and awarded the patient $1,024,266, of which $750,000 were punitive damages intended to punish the physician.[40]

IMPLICATIONS FOR NURSING PRACTICE

The liability for intentional tortious conduct rests squarely on the person performing the tortious acts. However, there may also be circumstances where the employer is held liable for the injuries as well. Except in cases of outrageous or malicious conduct, tortious conduct is most likely to result because the nurse is unaware that his or her actions are not protected by applicable laws. In order to avoid such liability, it is advisable to become familiar with the state and federal laws that are likely to apply to the practice of nursing. Such laws include reporting requirements relating to child abuse, elder or dependent-adult abuse, victims of crimes, and communicable diseases. It is especially important to become knowledgeable about state laws regarding the confidentiality of AIDS diagnosis and HIV antibody status. If the nurse is dealing with chemical-dependency patients, he or she should also be familiar with federal and state drug and alcohol treatment confidentiality laws. The mental health nurse should be knowledgeable about involuntary and voluntary treatment and confinement laws. The state laws relating to the release of patient information should also be reviewed. Avoiding intentional tort liability involves understanding what intentional conduct is permitted and what is considered improper and tortious in the jurisdiction where the nurse practices.

Points to Remember

▶ To successfully prosecute a lawsuit based on the allegations of an intentional tort, a person must prove that the act was committed with the intent to cause an injury, that the act was an invasion of a right, or that it was substantially certain that the injury or invasion would result from the act. It must also be shown that the person was damaged by the action in some way.

▶ To be considered defamatory, publications must be made to some third person and must injure the victim's reputation in some way. The statements must not be true or protected by some absolute or qualified privilege, and the disclosure of the information must not have been required by some state or federal law.

▶ Invasion of privacy can occur in a number of contexts in the health care setting. Unreasonably revealing the personal or private affairs of a patient may interfere with the solitude of the person and, if false, may also give rise to a cause of action for defamation.

▶ There is no legal obligation to disclose information of any kind about a patient to the news media.

▶ Administering treatment against the patient's will may be considered assault and battery.

▶ When force is used to detain a patient, liability for false imprisonment may also exist.

▶ Performing a medical or surgical procedure without the patient's consent may give rise to allegations of both negligence and battery.

▶ The nurse should become familiar with applicable state and federal laws relating to reporting obligations and requirements of confidentiality of patient information.

Study Questions

1. Define an intentional tort.
2. Distinguish an intentional tort from negligent conduct.
3. Give examples of and discuss the following torts:
   a. Defamation
   b. Invasion of privacy
   c. Assault
   d. Battery
   e. False imprisonment
   f. Trespass to land
   g. Intentional infliction of emotional distress

4. Relate how you can prevent invasion of privacy for your patients.
5. Define and give an example of a medical battery.
6. Discuss how informed consent relates to medical battery.

REFERENCES

1. *See* Keeton, WP, et al., *Prosser and Keaton on the Law of Torts,* § 1, at 1 & 2, ed 5, 1984.
2. Calif. Civil Code § 1708 (West 1985).
3. Good Samaritan statutes vary from state to state but generally absolve from liability the health care provider who in good faith provides emergency care at the scene of an emergency.
4. *See* Keeton, WP, et al., *Prosser and Keaton on the Law of Torts,* § 111, at 773, ed 5, 1984.
4a. Schessler v. Keck, 271 P.2d 588 (Cal. App. 1954).
5. 5 B.E. Witkin, *Summary of California Law, Torts,* § 493 at 580 (9th ed. 1988).
6. *Mickens v. Davis,* 132 Kan. 49 (1931).
7. *Bolling v. Baker,* 671 S.W.2d 559 (Tex. App. 1984).
8. *Murphy v. Herfort,* 528 N.Y.S.2d 117 (1988).
9. *Fairfield v. American Photocopy Equipment Co.,* 138 C.A.2d 82, 86 (1955).
10. *Miller v. National Broadcasting Co.,* 187 C.A.3d 1463 (1986).
11. *See Schloendorff v. Society of New York Hospital,* 211 N.Y. 125, 127 (1914).
12. *See* Mathieu, M, *Respecting Liberty and Preventing Harm: Limits of State Intervention in Prenatal Choice,* 8 Harv. J.L. & Pub. Pol'y 19 (1986); and Jonsen, A, *Transition from Fetus to Infant: A Problem of Law and Ethics,* 37 Hastings L.J. 697 (1986).
13. *See* Restatement (Second) of Torts § 652D cmts. a-k (1977).
14. *Bazemore v. Savannah Hospital,* 155 S.E. 194 (Ga. 1930).
15. *Id.* at 195.
16. *Prince v. St. Francis-St. George Hospital, Inc.,* 484 N.E.2d 265 (Ohio App. 1985).
17. *Vassiliades v. Garfinckel's, Brooks Bros.,* 492 A.2d 580 (D.C. App. 1985).
18. *Feeney v. Young,* 191 A.D. 501 (1920).
19. Calif. Civil Code § 56.16 (West 1982).
20. *Barber v. Time, Inc.,* 159 S.W.2d 291 (Mo. 1942).
21. *Roberson v. Provident House,* 576 So.2d 992 (La. 1991).
22. *Baca v. Velez,* 833 P.2d 1194 (N.M.App. 1992).
23. *Canterbury v. Spence,* 464 F.2d 772 (D.C. Cir. 1972), quoting *Schloendorff v. Society of New York Hospital,* 211 N.Y. 125 (1914).
24. 5 B.E. Witkin, *Summary of California Law, Torts,* § 358 (9th ed. 1988).
25. *See* discussion of the *Berkey* case by the California Supreme Court in *Cobbs v. Grant,* 8 Cal.3d 229, 239 (1972).
26. *Gaskin v. Goldwasser,* 520 N.E.2d 1085 (Ill. 1988).
27. *Patrich v. Menorah Medical Center,* 636 S.W.2d 134 (Mo.App. 1982).
28. *See Rennie v. Klein,* 102 S.Ct. 3506 (1982); and *Large v. Superior Court,* 714 P.2d 399 (Ariz. 1986).
29. *See* Calif. Bus & Prof. Code § 2397 (West 1990).
30. *Mattocks v. Bell,* 194 A.2d 307 (D.C.App. 1963).
31. *See* Restatement (Second) of Torts § 35 (1965).
32. *Cook v. Highland Hospital,* 84 S.E. 352 (N.C. 1915).
33. *Big Town Nursing Home, Inc. v. Newman,* 461 S.W.2d 195 (Tex.Civ.App. 1970).
34. *Blackman for Blackman v. Rifkin,* 759 P.2d 54 (Colo.App. 1988), *cert. den.* (1989).

35. *Maben v. Rankin*, 55 Cal.2d 139 (1961).

36. *Hapgood v. Biloxi Regional Medical Center*, 540 So.2d 630 (Miss. 1989).

37. 5 B.E. Witkin, *Summary of California Law, Torts*, § 604, at 704 (9th ed. 1988).

38. *See* Restatement (Second) of Torts § 158 (1977).

39. *Fardig v. Municipality of Anchorage*, 785 P.2d 911 (Alaska App. 1990).

40. *Adams v. Murakami*, No. C418409 (Los Angeles County Superior Court).

▶ ## ETHICS IN PRACTICE

Three days after his 81st birthday, Mr. E. was admitted to the medical unit with a diagnosis of metastatic cancer of the liver. He had had several full-course treatments of chemotherapy and radiation during the previous year with only temporary remissions of the disease. His condition had deteriorated rapidly during the previous month, and his family was no longer able to care for him at home. Dr. K., his physician, expected Mr. E. to die within a few weeks, if not sooner, and admitted him to the hospital primarily for pain control. On admission, Dr. K. ordered morphine sulfate (MS) 5 mg IV to be given every 2 hours around the clock.

Although this was a relatively large dose of a strong narcotic medication to be given this frequently, Mr. E. tolerated the treatment for the first 36 hours and reported a significant reduction in his pain. On the third morning after his admission, Mr. E. was difficult to arouse for his morning vital signs and breakfast. When his nurse, Joan F., RN, finally did get Mr. E. awake, he was confused, his blood pressure was 82/50 with shallow respirations at 10 per minute. He still complained of severe generalized body pain and asked for "more of that medication that helped so much the day before."

Joan did not give Mr. E. his scheduled 8 A.M. dose of MS. She phoned Dr. K. and reported her assessment of the patient, expressing her belief that continuing the medication at the previously prescribed dose and frequency would be fatal to this patient. Dr. K., who had been up most of the night with an emergency patient, stated sarcastically, "And Mr. E. has such a productive life to look forward to—give the medication like I ordered it! And don't call me any more about this—I'll be in after lunch!" and slammed down the phone.

What should Joan do? If she continues to give the medication at the prescribed dose and frequency and the patient dies, could she be held liable for an intentional tort? What are the ethical principles involved in this case? How could she best resolve the dilemma?

Professional Liability Insurance

ETHICAL CONSIDERATIONS

▼ From a historical viewpoint, litigation against health care providers is a very recent development. During the 1940s and World War II, in particular, health care made major strides forward in the use of antibiotics, psychotropic medications, surgery, and life-support equipment. Since then, health care has become technically sophisticated with an ever-increasing success level in the cure of serious diseases, treatment of critical injuries, and prolonging of life by medical and nursing interventions. With the advances in medical technology, nursing has become a skill-oriented practice working to enhance the life-saving efforts of medicine.

Unfortunately, as nursing and health care have become more dependent on technology, the treatment of patients has become less personalized. The public has begun to perceive the health sciences as infallible and health care as a person-to-institution relationship. Because these patients no longer feel the traditional close personal relationship between the health care provider and the sick, they have become more inclined to use litigation as a means of retribution for harm resulting from health care treatments, medications, or surgery.

During the 1970s the malpractice crisis exploded, and health care providers at all levels began to recognize the vast scope of potential lawsuits that could be filed against them. A medical malpractice lawsuit could be filed by any patient at almost any time.

Because physicians were the most common early targets of malpractice lawsuits, they quickly recognized the need to increase their liability coverage under their existing malpractice insurance. Nurses, however, were much slower to acquire malpractice coverage, perhaps because lawsuits against them were much less common and it was difficult to find insurance companies that would issue malpractice policies to nurses. Even today, nurses vacillate between acquiring and not acquiring individual malpractice coverage. Most nurses are covered to some degree by their employer's insurance policy, but these policies have as the primary goal protection of the employer, not the nurse.

In a perfect world where no mistakes were ever made, where every treatment was successful, where medications had no side effects, and where every patient was physiologically the same, there would be no need for malpractice insurance. But in the real world, nurses deal with increasingly complicated technology, as well as patients who are older and more critically ill, and things sometimes go wrong. The ethical principle of accountability is one of the key elements in the establishment of a profession. Nurses must be responsible for their actions as professionals, including actions that are sometimes in error. In accepting responsibility for their actions, nurses acknowledge the fact that they do make mistakes. In the litigious atmosphere of today's society, it would seem logical for malpractice insurance to be as much a requirement of nursing practice as uniforms, an automobile, a telephone, and a nursing license. If for no other reason, malpractice insurance will cover the cost of the lawyers who provide the defense. Often the cost of the defense alone, regardless of the outcome of the case, is sufficient to financially destroy a nurse.

OBJECTIVES

Upon reading this chapter, the reader will be able to:

1 Discuss the types of insurance policies available to professional nurses.
2 Discuss whether a specific policy matches an individual nurse's practice needs.
3 Define the issues that should be considered when deciding between employer-sponsored coverage and individual policy coverage.

Box 9–1   BASIC TYPES OF POLICIES

1. Occurrence basis: Covers injuries that occur during the period covered by the policy.
2. Claims-made: Covers injuries only if the injury occurs within the policy period *and* the claim is reported to the insurance company during the policy period or during "the tail."
   a. **Tail:** An uninterrupted extension of the policy period, also known as the *extending reporting endorsement.*

INTRODUCTION

Nurses cannot afford to be without liability insurance. However, the kinds of decisions that must be made—whether to purchase an individual or an institutional policy, an occurrence or a claims-made policy—can make the selection process confusing. This chapter looks at the issues nurses should consider when choosing a policy to ensure they have the type of coverage that will best protect them if they should be sued.

WHAT TO LOOK FOR IN AN INSURANCE POLICY

The **insurance policy** is an agreement by the insurance company stating that, in exchange for a premium, the company will pay money when certain injuries are caused by the person insured by the policy.

The Two Types of Policy Forms: Which Type Is Best?

There are two types of liability insurance policies: **occurrence basis policies** and **claims-made policies.** An occurrence basis policy covers injuries that occur during the period in which the policy is in effect, which is known as the *policy period.* Occurrence policies are recommended because once the coverage is in place, the nurse is insured regardless of when a lawsuit is brought or whether or not the policy has been renewed.

On the other hand, a claims-made policy is in effect only if the injury occurs within the policy period and the claim is reported to the insurance company either during that policy period or during an uninterrupted extension of that policy period (the "tail"). A **tail** provides coverage for periods when the nurse is exposed to certain professional liabilities but no longer has a claims-made policy in force. For example, if a nurse leaves the practice of nursing in 1994 and has a claims-made policy, a tail should be purchased to cover the possible lawsuits that could be filed for acts of negligence that occurred in 1994 or before. If the nurse has a claims-made policy, continuous coverage must be maintained to assure that protection will be available if a claim is made in the future.

Nurses practicing in such "long-tail" specialities as labor and delivery or pediatrics (where there may be a long period of time between an injury and an assertion of a claim) need occurrence coverage or the continuous renewal of a claims-made policy. Influencing this long tail period may be the length of the statute of limitations in the state. For example, if a nurse practices in a state in which the statute of limitations is tolled (suspended) for minors, then lawsuits may be filed on behalf of a child until the child reaches the age of 21.[1]

Occurrence coverage is rarely made available to hospitals, so hospitals typically carry claims-made policies as their institutional coverage. This practice can present difficulties for the nurse who relies solely on an employer-sponsored institutional liability policy. The institution can cancel the claims-made policy without buying the tail. That leaves no coverage for claims asserted after the policy is canceled, even for incidents that occur while the policy is in force. If the nurse is involved in one of those incidents, the institution's responsibility or even financial ability to defend him or her and pay for the injury can become a serious issue. The nurse being sued could have to pay for the defense of the suit or for the money judgment awarded to the plaintiff.

Occurrence basis policies are still available to individual professionals. Group policies that cover partnerships and professional corporations may also be available on an occurrence basis.

Box 9–2   WHAT TO LOOK FOR IN AN INSURANCE POLICY

1. Type of insurance policy
   a. Claims-made
   b. Occurrence
   c. Individual
   d. Institutional
   e. Group
2. The insuring agreement
3. Types of injuries covered
4. Exclusions
5. Who is covered
6. Limits of policy and deductibles
7. Financial strength of the insurance company
8. Right to select counsel
9. Right to consent to settlement or trial of suit
10. Cost of policy

The Insuring Agreement

A **liability policy** is a written agreement between the health care provider and the insurance company. The insurance company agrees to pay compensation to a person for injuries caused either by an act of omission or commission by the insured health care provider. The insurance company's promise to pay in exchange for premiums is called an **insuring agreement.**

In nursing liability policies, the insuring agreement takes one of two forms:

Form A

The Company will pay on behalf of the Insured all sums which the Insured shall become legally obligated to pay as damages because of injury to a *patient* or *client* [emphasis supplied] to which this insurance applies, caused by a *medical incident* [emphasis supplied] which occurs during the policy period (from Chicago Insurance Co., Nursing Professional Liability Policy, Form CIC-44-36 [6/87]).

Form B

The Company will pay on behalf of the Individual Insured all sums which the Insured shall become legally obligated to pay as damages because of injury arising out of the rendering of or failure to render *professional services* during the policy period by the Insured, or by any person for whose acts or omissions such Insured is legally responsible (from Transamerica Insurance Group, Professional/Personal Liability Policy, Form 518255).

Form A is limited because it covers only injuries to identifiable patients and only those injuries resulting from identifiable medical incidents. The coverage is limited to a narrow set of nursing activities: hands-on clinical care. Form B broadly covers injury to anyone in the scope of professional services.

Types of Injuries Covered

In addition to covering specified acts, both insuring agreements refer to certain injuries. The language is both broad *and* limiting. In both instances, compensable "injury" is not defined and is broad enough to include all types of injury: bodily injury, mental anguish, property damage, and economic injury. However, the insurance company will pay only if the insured nurse is sued for **damages,** which means *money.*

The "damages only" limitation becomes critical if the sole objective of the lawsuit is to force the nurse to do or avoid doing a certain act. This type of suit is called a *specific performance lawsuit* or *injunctive relief action.* An example would be a doctor suing a nurse to stop the "unlawful practice of medicine." The nurse's insurance policy with either of the insuring agreements (forms A or B) would not respond until a claim for *monetary* damages is also asserted.

Professional nursing associations, which support the expansion of nursing practice and sponsor insurance policies to ensure that their members are protected, should be aware of the limitations. They should also consider how to ensure that defense funds are available for the insured if an injunctive relief action that is excluded by an association-sponsored "damages only" policy is brought against a member.

Exclusions

Items not covered by a policy are called **exclusions.** If an alleged activity or circumstance is excluded, then the insurance company may take the position that the nurse's defense costs will not be paid if it is determined that the excluded activity occurred. This insurance company's position is called a *reservation of rights,* because the company reserves the right to deny coverage once the facts are determined. If it is ultimately determined that there is an excluded activity, then the insured must reimburse the insurance company for the defense costs. Other companies will expect the nurse to pay the bills and costs of litigation until the alleged activity is proved *not* to be excluded.

There are some professional liability policies that have recently added an exclusion for the transmission of AIDS from provider to patient. Of equal concern are exclusions for claims arising out of:

1. Sexual abuse of a patient.
2. Injury caused while under the influence of drugs or alcohol.
3. Criminal activity.
4. Punitive damages—damages awarded to "punish" the defendant for egregious acts or omissions.

More subtle are exclusions resulting from the very nature of the insurance policy: is it written to cover institutional or individual nursing liability? The broadest coverage available is provided by an individual liability policy in which only acts beyond the scope of nursing practice are excluded. Resolution of a dispute over the definition of the scope of nursing practice may require testimony to determine whether the acts alleged are taught as part of a nursing curriculum and therefore "nursing practice." So long as the allegations are found to be within the scope of nursing practice, and not otherwise excluded, the individual nursing professional liability policy covers the nurse. Naturally, all practices taught as part of a nursing curriculum should be considered within the scope of nursing practice.

Institutional liability policies offer less protection for the nurse; they exclude acts beyond the nurse's scope of employment. It is possible for an act to fall within the definition of nursing practice yet still be prohibited by an institution. For example, an institution could prohibit nurses from administering certain medications intravenously. For an institutional policy to cover an alleged act, two tests must be met:

1. The act is not excluded as beyond the scope of nursing practice.
2. The act is not excluded as beyond the scope of employment as defined in a specific institution.

Who Is Covered?

The party who purchases a professional liability policy is always covered by it. The purchaser is the *Named Insured,* who can be an individual, an institution, or a group.

In addition to the purchaser, who else is covered by the policy?

1. On an individual policy, the individual nurse's employees or agents may be covered.
2. On an institutional liability policy, usually employees and volunteers, perhaps even consultants to the organization, are covered.
3. On a group policy, a group of similarly licensed professionals and the business corporation which that group of professionals commonly owns are covered. Whether other types of professionals can be added, even as employees of the master policy owners, is a case-by-case inquiry.[2]

All three types of policies can be endorsed to cover not only "insureds," but "former insureds for acts committed while insureds." This can be verified with the institution so that the employee who leaves the hospital's employment can continue to be covered by the former employer's in-force insurance program.

Limits and Deductibles

In exchange for premiums, the insurance company agrees to pay up to a certain amount on behalf of an insured. This amount is called the policy's **limit of liability.** The policy limit is always expressed in two ways:

1. The amount that can be paid for one incident (the *per incident* or *per occurrence* limit).
2. The amount that can be paid in any one policy year (the *aggregate* limit).

Legal defense costs are always paid for by a professional liability policy company in addition to the policy limit of liability, or sometimes as part of the limit. The better policy is one that provides defense costs in addition to its limit of liability because then more funds are available to pay for a plaintiff's loss and damages.

Financial Strength of the Insurance Company

Beyond the specific terms of the insurance policy, it is important to evaluate the financial ability of the designated insurance company to pay claims when they are due. This is important for any "long tail" type of exposure, since there are usually a number of years between the time of the occurrence and the time the claim is paid—and a thinly capitalized carrier could go under in the meantime. Just as creditworthiness of business corporations is evaluated by firms such as Moody's and Standard and Poor's, the insurance industry relies on a firm named A.M. Best to evaluate both the financial size and the financial strength of insurance companies in the United States. An A.M. Best rating of A− or better should be a prerequisite for purchase of any insurance policy. This rating is even more important for a nursing liability policy where claims may not be made for many years. Annual editions of A.M. Best can be found in public and business libraries.

Right to Select Counsel

Some insurance companies allow nurses to select their own counsel to represent them in a medical negligence claim. Otherwise, their case is referred to a law firm or attorney previously retained by the insurance company. If this is important to nurses, they should ask specifically who determines the law firm or attorney that will represent them.

Right to Consent to Settlement or Trial

Some policies allow the nurse to refuse to settle a claim, whereas other policies do not permit this decision to be made by the nurse. Therefore, nurses should ask who has the right to decide if the case is settled or goes to trial.

IS IT NECESSARY FOR A NURSE TO BUY AN INDIVIDUAL LIABILITY POLICY?

Box 9–3   THE THREE TYPES OF INSURANCE POLICIES THAT COVER A NURSE'S PROFESSIONAL EXPOSURE
1. Individual liability policy   2. Institutional liability policy   3. Group liability policy

Individual policies offer nurses the broadest coverage. These policies offer 24-hour coverage so long as the nurse's acts fall within the scope of nursing practice. The institutional policy has narrower coverage and requires the nurse to practice within the defined scope of employment. The institutional policy can be expected by the nurse to extend to all employees.

Group liability and institutional policies are really extensions of individual liability policies because they cover a group of similarly licensed professionals and the business corporation that they commonly own. These policies require the most scrutiny by a nurse employed by a group to ensure that coverage is extended to the nurse as an employee. The nurse employee who is evaluating coverage under an employer-sponsored program (group or institution) can request that the employer show a certificate of insurance which explicitly states that employees are covered as "insureds."

Balancing the Costs and Benefits of Buying an Individual Policy

Once it is determined that coverage does indeed exist under an employer-sponsored insurance program, the next question to ask is whether to rely on the employer-sponsored insurance as the sole source of protection.

In a pamphlet entitled "Demonstrating Financial Responsibility for Nursing Practice,"[3] The American Association of Nurse Attorneys, Inc. (TAANA), states:

A. All professional nurses engaged in the practice of nursing should be insured against liabilities to third parties arising out of their professional practice.
B. The means by which a nursing professional elects to insure professional practice should be based on an informed decision.

Evaluating Individual Exposure

TAANA, along with others,[4] points to a number of important issues that should be considered when making a decision on purchasing insurance:

1. Will the employer seek indemnification (a monetary contribution) from a nurse employee whose professional services cause losses beyond the employer's insurance policy limits or within the employer's deductible?

The optimistic answer to this question is that the employer who faces a nursing shortage, or even one who is interested in maintaining good employee relations, will not seek indemnification from the nurse so long as the nurse acted within his or her scope of employment. However, there is little reported case law on this subject. Also, the unstable economic environment facing all hospitals today may lead a board of trustees to conclude that the best business decision is to seek indemnification from a nurse employee (or, more likely, a former employee) rather than face financial catastrophe. It is up to the individual nurse to assess both the economic climate and the quality of the employer-employee relationship in evaluating this issue. However, this issue alone should not determine the nurse's choice of coverage.

2. Does the nurse practice outside the primary employment setting?

At best, the institutional liability policy covers the nurse only for activities conducted while employed at *that* institution. If the nurse engages in private duty nursing, independent consulting, or voluntary service, or determines that his or her nursing activity is controlled by more than one "master," or employer, the nurse should consider an individual liability policy. This policy provides the nurse with 24-hour protection, regardless of job description and setting.

3. What state and federal laws affect the nurse's exposure?

All nurses employed by the federal government (the Public Health Service, the Veterans Administration, the military) are immune from work-related liability under the Federal Tort Claims Act. Some states still grant sovereign or charitable immunity to hospitals and usually (but not always) to the hospitals' employees.[5] Other states view hospitals as businesses and remove any charitable immunity protection.

In an attempt at tort reform, some states have sought to limit the economic liability of any one defendant. The result, ironically, could be more nurses being named as individual defendants in lawsuits, since more defendants implies deeper pockets. As the individual nurse's exposure increases, so does the need for individual liability protection.

What is the Nurse's Area of Clinical Practice?

Professional liability overall is a long tail exposure—it may be a long time between when an incident occurs and a claim is made. The purchase of individual liability policies is particularly advisable for obstetric and pediatric nurses who, depending on state statutes, are at risk for lawsuits until a child reaches 21 years old. These policies are also recommended for nurses who practice in what the insurance industry views as areas with a high risk of severe injury. These high-risk areas include the operating room, emergency room, critical care areas, and home health care.

Are There Circumstances When it May Not Be in the Nurse's Interest to Carry an Individual Liability Policy?

1. There is a belief that the availability of individual insurance converts a nurse into another "deep pocket" and makes the nurse more vulnerable to a lawsuit. However, there is no central data bank that has information regarding the insurance status of nurses.
2. A separate insurance policy means separate legal representation for the nurse. Some argue that this may make a joint defense with the employer more difficult and perhaps more costly.
3. There is the question of how multiple insurance policies respond to the same nursing incident. When both the employer and the

nurse purchase commercial policies, which policy pays first depends on each policy's "other insurance" language. The policy should specify how that insurance coordinates with other collectible insurance for the same loss. The most likely result is a pro-rata (even split) contribution by the available policies; however, there can be situations where the nurse's individual policy is required to pay first.[6]

When the employer is self-insured and the nurse has purchased individual commercial insurance, the result may be surprising. The nurse's policy pays first, to the extent of the employer's self-insured deductible. Self-insurance is not considered "other insurance" for the question of which insurance policy pays first.[7]

Cost

The final consideration in evaluating the nurse's exposure is the cost of the policy for individual protection. The cost must be compared with the amount of personal assets the nurse exposes without insurance protection.

Evaluating Individual Benefits

When evaluating individual benefits, the following items should be considered:

1. The purchase of an individual nursing liability policy acknowledges the nurse's responsibility for individual actions as a professional.

Purchasing individual coverage reinforces the concept of individual responsibility. Physicians purchase individual policies because they expect to take responsibility for their professional services. Nurses must also demonstrate individual responsibility for their professional services, both financially and otherwise.

2. The purchase of an individual nursing liability policy contributes to the establishment of nurse-specific claim data, which ultimately can be pooled for the development of credible nursing liability loss information.

Many nurses do not purchase individual policies. Instead, they rely on employer-sponsored insurance policies that do not identify nursing losses separately. The result can be higher premiums for nursing liability insurance.

Premiums are set by insurance carriers based on their perceptions of risk. The absence of credible nursing lawsuit information contributes to carriers' unacceptable conclusion that specialty nurses should pay the same rates as groups with worse, but documented, loss experience. If nurses cannot document their lawsuit experience, then it is not possible to demonstrate that nursing is less risky as a profession or as a practice specialty within the profession. Questions such as "Are nurse practitioners 'safer' than physician assistants or family practice physicians?" and "Are nurse midwives suffering because of the loss experience of obstetricians?" cannot be answered.

In the meantime, in an attempt to consolidate national nursing claims data, the American Nurses' Association has established a voluntary reporting system. For further information contact:

The National Nurses Claims Data Base
600 Maryland Avenue, S.W.
Suite 100 W
Washington, DC 20024
(202) 554-4444

3. The right to select counsel and control defense.

Professional liability insurance policies are usually written so that the Named Insured has the right to a defense attorney. The attorney is hired by the insurance company but represents the Named Insured. When the nurse is not the purchaser and not the Named Insured of the policy, there may be reluctance on the part of the insurance company to supply the nurse defendant with counsel of his or her own. There can be situations in which the employee and the employer conflict in their defense. By not having his or her own lawyer, a nurse's interests can become secondary to the Named Insured who purchases the insurance policy.

4. The nurse purchases an individual liability policy to assure that the state-by-state battles to broaden nurse practice acts are not in vain.

Written broadly to protect the nurse for *any professional service* deemed to be within the *scope of nursing practice,* the individual liability policy best enables nursing professionals to reap the benefits of what they sow from lobbying efforts to broaden state nurse practice acts.

Box 9–4   NURSING LIABILITY POLICY CHECKLIST

Before purchasing an individual nursing liability policy, the following questions should be answered:
1. Who is the Named Insured?
2. Is coverage provided for others than the Named Insured?
   a. Employee or agent?
   b. Volunteer?
   c. Consultant?
   d. Former insured?

Continued on the following page

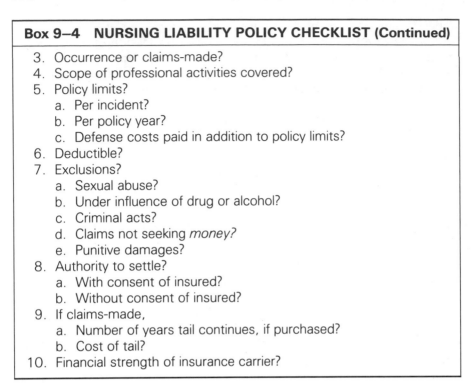

Box 9–4   **NURSING LIABILITY POLICY CHECKLIST (Continued)**

3. Occurrence or claims-made?
4. Scope of professional activities covered?
5. Policy limits?
   a. Per incident?
   b. Per policy year?
   c. Defense costs paid in addition to policy limits?
6. Deductible?
7. Exclusions?
   a. Sexual abuse?
   b. Under influence of drug or alcohol?
   c. Criminal acts?
   d. Claims not seeking *money?*
   e. Punitive damages?
8. Authority to settle?
   a. With consent of insured?
   b. Without consent of insured?
9. If claims-made,
   a. Number of years tail continues, if purchased?
   b. Cost of tail?
10. Financial strength of insurance carrier?

Points to Remember

▶ An insurance policy is an agreement by the insurance company which states that, in exchange for a premium, the company will pay money when certain injuries are caused by the person insured by the policy.

▶ Occurrence basis policies are preferable to claims-made policies and are available to individual professionals.

▶ Individual professional liability policies are broader than employer-sponsored policies.

▶ Not all individual professional liability policies are equally broad. Look for policies that cover injuries resulting from your "professional services," not from a "medical incident."

▶ An informed decision whether to rely solely on an employer-sponsored policy should weigh the cost of the individual policy against the benefits that a separate liability policy confers on the nurse individually and on the nursing profession generally.

▶ No available insurance ultimately means no practice. Therefore professional nurses' organizations have a responsibility to keep individual nursing liability insurance available.

Study Questions

1. Does the purchase of an individual liability policy make the nurse more likely to be sued?

2. An employed nurse is named individually in a lawsuit, along with the employer. Is the nurse automatically entitled to an attorney separate from the employer's attorney?

3. Discuss whether tort reform measures in your state have increased or decreased the nurse's exposure to tort liability.

4. A nurse works at only one job and the employer's policy indicates that the nurse is insured under it. Should the nurse purchase an individual policy as well?

5. Discuss the various sources, nursing associations, and companies that provide professional liability insurance for nurses. How are they similar and different?

6. Discuss the types of insurance policies available to professional nurses.

7. Discuss what specific items you should look for in an insurance policy.

8. Discuss "exclusions" as seen in insurance policies.

9. Explain the differences and similarities between individual, institutional, and group policies.

REFERENCES

1. For example, effective June 30, 1984, 42 Pa. C. S. 5533 (b) tolls the statute of limitations for minors in personal injury actions in Pennsylvania. Preceding June 30, 1984, there was no tolling.

2. See *Legler v. Meriwether*, 391 S.W.2d 599 (Mo. 1965) and *National Union Fire Insurance Com pany of Pittsburgh v. Medical Liability Mutual Insurance Co.*, 446 N.Y.S. 2d 480 (Sup. Ct. A.D., 3rd Dept. 1981). In both cases, the nurse employee was held not to be covered by the group liability policy of the employer. In the second case, National, the nurse also carried her own policy, which did respond.

3. Copies of the TAANA pamphlet are available at a nominal charge from:

   The American Association of Nurse Attorneys, Inc.
   720 Light Street
   Baltimore, MD 21230-3826
   Telephone (410)752-3318
   Fax (410)752-8295

4. See Northrop, C.: Buy liability insurance? Some factors to consider. The American Nurse 29, October 1987; *also* Feutz, S: Professional Liability Insurance, chap 7. In Northrop, C, and Kelly, M (eds): Legal Issues in Nursing. CV Mosby, St Louis, 1987, p 441.

5. For example, New Jersey limits the nonprofit hospital corporation's liability for negligence to $10,000, but then says "Nothing herein contained shall be deemed to exempt the said agent or servant individually from their liability for any such negligence" N.J.S.A. 2A: 53A-7 and 53A-8 (1959).

6. *See Jones v. Medox*, 430 A.2d 488 (D.C. App. 1981). Court stated that in harmonizing "other insurance" provisions, nurse's individual policy must pay first, since employer's policy stated explicitly that its limits applied "excess" of other valid and collectible insurance.
7. *American Nurses' Association v. Passaic General Hospital*, 471 A2d 66 (N.J. Super. A.D. 1984). Hospital's self-insured deductible deemed not to be "insurance" for purpose of harmonizing "other insurance" provisions in the nurse's individual policy and the hospital's policy.

▶ ETHICS IN PRACTICE

David B., 56 years old, was admitted to the intensive care unit (ICU) with severe chest pain and a diagnosis of an acute anterior myocardial infarction (MI). After several hours in the unit, he began to have short runs (5 to 10 beats) of ventricular tachycardia (VT) that ended without treatment. The physician was called, and an order for lidocaine was obtained.

Karen M., who was Mr. B.'s nurse, took the phone order for the medication. In writing down the order, she mistakenly wrote "1000 mg IV bolus, followed by drip at 2 mg per minute," rather than "100 mg IV bolus, followed by drip at 2 mg per minute." Amanda K., another RN who had been pulled to the ICU from the pediatric unit, offered to give the medication because Karen was so busy. Amanda gave the medication as the order was written, and Mr. B. promptly went into cardiac arrest. Resuscitative measures, including a pacemaker, proved futile in reviving him.

It was only after the code was over and Karen was completing her chart that she realized her error in writing down a dose that was 10 times more than the usual dose. If she had been giving the medication herself, she would have discovered the error immediately, but the pediatric nurse was unfamiliar with the ICU medications and had given the full dose. The patient had arrested so quickly after the medication was given that Amanda did not have time to chart it. Because Karen was the only one who had seen the chart and the order, it would be very easy for her to change it. Amanda had already gone back to the pediatric unit and did not even realize she had given a wrong dosage of this lethal medication. It is also likely that no one else would ever discover what really happened to Mr. B.

About that time, Mr. B.'s wife arrived to collect his personal belongings. She stopped at the desk where Karen was completing her chart to thank Karen for her care of her husband. Karen feels very guilty about the incident and wonders if she should tell Mr. B.'s wife what really happened.

What should Karen do? What would be the consequences of the possible choices of action? What ethical principle(s) should underlie Karen's decision?

Liability of Nursing Supervisors

ETHICAL CONSIDERATIONS

New graduate nurses, as well as nurses who are in their first few years of practice, rarely consider the possibility of becoming a nursing manager. If asked, most of these nurses would most likely answer that they had neither enough knowledge nor a high enough level of skills to be a supervisor or head nurse, and were not ready to assume the increased responsibility of such a position. Most likely they would be correct in their assessment of the situation. However, the reality of the workplace is that many good bedside nurses do go on to become nursing managers in a variety of different roles ranging from assistant head nurse to director of nursing.

In the patient care setting, nurse managers are primarily problem solvers. When difficult or unusual situations arise that the floor nurses are unable to deal with, the nurse manager is called upon to resolve the difficulty. Nurse managers also function as organizers and disciplinarians. They are often responsible for staffing, giving permission for vacation days and days off, and arranging the work schedule to ensure adequate patient care. When a problem arises with a nurse who is not providing care at an acceptable level, it is the responsibility of the nurse manager to determine the exact problem and then take a course of action to resolve it.

The ethical concept of *accountability* means that the nurse is answerable or responsible for his or her actions. Accountability in nursing takes two forms. *Personal accountability* is the responsibility that the nurses have to themselves and to the patient or patients entrusted to their care. *Public accountability* is the responsibility the nurse has to the employer and to society in general. The primary goals of professional accountability in nursing are to maintain high standards of care and to protect the patient from harm.

All nurses are accountable for the proper use of their knowledge and skills in the provision of care. Nurse managers have an additional accountability to those whom they supervise. A key element in accountability is the nurse's willingness to accept the consequences for decisions made and actions taken. As professional autonomy increases, so does the level of accountability.

Nursing managers practice with a high degree of professional autonomy. Therefore, their accountability is also greatly increased. Because nursing managers function to guide the nurses under their supervision, solve difficult problems, and make decisions about a variety of patient care issues, they should possess good decision-making skills, as well as a high level of theoretical and technical knowledge. Both ethically and legally, nursing managers are held to higher standards than the nurse who is not in a nursing management role. What would be acceptable as a reasonable and prudent course of action for a non-nurse manager may not be acceptable for a nurse manager. Indeed, because of their presumed greater level of knowledge, nurse managers are often called upon to be expert witnesses in malpractice suits.

OBJECTIVES

Upon completing this chapter, the reader will be able to:

1. Describe in detail the nurse manager's role in establishing and maintaining hospital standards of care.
2. Identify situations in which a nurse supervisor is liable for the actions of another.
3. Describe the difference between vicarious and direct liability as they affect the nurse supervisor.
4. Describe the common areas of direct or personal liability of the nurse supervisor, including the duty to train, orient, and supervise.
5. Describe how potential liability from the effects of short staffing can be minimized by determining the reasonableness of actions under the circumstances.
6. Describe the nurse supervisor's role in minimizing potential liability situations.
7. Define abandonment and wrongful discharge or transfer, and discuss how they can arise in the hospital setting.

INTRODUCTION

Whenever there is a problem on a hospital unit, such as an unexpected change in a patient's condition, medication that is not received from the pharmacy, a laboratory that fails to send results STAT, or a difficult physician, there is one cry that is heard: "Call the supervisor in charge." Nursing supervisors have unique positions in hospitals. Although they do not provide direct patient care, they are in charge of groups of professionals who do. Their supervisory responsibility, and the potential legal liability inherent in it, concerns many managers.

In this chapter, the term *supervisors* is used generically to include all levels of nurse managers from head nurses, to directors of nursing, to vice-presidents of patient services. This chapter addresses several areas of potential liability for the nurse supervisor.

SUPERVISORS ESTABLISH HOSPITAL'S STANDARD OF CARE

In Chapter 1, the four basic elements of nursing malpractice were discussed in detail. They are:

1. Standard of care (duty)
2. Breach of the standard of care
3. Proximate or legal cause or causal connection
4. Damages

A plaintiff must prove all of these elements to establish malpractice.

In their role as nurse managers, supervisors have the primary responsibility for establishing and maintaining standards of care that the staff must follow. Although nurses must meet basic national, state, and perhaps specialty group standards, each individual hospital establishes standards for its nursing service personnel that are spelled out in its nursing service policy and procedure manuals.

In a malpractice lawsuit, the plaintiff's counsel tries to show that the nurse failed to meet a standard adopted by his or her institution. If asked under oath, hospital nurses must admit that the staff is bound to follow the policies and procedures adopted by their institution and that they are required to be familiar with institutional policies and procedures. The nursing supervisor must make sure that the nursing standards described in the policy and procedure manuals are reasonable.

THE IMPORTANCE OF LANGUAGE

Supervisors must avoid language that creates unrealistic expectations or "ensures" patient safety when drafting policies and procedures. The law requires that nurses be reasonable under the circumstances, not that they be perfect. Although nurses try to provide optimum care and follow the highest standards, it can be argued that when less than optimum care occurs, a breach of the policy has taken place. If a patient is injured, then the policy may have established a higher standard of care than the law would otherwise recognize or impose. Even if lower standards apply to a specific situation, if the hospital policy establishes a higher standard, then that applies in the individual case. The language used and the responsibilities outlined in policy and procedure manuals must be reasonable and generally accepted within the nursing profession.

It is a common misconception that policies and procedures are reviewed by legal counsel to determine whether they are reasonable from a legal standpoint. It is suggested that all policies and procedures be reviewed by legal counsel in an effort to avoid unrealistic expectations.

Nursing supervisors have an obligation to make certain that manuals are available on each nursing unit; that staff members periodically review the manuals; and that staff members perform procedures in accordance with the manuals.

In *Parker v. Southwest Louisiana Hospital Association,*[1] the hospital's policy exceeded national standards; however, this policy was not followed by the staff. An apparent "well baby" had a cardiac and respiratory arrest approximately 24 hours after birth. Even though resuscitative procedures were instituted immediately, the infant sustained severe brain damage and died 9 months later.

Hospital policy required that well babies be visually observed every 10 to 15 minutes, even though the American Academy of Pediatrics standards required visual observation only every 20 to 30 minutes. Because the hospital required a more rigorous standard in its written policies, the staff's failure to adhere to those policies resulted in hospital liability for this tragic death.

IMPORTANT POINT TO REMEMBER:

The words and expectations expressed in your hospital's policy and procedure manual establish your institution's standard of care. Make certain that the standard is reasonable and does not promise a higher standard than the law requires.

LIABILITY FOR OTHERS

The most often asked question from nursing supervisors is: "Can I be held personally liable if a nurse I am supervising commits malpractice?" The short answer is: "It depends."

While everyone is held responsible for their own acts of negligence, there are certain limited instances when the law imposes liability for the acts of another. This is known as **vicarious liability.** Under the theory of ***respondeat superior,*** the employer is held responsible for injuries that occur when the employee is negligent in carrying out duties in the "course and scope of employment."

Based on this theory, if a nurse commits an act of malpractice while on duty, the hospital, not the nursing supervisor, is liable for the damage. As long as the nursing supervisor carries out the responsibilities as supervisor and does not employ the nurse, liability under a theory of *respondeat superior* is not imposed.

The case of *Bowers v. Olch*[2] illustrates this point. A surgical nursing supervisor assigned two nurses to assist in the patient's operation, one as a circulating nurse and the other as a scrub nurse. Several days after the surgery, a needle was discovered in the patient's abdomen. The patient sued the supervisor, the hospital, the operating room nurses, and the physicians. The court dismissed the nursing supervisor from the lawsuit because the theory of *respondeat superior* was not applicable to her. The supervisor did not employ the nurses she supervised and was not legally responsible for their actions.

If, however, a nurse owns a service which supplies sitters and employs and supervises individuals to sit with patients in the hospital or in the home, liability may attach. For example, if one of the sitters falls asleep on duty and the patient falls out of bed and fractures a hip, the nurse employer can be held liable. Even if the owner-employer–nurse supervisor is not present, the nurse employer is liable under *respondeat superior.*

UNLICENSED PERSONNEL AND THE SUPERVISOR'S LICENSE

A frequently asked question is: "Am I at risk of losing my license if the unlicensed personnel I supervise are negligent?" The answer is: "No." Only the person awarded the license can lose the license. Student nurses, aides, orderlies, technicians, assistants, or any other nonlicensed personnel do not work under the protection of the supervisor's license. They are working within the confines of a health care facility and under the license of the facility, not of a specific nurse.

The supervisor has an obligation to guarantee that unlicensed personnel do not perform functions which require a license and to safeguard that tasks assigned to subordinates are appropriately carried out. For example, a supervisor allows a nurse's aide to administer medication, but the aide administers it to the wrong patient. Most likely, the supervisor will be found negligent and the hospital, as the employer of both, will be held responsible. The supervisor is responsible for making sure that untrained and unlicensed personnel do not administer medication. The supervisor breached that duty and is also liable for failure to provide adequate supervision.

Even if the tasks assigned are appropriate to the training of the personnel, it is the supervisor's obligation to monitor that the tasks are performed correctly.

In *Hicks v. New York State Department of Health*,[3] a nurse was found guilty of patient neglect because of her failure to properly train and supervise the aides working under her. A security guard found an elderly nursing home patient lying in the dark, partially in his bed and partially restrained in an overturned wheelchair. He was undressed and covered in dried urine and feces. The court found that the nurse failed to assess whether the nursing aides had delivered proper care to the patient, which led to inadequate care of the patient.

IMPORTANT POINT TO REMEMBER:

Supervisors must be sure that unlicensed personnel:
1. Do not perform functions that require a license.
2. Perform assigned functions in an appropriate manner.

PERSONAL LIABILITY

Failure to Render Direct Patient Care

While nursing supervisors are not usually held responsible for the acts or omissions of the staff that they supervise, they are always held responsible for their own acts or omissions. This is known as *direct liability*. Since the job description of a supervisor includes many more "acts" to be performed than the job description of a staff nurse, there is more opportunity for the supervisor to "fail" to do something. The clearest example of personal liability occurs when a supervisor renders direct patient care and causes an injury.

In *Norton v. Argonaut Insurance Co.*,[4] an assistant director of nursing made the rounds on a busy pediatric unit and offered to transcribe physician's orders and carry them out. The physician's order for a 3-month-old infant was "Lanoxin 3 c.c.," but the order did not indicate PO (per os, by mouth) or IM (intramuscular). This supervisor was unaware that a pediatric elixir of Lanoxin existed and knew only of the injectable liquid.

The supervisor questioned the order with two physicians but never called the physician who ordered the medication. She also failed to check the *Physician's Desk Reference* or call a pharmacist to determine the correct dosage. She administered 3 cc (mL) of IM Lanoxin to the 3-month-old, who died from an overdose. The supervisor was found negligent and the hospital's insurer was held liable.

The supervisor was found negligent not in her supervisory duties, but because she failed to know the appropriate pediatric dosage and did not take appropriate actions to determine the correct dose.

Failure to Perform Duties as a Supervisor

Supervisors can also be held liable for a failure to carry out their supervisory responsibilities. For example, certain institutions require staff nurses to notify the supervisor of unfavorable patient responses. It is then the supervisor's responsibility to notify the attending physician. This procedure is followed especially during the night shift. If the supervisor's failure to notify the physician of an important change results in injury to the patient from delayed treatment, then the supervisor may be liable.

Duty to Train, Orient, and Evaluate

Another area of expanding nurse supervisor liability arises from the supervisor's obligation to train, orient, and evaluate the ability of staff nurses to perform specific functions and procedures. Most major hospitals have in-service education departments to orient new nurses and assist in the continuing education of nurses. The supervisor's responsibility is to determine on a day-to-day basis whether nurses are capable of performing necessary procedures.

The key to the supervisor's functioning is reasonableness. It is considered reasonable to check periodically to make certain that procedures are being followed and that the nurses working in an area know the procedures used routinely.

An unreported case involved a 1-day-old infant who became a paraplegic when air was pumped into a scalp vein, crossed the infant's patent foramen ovale, and lodged in vessels in his lower spine. At least five nurses who rotated through the neonatal intensive care unit II (NICU II) checked the pump and IV and failed to place an end-line filter on the IV tubing as it entered the child. The pump had neither an alarm nor an automatic shut-off device in case the fluid ran out. The only mechanism to prevent air from being pumped into the patient if the fluid ran out was the end-line filter. When wet, the filter became an air barrier.

The nursing procedure manual for the operation of the pump clearly stated that this end-line filter must be used during the set up of the pump and at all times when the pump was in operation. Five nurses who took care of the infant did not know that, when using the pump, the end-line filter was required. None of the five nurses who worked in the NICU II knew that the procedure existed or how to operate the pump.

The head nurse of the unit and the supervisor were found negligent for failing to make sure that the staff nurses knew the procedures for their unit and could implement them safely. The jury concluded that it was not reasonable for so many nurses to be ignorant of the safe operation of the pump. Following the incident, a procedure was developed to determine each nurse's knowledge of the use of the pump.

SHORT STAFFING

Of most concern to nursing supervisors, however, may be liability caused by inadequate staffing. Units are constantly functioning with fewer than the optimum number of nurses. Nurses must be "pulled" or "floated" to areas where they have little or no expertise, and where hospitalized patients are sicker and require more intensive care.

To avoid potential liability situations caused by short staffing, the supervisor must be reasonable and staff nurses must be flexible. The law requires that a nurse's actions be reasonable under the circumstances. Whether an action is reasonable is always the central question in determining liability in short staffing situations.

Reasonableness under the circumstances requires close attention in any situation involving patient safety. While there may not be sufficient staff to monitor patients constantly, there are reasonable alternatives that would lessen the risk of injury to the patient. A medicated patient has special safety concerns. Side rails must be up, the patient must be instructed not to get out of bed, and the call light must be placed within the patient's reach. These are all simple measures, but they were not applied in a Louisiana hospital.

In *Bossier v. DeSoto General Hospital*,[5] a patient who had been given a narcotic sustained injury when she fell on her way to the bathroom. Only half side rails were in use, and no one had told the patient not to get out of bed. No one suggested to the family that the patient needed constant supervision while receiving the medication. Reasonable measures under the circumstances were not employed, and the hospital was held liable.

One measure of reasonableness is how closely accepted guidelines and standards have been followed. The nursing supervisor must be aware of the guidelines concerning staffing requirements. The Joint Commission on Accreditation of Healthcare Organizations (JCAHO) provides certain standards for staffing that generally require "a sufficient number of qualified registered nurses ..." and "sufficient nurses to assure prompt recognition of any untoward change."[6] As yet, no specific numbers have been assigned by the JCAHO as to what constitutes a sufficient number of qualified staff; however, this may change. Courts have not been able to provide "numbers" because what is reasonable under one set of facts may not be reasonable under another.

Similarly, most health care organizations have been reluctant to say precisely what number constitutes an adequate staff. Certain specialty areas such as obstetrics have established standards requiring specific staff-patient ratios. These standards must be consulted in determining staffing requirements in these specialty areas.

Factors Affecting Reasonableness of Staffing

1. Acuity of the patients
2. Intensity of care
3. Qualifications and experience of the staff available
4. Attempts to secure adequate staffing
5. Utilization of alternatives (such as family members, friends, and outside nurses)
6. Use of ancillary staff
7. Clear documentation of efforts to bring in additional staff
8. Utilization of safety measures (side rails, posey jackets, or, in certain limited circumstances, restraints)
9. Increased frequency of rounds

Floating

Because of the need to provide competent care, not just bodies, floating, as a means of relieving short staffing of units, raises questions for supervisors. A nurse "pulled" to another unit must be competent to perform the duties assigned. For example, it may not be appropriate to float an RN applicant with no intensive care experience to a pediatric ICU. However, an experienced RN working in an unfamiliar area is still better qualified than no nurse at all.

Perhaps the best solution to floating is to cross-train nurses in specific, related areas, such as labor, delivery, and post partum; surgery and post anesthesia; pediatrics, nursery, and NICU. Cross-training increases the number of nurses who can perform in a patient care area, while increasing the confidence of the nurses providing care in these areas.

Agency or Pool Nurses

Other reasonable alternatives are the use of agency or outside pool nurses and in-house pool nurses. Outside pool nurses are not employees of the facility; they are employed by an agency whose function it is to provide nurses to hospitals with short-staffing problems. In-house pool nurses are employed by the facility, are not assigned a permanent unit, and agree to float. They may also be part-time employees or nurses seeking overtime work who are willing to work on any hospital unit. Pool nurses must be oriented to units and must be evaluated by supervisors to determine whether they meet hospital requirements for the position. Pool nurses should not be made charge nurses, except in rare circumstances, and only after there has been adequate orientation to hospital policies and procedures. Because charge nurse responsibilities include supervising other personnel, qualifications and training must be well documented before a nurse is allowed to assume those responsibilities.

In-house pool arrangements can provide nurses familiar with the institution; however, the number of shifts a registered nurse works should be monitored. Guidelines should be put in place limiting the number of additional shifts an in-house person can work as a pool nurse. Tired nurses make mistakes that can harm or endanger patients. The same concerns apply when supervisors ask nurses to work overtime.

IMPORTANT POINT TO REMEMBER:

The law does not require that optimum care be provided. The care must be reasonable under the circumstances.

Supervisors and Independent Contractors

Outside pool nurses who work in hospitals are not employees of the hospital, but independent contractors. In some instances, the nurse is hired by the patient or the patient's family.

Vicarious liability is another term for liability imposed because of the relationship between the persons. As discussed previously, *respondeat superior,* or "let the master answer," theory is a form of vicarious liability. In a true independent contractor situation, there is no vicarious liability.

If a nurse is employed by an outside agency or pool and injures a patient in the hospital, then, in general, the employer (the pool agency) is liable. There are situations, however, where the hospital may be held liable for the pool or contract nurse. For example:

- If the supervisor fails to orient the nurse to the unit and this leads to injury, the hospital is liable for breaching its duty to provide the necessary training.
- If the hospital or agency fails to ensure that the nurse is licensed and is competent to perform procedures, then the hospital and agency may be held liable if the pool nurse injures a patient.
- If the supervisor fails to make the necessary rounds and provide assistance to the pool nurse and this failure results in patient injury, then the hospital will most likely be held responsible.

The nurse's employer may also be held liable under a theory of *respondeat superior* for the actions of its employee. Even if a pool nurse is involved as an independent contractor, the patient may successfully sue the hospital. The patient may allege that the hospital "vouched" for the pool nurse or that the pool nurse was an "apparent agent or employee" of the hospital. While the agency may ultimately pay the monetary damages in the case, the existence of an independent contract does not necessarily shield the supervisor or the hospital from being named in a lawsuit and defending it.

In *Briggins v. Shelby Medical Center,*[7] the Supreme Court of Alabama ruled that whether a hospital was vicariously liable for the acts of a certified registered nurse anesthetist employed by an independent contractor was a question to be decided by the jury.

A certified registered nurse anesthetist (CRNA) employed by Alabama Anesthesia Associates administered anesthesia to Ms. Briggins, who aspirated during the course of surgery and died a few days later. The decedent's husband sued both the hospital and the anesthesia group as the employers of the CRNA. The hospital filed a motion for summary judgment alleging that since it was not the employer of the CRNA, it could not be held vicariously liable for his actions. The Alabama Supreme Court ruled that the inquiry as to whether the hospital could be liable went beyond the mere fact of employment and sent the question to the jury to decide. The jury ruled that the existence of the independent contract was not enough to insulate the hospital from potential liability for the acts of an employee of an independent contractor.

Contracts between the pool agency and the hospital must provide that the agency will indemnify or reimburse money to the hospital if the hospital is found liable for the actions of the pool nurse.

ABANDONMENT

Traditionally, **abandonment** is a premature termination of the professional treatment relationship without adequate notice to the patient. Claims for abandonment are generally made against physicians. It is much harder for a plaintiff to sustain an abandonment cause of action against a hospital providing in-patient services. However, situations can and do exist where abandonment claims are successful.

The emergency room, especially at large inner-city hospitals, can be a source of abandonment claims, since patients can "fall through the cracks" in the system. For instance, a patient could be triaged, placed on a gurney, put in the hall, and not seen again until some staff or visitor notices that he or she is not breathing. It is vital that supervisors in emergency rooms know that once a patient is in the hospital's system, it is their responsibility to be sure the system provides adequate follow-up. Even when triage determines that a patient can wait to be seen, the patient must not be left without someone responsible for reasonable, periodic follow-up.

The failure to adequately monitor patients on in-patient units may lead to allegations of abandonment. For example, if a nurse leaves a unit without adequate coverage or before relief arrives and something happens to a patient, an abandonment argument can be made.

In *Eyoma v. Falco*,[8] a jury exonerated an anesthesiologist and held a postanesthesia nurse 100% at fault for the death of a patient. The nurse on duty left the unit, asking another nurse to "keep an eye" on her post-op patient, but there was no indication that this second nurse heard the nurse or observed the patient. When the anesthesiologist made rounds, he saw that the patient was not breathing and resuscitative efforts were started. The patient remained in a coma for 1 year and then died.

Transporting patients for in-house testing, X-rays, or surgery can also lead to situations where the patient is left alone. Supervisors must be sure that hospital transportation departments are not leaving patients after transport without adequate supervision. It is not reasonable to leave an unattended patient waiting anywhere in the hospital. If that patient falls, the hospital will probably be held responsible for the injuries.

Related to the theory of abandonment is the theory of wrongful discharge or wrongful transfer. This situation can arise when a person with no health insurance goes to the emergency room of a private hospital. Even though it is likely that the hospital will not recoup payment for services, those emergency services must be provided if the patient arrives in an unstable condition.

Under the **Consolidated Omnibus Reconciliation Act (COBRA),** hospitals receiving federal monies (Medicare) that provide emergency services are required to provide a screening examination and all services necessary to stabilize serious medical conditions, including active labor, before the hospital may discharge or transfer the patient.

Known as the *antidumping act,* this Emergency Medical Treatment and Active Labor Act, found in 42 U.S.C. 1395 Section (dd), was intended to relieve the tremendous burden on charitable institutions by requiring private institutions to provide necessary emergency services without regard to an individual's ability to pay. This statute specifically authorizes civil suits for damages; loss of Medicare monies for noncompliance; access to federal court; and a 2-year statute of limitations in which to bring any action.

At a minimum, hospitals must adopt a written policy that reflects the language of the statute. Each transfer from the emergency room should be reviewed to determine compliance. If the institution does not provide maternity services, this fact should be clearly posted in the emergency room. Even without maternity services, if a pregnant woman, in the late stages of active labor, enters the emergency room, a physician must certify that the patient is stable before a transfer can take place.

IMPORTANT POINT TO REMEMBER:

Many states have passed antidumping statutes. Before implementing any procedure, your state's law should be consulted.

MINIMIZING POTENTIAL PROBLEMS—THE NURSE SUPERVISOR'S ROLE

Each hospital accredited by the JCAHO has to implement an overall quality assurance (QA) program. The standards require evaluations of the quality and appropriateness of patient care, suggestions on how patient care can be improved, and resolutions of identified problems (see Chapter 10).

Generally, supervisors are required to implement the QA program. In their unique positions, they can act as liaisons between nurses, other departments within the hospital, and the medical staff.

Quality Assurance Programs Developed by Hospitals May Include the Following:

1. Nursing orientation programs, continuing education requirements for nurses, and periodic monitoring of continuing education hours by supervisors.
2. Identification of high-risk areas for patient injuries.
3. Identification of high-risk areas for potential liability.
4. In-service education programs on adequate and appropriate documentation in the medical record.
5. Periodic chart audits to determine whether staff nurses as well as physicians are charting appropriately and actually communicating the medical information necessary for good patient care.
6. Effective communication mechanisms to handle complaints made by patients, their families, physicians, and other departments within the hospitals.
7. Findings from the programs should not be used to punish health care workers.

The effectiveness of any QA program is a three-step process: development, implementation, and follow-up. Supervisors are in the best position to coordinate the efforts of any QA and risk management program.

CONCLUSION

The first goal of any health care facility is to provide good patient care. Because of their roles as teacher, manager, and nurse, supervisors are often the first to recognize how patient care can be improved and what steps are necessary to accomplish those changes. Very often, supervisors are faced with conflicting concerns about the delivery of good patient care and the reality of financial constraints imposed either by their institution or by third party payors. It is the skillful supervisor who can recognize how to effect reasonable change without increasing cost. No one can prevent all adverse outcomes. The goal is to recognize the ones that can be prevented. Striving for the optimum patient care should be the goal of the health care system in this country.

Points to Remember

▶ Supervisors have the primary responsibility for establishing and maintaining standards of care that the staff must follow.
▶ The language used and the responsibilities outlined in policy and procedure manuals must be reasonable and generally accepted within the nursing profession.
▶ If a nurse is an employer/owner/supervisor, the nurse employer can be held liable for negligent acts of employees under the theory of *respondeat superior.*
▶ Nursing supervisors are not at risk for losing their licenses if the unlicensed personnel they supervise are ngeligent.
▶ Supervisors must be sure that unlicensed personnel do not perform functions that require a license or perform assigned functions in an appropriate manner.
▶ Nursing supervisors can be held personally liable if they fail to render direct patient care.
▶ Supervisors can also be held liable for failure to perform duties of a supervisor and failure to train, orient, and evaluate staff.
▶ Floating or "pulling" a nurse to another unit can be dangerous if the nurse does not have the experience and knowledge required to care for that type of patient.
▶ Abandoment is a premature termination of the professional relationship without adequate notice to the patient.
▶ COBRA stands for the Consolidated Omnibus Reconciliation Act and affects hospitals receiving federal monies that provide emergency services.

Study Questions

1. Discuss how the hospital's policy and procedure manual can be used by plaintiff's counsel to establish negligence.
2. Define the concept of *respondeat superior* and describe under what circumstances it is applicable.
3. What are the nurse manager's responsibilities in supervising unlicensed personnel?

4. Discuss the nurse manager's duty to train, orient, and evaluate staff and how the breach of these duties can result in liability.

5. Name five factors that affect the reasonableness of the nurse manager's actions in a short staffing situation.

6. Before determining whether a nurse should be floated to another floor, what factors must the nurse supervisor consider?

7. Define vicarious liability and give an example of it.

8. Define abandonment and give examples of situations where a claim for abandonment may be made in a hospital setting.

9. What criteria must be met under COBRA before an emergency room patient may be transferred to another institution or facility?

10. List three programs hospitals should include in their QA or risk management programs.

REFERENCES

1. *Parker v. Southwest Hospital Association*, 540 So.2d 1270 (La. App. 3d Cir. 1989).
2. *Bowers v. Olch*, 120 Cal. App. 2d 108, 260 P.2d 992 (1953).
3. *Hicks v. New York State Department of Health*, 570 N.Y.S.2d 395 (A.D. 3 Dept. 1991).
4. *Norton v. Argonaut Insurance Co.*, 144 So.2d 249 (La. App. 1st Cir. 1962).
5. *Bossier v. Desoto General Hospital*, 442 So.2d 485 (La. App. 2d Cir. 1983).
6. JCAHO Nursing Services N.R. 4.1 and N.R. 4.2.
7. *Briggins v. Shelly Medical Center* 585 So.2d 912 (Ala. 1991).
8. *Eyoma v. Falco*, 589 A2d 653 (N.J. Super. A.D. 1991).

▶ **ETHICS IN PRACTICE**

Maggie C., RN and head nurse of a busy neurological intensive care unit, was reviewing the weekend staffing for the unit on a Friday afternoon. As usual, the unit's nine beds were full with patients in various levels of recovery from brain surgery or head injuries. The staffing on the weekend was "short," with only enough staff to safely care for eight patients. After spending a great deal of time reworking the schedule, calling nurses on the phone, and trading days off, Maggie finally managed to arrange sufficient coverage for the unit.

As Maggie was closing her office for the weekend, Dr. West, a neurosurgeon, approached her and related the following situation. Mrs. P., a 63-year-old patient with a brain tumor, had been scheduled for surgery 3 days earlier. Because she had a very rare blood type that was difficult to match, the surgery had been delayed. Although a few days' wait was not expected to worsen her condition drastically, Mrs. P. had become anxious when informed about the delay. Although the blood bank had just obtained the necessary units for the surgery and had informed Dr. West that he could now operate, Dr. West was wondering if the neurological unit would be able to safely care for Mrs. P. over the weekend.

This unit was the only unit in the hospital equipped to monitor brain surgery and provide appropriate nursing care for this type of patient. Because the neurological step-down unit was also full, it would be difficult to transfer one of the patients on the neurological unit to make a bed available for Mrs. P. Mrs. P. would most likely require one-to-one care for 18 to 24 hours after surgery.

Should Maggie tell Dr. West that he can go ahead with the surgery and that she will make the adjustments to provide care for this patient? What ethical obligations does Maggie have to the patient? How about her obligations to Dr. West and the hospital?

Hospital Liability— Employment Issues

ETHICAL CONSIDERATIONS

▼ When an employment arrangement is created, both the employee and the employer are bound by certain ethical rights and obligations. In the health care system, the majority (approximately 75%) of all nurses are employed in hospitals or nursing homes. The employer-hospital's legal rights are outlined clearly in the legal system under such principles as *vicarious liability* (a type of substitute liability in which the employer is responsible for the actions of an employee) and the older common-law principle of *respondeat superior* (which implies a master-servant relationship between the hospital employer and the nurse employee). The hospital's obligations to the nurses it employs are not as clear in the legal system, and it may seem that the nurse-employees have few legal or ethical rights to defend themselves against the power of the institution.

In an ideal world, the nurse's primary and only responsibility would be to provide quality care to the assigned patients. The reality of the situation in the hospital setting is that the nurse has a triangle of responsibilities: responsibility to the patient, responsibility to the hospital, and responsibility to the physician. Nurses experience continual conflict among these three responsibilities. This conflict takes many forms. Nurses are taught as students that they should develop high ideals and standards. One of the primary focuses of nursing as a profession is health maintenance and patient education. The hospital setting, however, is one of the worst places to express high ideals, or to attempt to implement health maintenance and patient education. Nurses have little time to deal with patients individually because of poor staffing, shortened hospital stays, and restrictive hospital policies that prevent the nurse from carrying out these important activities. Nursing as a profession has a strong tradition of humanizing health care through a holistic, personal approach to patient care that includes all of the patient's problems as well as the patient's family. Yet, the health care

189

system tends to place a high value on and reward those nurses who master the new technology, develop more advanced medical skills, and spend less time with patients and their families. Nursing students are taught that they are colleagues with physicians in the provision of care for patients, yet the physician's role contains more power and prestige.

The employer-hospital's obligations toward the nurses it employs appear to be rather limited. In general, these obligations fall into two categories: to provide a safe and secure environment for nurses to perform duties, and to provide a fair wage. While these categories can be expanded to include other factors, such as health care insurance, time off for maternity leave, hepatitis B vaccine, and so on, the extension of benefits appears more often to be an issue of recruitment and retention of nurses rather than an ethical issue of justice in employment.

All nurses are familiar with the Patient's Bill of Rights. In many hospitals, patients are provided with a copy of this document upon admission. While this document is not legally binding, it does provide some sense that patients are important individuals and recognizes their autonomy in the often impersonal health care system. In addition, the Patient's Bill of Rights gives patients a feeling that they are "owed" certain elements of care and respect from the institution as well as the institution's employees.

Are nurses ever given a Nurse's Bill of Rights when they are hired by a hospital, nursing home, or some other agency? Most nurses probably do not even know that such a document exists (see Box 11–1). Like the Patient's Bill of Rights, the Nurse's Bill of Rights has no legal means of enforcement, but it does outline some fundamental ethical rights for nurses that should be recognized by the hospital, nursing home, or other employing agency. Nurses work in extremely difficult circumstances because of their central role in patient care, close contact with families, dominance by the medical professions, and limitations from institutional policies. Yet, without nurses to provide the hands-on, 24-hour-a-day care, hospitals would have no way to deliver their much advertised services. Nurses must be recognized as the valuable elements of the health care system that they truly are.

Box 11–1 NURSE'S BILL OF RIGHTS

1. The right to be treated with respect.
2. The right to a reasonable work load.
3. The right to an equitable wage.
4. The right to set your own priorities.
5. The right to ask for what you want.
6. The right to refuse without making excuses or feeling guilty.
7. The right to make mistakes and be responsible for them.
8. The right to give and receive information as a professional.
9. The right to act in the best interest of the patient.
10. The right to be human.

Source: Chenevert, M: Pro-nurse Handbook, ed2. CV Mosby, St Louis, 1993, p. 113, with permission.

OBJECTIVES

Upon completing this chapter, the reader will be able to:

1 Describe how a hospital can be held liable for the actions of its employees, independent contractors, and professionals.
2 Interpret events and issues in hospitals, nursing homes, or other health care facilities that pose personal liability risks for nurses.
3 Identify the major protected groups in antidiscrimination statutes.
4 Discuss the rationale for developing and maintaining employee records, evaluations, and hiring applications.
5 Define the Americans with Disabilities Act (ADA).
6 Define the types of sexual harassment.

INTRODUCTION

In the majority of medical malpractice claims filed, the hospital where the nurse or physician treats or cares for the patient is usually named as a defendant under various legal theories. Hospitals are named as defendants because of their "deep pockets"—meaning that they can pay larger settlements or judgments.

The first recognized legal duty of a hospital is its responsibility for the acts of its employees under the doctrine of *respondeat superior*. The courts have also developed two other areas of liability for hospitals, ostensible authority and corporate negligence.

Box 11-2 ELEMENTS OF DOCTRINES OF HOSPITAL LIABILITY

Respondeat Superior

1. Act of employee
2. During employment relationship
3. Negligent act occurred within the scope of employment

Ostensible Authority

1. Patient looks to hospital for treatment
2. Hospital assigns physician or nurse to treat
3. Negligence of physician or nurse causes injury

Corporate Negligence

1. Hospital knew or should have known
2. Physician or nurse provides substandard care

RESPONDEAT SUPERIOR

Respondeat superior is a Latin term handed down from English common law that means, "Let the master answer." When a nurse is hired by a hospital, agency, nursing home, individual, or other entity, the nurse owes a "duty of care" to the individuals under the care of the employer while he or she is on duty and acting within the "scope of employment," that is, performing the tasks necessary to accomplish the employer's goals.

If the nurse breaches a duty or standard of care owed to the patient and causes injury, the hospital may be held legally liable under the doctrine of *respondeat superior.* The nursing act in question must occur while the nurse is on the institution's premises, during the time of employment, and while performing the duties required by the employer for the action to be considered within the nurse-employer relationship.

In *Pisel v. Stanford Hospital,* a high-level nurse manager altered a patient's medical records. The hospital was held liable for her actions since she was working in the scope of employment.[1]

Similarly, if an untrained nurse or technician makes an error that causes an injury, a hospital may be held directly responsible.[2]

Examples of acts outside of the nurse-employer relationship that do not fall under *respondeat superior* include providing nursing care outside of the facility, giving advice to neighbors, or responding to an emergency on the street. In addition, any procedure performed by a nurse that should only be done by a physician or nurse practitioner is also considered outside the nurse's scope of employment and the hospital is not liable.

Box 11-3   FACTORS ESTABLISHING AN ACT WITHIN SCOPE OF EMPLOYMENT

1. The time, place, and purpose of the act
2. Its similarity to what is authorized
3. The extent of departure from normal methods
4. Past dealings between the employer and employee
5. Whether the employer had reason to expect that such an act would be done

---

Liability

Under the doctrine of *respondeat superior,* the nurse as well as his or her employer can be held liable. The employer may be named in a suit with or without the employee and may be held liable because of the employer-employee relationship.

In *Willinger v. Mercy Catholic Hospital,* the hospital was held liable for the brain damage of a 5-year-old caused by the failure of the nurse anesthetist to properly monitor anesthesia during a tonsillectomy. The nurse anesthetist, an employee of the hospital, induced anesthesia under the supervision of the anesthesiologist. The anesthesiologist was then called to an emergency operating room to treat another patient. When the anesthesiologist returned, he found the patient without a heartbeat and the "color of a cadaver." The nurse anesthetist was still administering a full dose of anesthesia and was not using a stethoscope to monitor the heartbeat.[3]

OSTENSIBLE AUTHORITY

Under the doctrine of **ostensible authority,** a hospital is liable for the negligence of an independent contractor if the patient has a rational basis to believe that the independent contractor is a hospital employee. Hospitals may be held liable for the acts of independent contracting nurses, just as they are found liable for the wrongful acts of physicians who are independent contractors.

The courts have used the following criteria to establish ostensible authority:

1. Subjective
2. Inherent function
3. Reliance
4. Control

Subjective

In *Grewe v. Mt. Clemens General Hospital,* a Michigan court held that the critical question was whether the patient, at the time of the admission, looked to the hospital for treatment of his physical ailments or merely viewed the hospital as a place where his physician would treat him for his problem.[4] A factor was whether the hospital provided the physician to the patient or whether the patient and the physician had a patient-physician relationship apart from the hospital setting. When a patient looks to the hospital for his or her treatment and is treated by medical personnel who are "ostensible agents" of the hospital, the hospital is held liable.

Inherent Function

Ostensible authority is applied most frequently to emergency room physicians, even though the contract between the physician and hospital usually identifies the physician as an independent contractor. However, some courts have held that the physician is an agent of the hospital because the emergency room physician performs an inherent function of the hospital in providing emergency care.[5] An *inherent function* is one that exists in and is inseparable from the hospital.

Reliance

A court may hold the hospital liable if the patient relies on the hospital's judgment (by choosing to be admitted to that hospital for surgery rather than another), but is injured because of something the hospital did or omitted doing.

Control

In certain circumstances, a hospital may be liable for an independent contractor, depending upon the degree of control exercised by the hospital. To identify whether or not control exists, a court examines and balances many factors such as:

1. The extent to which the employer determines the details of the work
2. The kind of occupation
3. The customs of the community
4. Whether the work is generally supervised by the employer
5. Who supplies the place to work
6. Who supplies the instruments to work
7. The method of payment

In *Rivera v. Bronx Lebanon Hospital Center*, the court held that hospitals may be liable for the acts of independent physicians who are staff members of the defendant hospital and who are assigned as the patient's attending physician by the hospital.[6]

Box 11–4   FACTORS ESTABLISHING CONTROL OVER AN INDEPENDENT CONTRACTOR

1. Who determines details of work
2. The kind of occupation
3. Customs of the community
4. Whether or not the work is supervised
5. Who supplies the place of work
6. Who supplies the instruments necessary to work
7. Method of payment: hourly, salary, piece work, and so on

CORPORATE NEGLIGENCE

The courts have developed two separate and independent hospital responsibilities that they consider under the doctrine of **corporate negligence.** (1) First is the hospital's responsibility to monitor or supervise all medical and nursing personnel within the facility, including the quality of care, whether the personnel are employees or independent contractors. The hospital is then liable for any injuries the patient suffers because of the hospital's failure to monitor or supervise the physicians and nurses. The courts also expect the hospitals to periodically review staff competency.[7] (2) Second, a hospital is held liable for failing to investigate a physician's credentials before granting staff privileges. This is likely to be applied to nurses in advance practice who may be required to apply for privileges to perform their duties, such as nurse-midwives and nurse-anesthetists.

Corporate Negligence Case

In an Illinois case, plaintiff Darling, an 18 year-old man, was treated in an emergency room for a broken leg by an orthopedic surgeon. The patient charged that the resulting amputation was caused by the negligence of the physician and nurses.

The patient brought a suit against the hospital and the doctor under the theory of *corporate negligence.* At trial, the patient proved that the hospital did not require the following:

1. Orthopedic surgeons to review and update their surgical skills
2. Consultation in the event of surgical complications
3. The nursing staff to regularly check and examine the patients recovering from surgery

He also showed that the hospital failed to enforce its policies requiring immediate reporting of patient complications by the nursing staff to the hospital administrator.[8]

In *Darling v. Charleston Community Memorial Hospital,* the court clearly stated that, because of its failure to monitor the care provided by its attending physicians and nurses through control of staff membership and clinical privileges, the hospital was liable for the type of care provided.[9]

In *Bost v. Riley,* the court interpreted *Darling* as holding that a hospital could be held negligent for "*failing to have a sufficient number of trained nurses* attending the plaintiff, failing to require a consultation or examination by members of the hospital staff, and failing to review the treatment rendered to the plaintiff."[10] The court held that a hospital has a duty to make a reasonable effort to monitor and oversee the treatment that is prescribed and administered by physicians and nurses practicing in the facility.

Credentials

Not only does the hospital have the duty to monitor the ability of the physicians and nurses, but it also has a duty to enquire about the credentials of the physician and nurse prior to hiring. In *Johnson v. Misericordia Community Hospital,* the Wisconsin Supreme Court found that there was sufficient evidence showing the hospital's knowledge of a physician's incompetence for the jury to find the hospital liable for granting the physician privileges and allowing him to practice orthopedic surgery.[11]

The court held that the duty of the hospital to reasonably investigate an applicant required that the hospital check the physician's references, educational credentials, former practice, and prior claims. It should also call the physician's former and prior associates, as well as professional associations the physician is affiliated with, and ensure that the physician is licensed in the state. Failure to scrutinize a physician's credentials could foreseeably result in appointing an unqualified physician to the staff, creating an unreasonable risk of harm to the hospital's patients.

As discussed in Chapter 3, the National Practitioner Data Bank, which became operational on September 1, 1990, is a central repository for all actions taken by a state regarding a licensed health care practitioner. It was established to address problems caused by health care providers who, after losing their license or hospital privileges, or being disciplined by the state licensing board or their hospital, move out of the state and practice in their new residence. Each state and health care facility or provider is required to inform the Data Bank of actions taken regarding a licensee. This information is available to any facility requesting information about a practitioner.

State medical boards are required to report disciplinary actions, revocations of licenses, on other actions restricting a physician's right to practice. Self-insurers and insurance carriers are also required to report settlement payments or payments made as a result of a judgment. Failure to report can result in fines up to $10,000.[12]

ISSUES IN HIRING, EVALUATION, AND TERMINATION

Hiring Process

The reasons for hiring personnel must be unbiased and fair and cannot be based on the individual's race, religious preference, age, or handicap.

Except for a few jurisdictions, all employment is employment at will, meaning there is no written contract specifying a term of employment. This permits either the employer or the employee to terminate employment without cause or notice.

Higher level nurses are more likely to be delivering services under a written contract. For employees working under contract, any reason used to terminate or discharge them may be considered unlawful because the contract specifies the term of employment and the only way to terminate the employee is by the terms of the contract. If no terms for termination are provided in the contract, then termination may occur only at the expiration of the specified years or when the employee breaches the terms of the contract.

Courts have found that contracts exist based on specific promises or words used in job announcements, application forms, and interviewing questions. Special care should be given to what is said in advertisements and applications. The nurse should understand that interview questions may be drafted in advance. Open questions are used to encourage the nurse applicant to talk and may call for a statement of position. Closed questions permit "yes or no" answers.

> Open: What are your feelings about occasionally being asked to work on another floor?
>
> Closed: Do you mind working on another floor on occasion?
>
> Open: How is this position related to your goals and ambitions?
>
> Closed: Would this position help you achieve any of your goals and ambitions?

"Why" questions used by the interviewer can make a question sound like a challenge and create unwanted defensive reactions. The question may be reworded in an open format to obtain the information.

> Poor: Why do you think you can handle this job?
>
> Better: What skills and management abilities do you have that would make you successful in this position?

When closing an interview, the interviewer should indicate how or when the decision will be made and how the applicant will be notified. The interviewer should not indicate approval or disapproval with an applicant's responses.

Contract Arising after Employment

Handbooks and personnel and policy manuals can create an employment contract.[13] Statements in employee manuals or company policies can be contractually binding and alter an underlying employment-at-will status. An aggrieved nurse may successfully assert that the employment manual is a part of the contract, and the employer can be bound by it. For example, an employee who is terminated without notice or severance pay may allege that the employer did not abide by the employment manual, which provides for progressive disciplinary reviews and 2 weeks' notice of the termination.

Generally, there are three theories used to determine whether an employee manual is contractually binding: employees' expectations, a combination of employees' and employers' expectations, or unilateral contract theory. The employees' and employers' expectations can be inferred by the court from all the surrounding circumstances. A unilateral contract may be found as an offer of continued employment by the employer, and the employee's continued work converts the offer to a formal contract.

Box 11–5   THEORIES USED TO DETERMINE IF EMPLOYMENT MANUAL IS A CONTRACT

1. Employee's expectations
2. Employee's and employer's expectations
3. Unilateral contract theory

Manuals may state that they are subject to change. Words such as "fair," "satisfactory," and "reasonable" are subject to personal and legal interpretation because they are subjective and vague. If there is a correction to a current version of the manual, it should be referred to as a restatement, not a revision. All corrections or restatements should be distributed to hospital employees. Employees should sign and date documentation to show that they have received notice of the changes.

Independent Consideration

Most jurisdictions uphold disclaimers in policies and procedures that they do not represent an employment contract. In *Thompson v. St. Regis Paper Co.*, the court stated that employers are not always bound by statements in employment manuals.[14] An employer can specifically state in a conspicuous manner that nothing contained in the manual is intended to be part of an employment relationship and are merely statements of company policy. The employer may also specifically reserve the right to modify the policies.[15]

However, even when an employment contract or the policies and procedures appear to provide for termination at will, if an employer gives the employee extra or independent consideration (such as salary or benefits) beyond what is stated in the contract and in the policies and procedures, then that employment may not be terminable at will.

A plaintiff nurse moved from Michigan to North Carolina to accept a position at Duke Hospital after she was told she could only be discharged for incompetence. While she was employed at Duke, she refused to administer a drug that she believed would injure a patient. The patient was severely injured as a result of being given the medication by others. During a malpractice suit and prior to being deposed, the hospital and physicians who administered the drug warned the nurse "not to tell all." She testified truthfully and was fired immediately. She filed a suit for wrongful discharge.

At trial, she claimed wrongful discharge under two theories of law: contract and tort. In contract, she argued that assurances by Duke Hospital induced her to move from Michigan to North Carolina to take the position. The court held that the move constituted additional consideration which removed her employment contract from one at-will to one at-contract.[16]

Performance Reviews

Failures to undertake appropriate performance evaluations and promote an individual based on those evaluations have been the bases of discrimination actions. To avoid claims of discrimination in promotions, performance reviews must support the decision on promotion. Periodic employee evaluations are advisable. Any forms used should list objective information and evaluation rather than subjective information and evaluation. Be aware, however, that providing for periodic evaluations may give rise to a "just cause" requirement for termination, and, if the evaluations do not reflect the reasons for termination, those reasons, which would be used as defenses to a discrimination charge, can be destroyed.

"Good cause" requirements can be developed directly from the policy and procedure manual of the employer. An employer should spell out the types of offenses that will be disciplined, the types of warnings that are given, and the appropriate discipline to be administered such as verbal or written notices. If the employer immediately terminates the employee, rather than following written procedure, there is no "good cause" for the termination.

Certain offenses may be established as cause for immediate termination. These offenses are generally lying, stealing, cheating, illicit drug use on the premises, and striking an employee or patient. If an employee is terminated for one of these offenses, the employer has "just cause" to do so.

Employee evaluations should describe significant performance problems and clearly state what kind of improvement is expected. Evaluations should be reviewed, signed, and dated by the appropriate superiors. A copy of the evaluation should be maintained in the files of the head nurse or supervisor, and the nurse should be given a copy. The evaluations should be based on observed and recorded employee performance during the period of the review. Feedback should be provided on a continuing basis and not merely at the time of the review. Documentation should reflect feedback, record the achievement of set goals, and note discrepancies.

To ensure that performance evaluations are objective, specific job-related standards, guidance to evaluators, and review by higher level management or personnel department should be established. A word of caution: Place a copy of a disciplinary evaluation in a separate file from the nurse's personnel file. Personnel files can be requested by a plaintiff's attorney in a nursing malpractice case, and a disciplinary evaluation can be damaging and used against the nurse or hospital in a malpractice suit.

**Box 11–5   FACTORS SHOWING RELIABLE AND
OBJECTIVE PERFORMANCE EVALUATIONS**

1. Specific job-related standards
2. Guidance given to the evaluators
3. Review by higher level management or personnel department

Terminating Problem Employees

How an employee is handled during the termination process can make a significant difference in his or her attitude and whether or not a lawsuit will be filed. A terminated employee may file suit because of negative feelings surrounding how the situation is handled, how the decision is made, or how the news is conveyed face-to-face.

If the employee belongs to a protected group (a member of one of the groups protected in the antidiscrimination acts), the likelihood of legal action may be increased. The hospital file must reflect the actions taken and the reasons for the termination. Detailed documentation should record the facts and actions supporting the termination decision. In addition, a review of how other employees have been handled should be conducted. If an individual has been handled differently, these differences must be justified.

The reasons for terminating the employee should be outlined during the termination interview. Any hint of cover-up or unfair treatment could result in the employee taking legal action. A hospital policy may also be developed that requires the employer to give written notice and the reasons for termination so that there is no room for misunderstanding.

Standards for Dismissal

In *Toussaint v. Blue Cross and Blue Shield of Michigan*, the court indicated that an employer should be permitted to establish its own standards for job performance and dismissal for nonadherence to those standards, even though another employer or a jury might have established lower standards.[17]

In *Pugh v. See's Candies, Inc.,* another court suggested the following:

In *Pugh,* a corporate vice-president with 32 years service was terminated without explanation. The court found an implied agreement that good cause was required for the termination, based on the extreme length of service, chain raises, bonuses and promotions, the president's repeated assurances that employment would continue if a good job was done, the company's acknowledged practice of not terminating executive personnel except for cause, and the company's failure to ever formally criticize or warn the plaintiff that his job was in jeopardy.[18]

Good cause is also found when an employer lays off an employee because of depressed market conditions or a need for the business to reorganize and relocate operations.[19] Open defiance and insubordination are also sufficient reasons for termination without the employer having to follow the contract rights, duties, and employee protections. Other examples include employee discharges for fighting,[20] for insubordination,[21] and for excessive absenteeism.[22] Further, clear violation of a company policy is a question for the court and not for the jury.[23]

Executives, managers, supervisors, and creative employees are generally evaluated by more subjective considerations that can frequently be difficult to quantify, measure, or objectively compare, particularly in a small company. Although cases do not tend to require broader company discretion for terminating higher-level or special employees, there appears to be some recognition that a different standard applies.[24]

Exception to At-Will Employment

The general rule in the United States is that there is no contract for employment; an employer is free to terminate an employee at any time for any reason or for no reason. The employee also has the right to leave the employer without notice or cause. When an employee cannot show that a contract was formed, there are still several exceptions to the strict at-will rule. The two major categories of exceptions are:

1. Implied covenant of good faith and fair dealing
2. Public policy

Implied Covenant of Good Faith and Fair Dealing

Termination itself does not constitute a breach of the covenant of "good faith and fair dealing," unless it is done specifically to deprive the employee of earned compensation. Several jurisdictions hold that employment relationships, like commercial relationships, require an obligation between the parties. This obligation prevents an employer from terminating an employee for the sole reason of depriving the employee of earned but not received compensation (commissions, salary, company benefits) for services already performed.[25]

Public Policy

An employee at-will may not be terminated for reasons inconsistent with established "public policy." Termination is prohibited by public policy if it is done "in retaliation for performing an important and socially desirable act, exercising a statutory right, or refusing to commit an unlawful act."[26] Employees have a claim if they are terminated: (1) for asserting a statutory right, such as filing a worker's compensation claim; (2) for doing what the law requires, such as serving on a jury; or (3) for refusing to do what the law forbids, such as committing perjury.

Under public policy theory, many states have laws that protect "whistle blowers." These laws protect employees who disclose alleged illegality and then are terminated by the employer.

A psychiatric nurse provided information to a state agency about a patient confined in a state hospital. She also testified on behalf of the patient at his commitment hearing. The employer said it terminated the nurse for failure to support hospital programs, insubordination, insults to superiors, mistreatment of patients, and failing to limit her damages by refusing to take a demotion. The court found that the nurse had been terminated because she had provided information to the state agency.[27]

Posttermination

Once an employee has been terminated, the issue of references arises. An employer must have a definite policy to prevent potential liability for defamation or negligence.

Defamation

Defamation occurs when the plaintiff is exposed to public hatred, ridicule, or contempt, through oral or written publication of false statements (see Chapter 8). The public is generally considered to be the more limited, professional community in which the plaintiff works. *Publication* occurs when there is any kind of communication to any individual other than the plaintiff. The person to whom the defamatory statements are made must have heard and understood the remarks to be directed to or about the plaintiff. The employer who knows that a published statement is false may be liable for defamation. Even when the employer disseminates information with reckless disregard to its truth or falsehood, he or she may be liable. Half-truths may be as misleading and are as actionable as whole lies.[28]

Negligence

An employee about whom the reference was given may not only have an action under defamation but may also have a separate negligence claim. The employer may not be legally obligated to provide references, but is bound to exercise due care in providing references it gives voluntarily. If due care is not used and causes damages to the former employee, the elements of negligence are met.

Qualified Privilege

An employer may have a conditional privilege to disclose defamatory information concerning an employee. A conditional privilege makes an employer's statements concerning the character and abilities of former employees, if directed either to his other employees or toward a prospective employer, nondefamatory.[29] This defense usually applies when information is sought from an employer as to the qualifications or character of a former employee.[30] Similarly, entries on internal personnel documents are generally considered conditionally privileged.

Loss of Privilege

A conditional privilege by the employer can be lost if the employee can prove recklessness. Recklessness includes reckless dissemination of statements or reckless disregard for truth or falsity of the information. Recklessness is also shown by failing to verify information, where it is practical, to safeguard against error.

Actual bad faith, ill will, or improper purpose or motive inconsistent with social policy or interests may constitute actual malice and prevent a qualified or conditional privilege from forming. Willful, false statements destroy the conditional privilege and constitute malice. An employer's reasonable belief in the truth of a statement will negate any finding of malice. Today, many hospitals develop policies to avoid any potential problems or litigation when discussing former employees or other sensitive information.

General Guidelines

Specific information about the plaintiff's length of employment and duties generally prevent disqualification of privilege. During the termination interview, the reference policy should be discussed. The policy should indicate only that the employee worked for the employer for a specific period of time and performed a particular type of work. Under some circumstances, the employer might agree to tell a prospective employer that a person was terminated but had specific skills and abilities that could be offered to the new employer.

EMPLOYMENT ISSUES

As more nurses become employers or those who are responsible for employment decisions within a facility, they have increased liability for employment decisions. Nurses' actions on behalf of their employers, or on their own behalf, raise the possibility of nurses being held liable for wrongful termination, wrongful failure to hire, or wrongful failure to advance employees.

Antidiscrimination statutes protect employees and employee management procedures, including hiring, planning and conducting performance reviews of employees, managing problem employees, and terminating unacceptable employees.

Box 11–7   OVERVIEW OF ANTIDISCRIMINATION STATUTES

Protected Groups

1. Race
2. Color
3. Religious preference
4. National origin
5. Pregnant women
6. Ages 40 and older
7. Handicapped

Continued on the following page

**Box 11-7   OVERVIEW OF ANTIDISCRIMINATION
            STATUTES (Continued)**

Exceptions

1. Religious entity may consider religious background
2. Bona fide occupational qualification
3. Business necessity

Title VII

Title VII 42 U.S.C. §2000 e-1 et seq. (the Civil Rights Act of 1964) protects employees from discrimination based on *race, color, religion, sex,* or *national origin,* and provides that *pregnant women* receive the same protection as other employees and applications. The **Equal Employment Opportunity Commission** (EEOC), which enforces Title VII, has guidelines that provide protection from sexual harassment, including conduct where:

1. Submission to sexual advances is implicitly or explicitly considered a condition of employment.
2. Submission to sexual advances is used as a basis for employment decisions.
3. Sexual harassment interferes with job performances even if it only creates an intimidating, offensive, or hostile atmosphere.

(See Appendix 3—Sexual Harassment.)

**Box 11-8   TITLE VII—PROHIBITED SEXUAL
            HARASSMENT**

---

1 Submission to sexual advances is implicitly or explicitly considered a condition of employment.
2. Submission to sexual advances is used as a basis for employment decisions.
3. Sexual harassment interferes with job performance even if it only creates an intimidating, offensive, or hostile atmosphere.

While Title VII covers most employers and employees, from hourly workers to executives, it allows some exceptions. The act permits religious institutions to consider religion in employment decisions. Two other exceptions permit an employer to discriminate for:

1. A bona fide occupational qualification (BFOQ)
2. A business necessity

An example of a BFOQ is demonstrated in an Illinois case. In *Garcia v. Rush-Presbyterian Medical Center,* the court found that employment at a complex medical center required the ability to speak English.[31]

Filing a Claim

The plaintiff must first exhaust all state and federal administrative remedies prior to filing a civil court action. Sixty days after filing with the state authority, the plaintiff may file a complaint with the EEOC, although some states permit filing in both the state agency and the EEOC at the same time. An EEOC complaint must be filed within 180 days of the alleged violation. The EEOC then investigates and resolves the violation through conciliation or court action. If the employee is not satisfied with the EEOC resolution, then the employee may file a claim with the trial court.[32]

Proof

In a Title VII claim, the plaintiff has the burden to prove, by a preponderance of evidence, a prima facie case of discrimination. A *prima facie case* is one that is found in the employee's favor if no conflicting evidence is offered by the employer. A prima facie case of discrimination is developed in one of two ways:[33]

1. There is direct evidence that there is discrimination such as a "smoking gun" or a letter stating a discriminatory reason for failing to hire or to terminate the employee.
2. Discriminatory treatment can be inferred by the plaintiff employee showing that:
   a. The plaintiff is a member of a protected group.
   b. The plaintiff is qualified for the job for which the plaintiff applies or from which the plaintiff is discharged.
   c. The plaintiff is rejected or terminated.
   d. The position remains open or someone outside the protected group has replaced the plaintiff.

Allocation of Proof

If an employee provides sufficient evidence that clearly shows a discriminatory reason for the employer's action, then the employer must defend against the charge by providing evidence that there was no discrimination. The plaintiff may then argue against the employer's defense with evidence that shows the employer's defense and reasons are untrue.

Box 11–9   ESTABLISHING A PRIMA FACIE CASE OF DISCRIMINATION

---

1. Direct evidence of discrimination.
2. Inference based on a showing that:
   a. Plaintiff is a member of a protected group.
   b. Plaintiff is qualified for the job.
   c. Plaintiff is rejected or terminated.
   d. The job remains open or someone outside of the protected group replaces the plaintiff.
3. In age discrimination, statistical patterns from which an inference of discrimination may be drawn.

The Age Discrimination and Employment Act

The **Age Discrimination and Employment Act** (ADEA), 29 U.S.C. §621 (1967), also enforced by the EEOC, prohibits discrimination by an employer against anyone 40 years old or older in decisions regarding hiring and promotions. It exempts public safety employees, top managers, and, until 1994, tenured college professors over 70 years old. The ADEA applies to industries that affect commerce and have 20 or more employees for each of 20 or more calendar weeks. It also applies to some labor unions and state and local governments. The proof and allocation of proof in an ADEA matter are similar to a Title VII case. Besides the "smoking gun" and "inferred" proof of discrimination, statistical patterns can establish proof from which a reasonable inference of discrimination can be drawn.[34]

The Civil Rights Acts

The Civil Rights Act of 1866 (42 U.S.C. §1981) prohibits discrimination on the basis of race, alienage, and national origin, in the formation and enforcement of employment contracts. On-the-job racial harassment is not included because the act does not apply to discrimination that does not impair the formation of the contract. There must be proof of "purposeful discrimination," and the burden of proof is the same as in Title VII.

The Civil Rights Act of 1871 (42 U.S.C. §1983) provides the right to sue a person who deprives another of a right under the Civil Rights Act of 1866 (42 U.S.C. §1981). The deprivation must occur "under the color of statute, ordinance, regulation, custom, or usage." "Under the color of statute" essentially means that there must be some action by the state or a state-supported entity that deprives another of the right to form and enforce an employment contract. Receipt of federal or state financial assistance, such as a college receiving federal funding, may be sufficient to be considered acting "under the color of statute."

The Rehabilitation Act of 1973

The Rehabilitation Act of 1973 outlaws discrimination based on handicap. According to the Rehabilitation Act, a **handicap** is a physical or mental impairment which substantially limits one or more major life activities. The handicap does not necessarily have to be a long-term disability; it can be a short-term handicap. The Rehabilitation Act applies to employers who receive *federal* financial assistance or who have contracts with the *federal* government.

The Americans with Disabilities Act

The **Americans with Disabilities Act** was passed by Congress in 1990 to eliminate discrimination against Americans with physical or mental disabilities (see Appendix 2). They do not have to be employed by employers who receive federal funding or have governmental contracts as required in the Rehabilitiation Act of 1973.

Points to Remember

- ▶ Three theories of hospital liability are:
  - ▷ *Respondeat superior*
  - ▷ Ostensible authority
  - ▷ Corporate negligence
- ▶ *Respondeat superior* means "let the master answer."
- ▶ *Scope of employment* refers to acts that describe what an employee is hired to do in order to accomplish the employer's goals.
- ▶ Ostensible authority is when the hospital is held liable for the negligence of an independent contractor if the patient has a rational basis to believe that the independent contractor is a hospital employee.
- ▶ Antidiscrimination statutes protect people from discrimination based on race, color, religious preference, national origin, as well as pregnant women, people ages 40 and older, and the handicapped.
- ▶ The Age Discrimination and Employment Act does not protect public safety employees, top managers, and tenured college professors over 70 years old. (By 1994, tenured college professors over 70 years old will be protected.)
- ▶ In interviews, there are two types of questions:
  - ▷ *Open,* which encourage the applicant to talk and may call for a statement of position.
  - ▷ *Closed,* which permit "yes" or "no" answers.

▶ The general rule is that in the United States if there is no employment contract, then an employer is free to terminate an employee at any time for any reason or for no reason (that is, fire at will).

▶ Whistle blowers are defended in many states by laws that protect employees who disclose illegality and then are wrongfully terminated by the employer.

▶ The Americans with Disabilities Act's goal is to eliminate discrimination against Americans who have physical or mental disabilities so that they can participate more fully in the work place and social life.

Study Questions

1. Compare and contrast the legal duties and responsibilities of a hospital under the various doctrines holding hospitals liable for acts occurring in the facility.

2. When can the hospital be liable for the acts of a nurse even if the nurse is not sued?

3. How can a hospital be held liable for the acts of a nurse who is an independent contractor?

4. Identify and describe the legal theories that a court may use to extend liability to a hospital for a nurse's actions.

5. Define the roles and positions that nurses have or may develop that lead to increasing liability in employment decisions.

6. What type of questions should never be on an interviewer's list?

7. Describe three situations that illustrate a policy that appears neutral but has a discriminatory impact.

8. When, if ever, can an employee with a drug or alcohol problem be terminated?

9. What are the advantages and disadvantages of being an "employee at will?"

10. What steps can a hospital take to prevent a terminated employee from filing a wrongful termination suit?

REFERENCES

Note: Cites to American Law Review, 4th edition (A.L.R. 4th) have been provided as a potential source for identifying the law in individual jurisdictions.

1. *Pisel v. Stanford Hospital,* 430 A.2d 1 (1980).
2. *Hamburger v. Henry Ford Hospital,* 91 Mich. App. 580, 284 N.W.2d 155 (1979).
3. *Willinger v. Mercy Catholic Hospital,* 362 A.2d 280 (Penn. Supp. 1976).

4. *Grewe v. Mt. Clemens General Hospital,* 273 N.W.2d 429 (Mich. 1978); 51 A.L.R. 4th 235 (1990).
5. *Adamski v. Tacoma General Hospital,* 20 Wash. App. 98, 579 P.2d 970 (1978); 51 A.L.R. 4th 235 (1990); *Mduba v. Benedictine Hospital,* 52 A.D. 450, 384 N.Y.S.2d 527 (1978).
6. *Rivera v. Bronx Lebanon Hospital Center,* 417 N.Y.S.2d 79 (A.D. 1979); 51 A.L.R. 4th 235 (1990).
7. *Park North General Hospital v. Hickman,* 703 S.W.2d 262 (1985); 12 A.L.R. 4th 57 (1990).
8. *Darling v. Charleston Community Memorial Hospital,* 33 Ill.2d 326, 211 N.E.2d 253, 14 Atl.3d 860 (1965).
9. *Id.*
10. *Bost v. Riley,* 262 S.E.2d 391 (N.C. App. 1980); 51 A.L.R. 4th 235 (1990).
11. *Johnson v. Misericordia Community Hospital,* 99 Wis.2d 708, 301 N.W.2d 156 (1981).
12. American Medical Association and National Health Lawyers Association: Physician's Survival Guide—Legal Pitfalls and Solutions. AMA, NHLA, Washington, DC, 1991, pp 41–60.
13. *Liekvold v. Valley View Community Hospital,* 141 Ariz. 544, 688 P.2d 170 (1984); *Mau v. Omaha National Bank,* 207 Neb. 308, 299 N.W.2d 147 (1980); *Roulon-Miller v. IBM Corp.,* 162 Cal. App. 3d 241, 208 Cal. 524 (1984); 33 A.L.R. 4th 120 (1990).
14. *Thompson v. St. Regis Paper Co.,* 102 Wash. 2d 219; 685 P.2d 1081 (1984).
15. 79 Mich. App. 93; 261 N.W.2d 222 (1977), *rev'd,* 402 Mich. *See also Karie v. General Motors Corp.,* 282 N.W.2d 925 (1978).
16. *Sides v. Duke,* 74 N.C. App. 331, 328 S.E.2d 818 (1985); 75 A.L.R. 4th 13 (1990).
17. *Toussaint v. Blue Cross and Blue Shield of Michigan,* 408 Mich. 579, 292 N.W.2d 880 (1980); 33 A.L.R. 4th 129 (1990).
18. *Pugh v. See's Candies, Inc.,* 116 Cal. App. 3d 311, 171 Cal. Rep. 917 (1981), *modified on other ground,* 117 Cal. App. 3d 502a (1981).
19. *Cutterham v. Coachman Industries, Inc.,* 169 Cal. App. 3d 1223, 215 Cal. Rep. 795 (1985); 677 F. Supp. 1021 (N.D. Cal. 1988).
20. *Grozek v. Ragu Foods, Inc.,* 63 A.2d 858, 406 N.Y.S. 2d 213 (4th Dept. 1978).
21. *Johnson v. National Beef Packing Co.,* 220 Kan. 52, 551 P.2d 779 (1976); 33 A.L.R. 4th 125 (1990).
22. *Shah v. S.S. Kresge Co.,* 166 Ind. App. 1, 328 N.E.2d 775 (1975); 33 A.L.R. 4th 120 (1990).
23. *Helsby v. St. Paul Hospital and Casualty Co.,* 195 F. Supp. 385 (D. Minn. 1961), *aff'd,* 304 F.2d 758 (8th Cir. 1962); 80 A.L.R. 4th 421, 433 (1990).
24. *Supra* at 19.
25. *Maddaloni v. Western Massachusetts Bus Lines, Inc.,* 386 Mass. 877, 438 N.E.2d 351 (1982); 44 A.L.R. 4th 1145 (1990).
26. *King v. Mannesmann Tally Corp.,* 847 F.2d 907 (1st Cir. 1988).
27. *Witt v. Forest Hospital,* 450 N.E.2d 811 (Ill. 1983).
28. *Glaz v. Ralston Purina Co.,* 24 Mass. App. Ct. 386, 509 N.E.2d 297 (1987) 12 A.L.R. 4th 544 (1990); *Tameny v. Atlantic Richfield Co.,* 27 Cal. 3d 167; 164 Cal. Rptr. 839 (1980).
29. *Doane v. Grew,* 220 Mass. 171, 107 N.E. 620 (1915).
30. *Sheehan v. Toban,* 326 Mass. 185, 93 N.E.2d 524 (1950).
31. *Garcia v. Rush-Presbyterian Medical Center,* 660 F.2d 1217 (7th Cir. 1981).
32. EEOC, 2401 E Street, N.W., Washington, DC 20210.
33. *McDonnell Douglas Corp. v. Green,* 411 U.S. 792 (1973).
34. *Marshall v. Sun Oil,* 605 F.2d 1331 (5th Cir. 1979); *Schultz v. Hickok,* 358 F.Supp. 1208 (N.D. Ga. 1973).

▶ ETHICS IN PRACTICE

Julie C., RN, had worked the 11 A.M. to 7 P.M. shift in the NICU for 2 years. Today, as she finished her last entry in the progress notes for Baby

L., a 1-pound, 4-ounce premature infant, she could hear the sounds of her nurse colleagues outside the window as they prepared to picket the hospital in a strike for better pay, better working conditions, and better staffing.

Over the past several months, the nursing staff had organized as a group and attempted negotiations with the hospital administration. The very traditional hospital administration had always viewed any attempt to organize any of the staff, but particularly the nurses, as unprofessional and insubordinate. The history of the hospital was replete with stories of nurses who had been fired because they had attempted to unite the nurses in an organized manner to seek better working conditions. Consequently, the administration viewed this strike as a major violation of their unwritten policy and threatened all the nurses who participated in the strike with employment termination.

Although Julie C. recognized that the working conditions were poor and that the pay scale was the lowest in the relatively small city, she still felt a strong obligation to the hospital and the patients. Many of the patients who could be discharged or moved to other facilities were already gone from the hospital, but a small number of the patients, such as Baby L., could not be moved without extreme risk to their health and lives.

The leader and organizer of the strike was one of Julie L.'s classmates and best friends. She had stressed to Julie that without the support of 100% of the nursing staff, the strike would be a failure and the hospital would win again. The hospital had already begun hiring some "aides" to provide care while the nurses were on strike. Julie felt that the care provided by these untrained aides was substandard and probably dangerous to the patients' lives. Julie's friend made the point that it was really the hospital's responsibility to provide adequate care for the patients and that the administration could have the whole nursing staff back as soon as they began negotiating in good faith.

Julie was tempted to sign out her charts and join the strike at the end of her shift. Yet she felt an obligation to stay for another shift and care for Baby L. and the several other infants who could not be moved. What should she do? What ethical issues are involved in her decision?

CHAPTER

12

The Nurse and the Contract

ETHICAL CONSIDERATIONS

▼ To many nurses, the term *contract* evokes visions of the murkier side of the legal system. Indeed, contract law can be complicated, confusing, and fear evoking to those not familiar with the terminology. But the reality is that nurses enter into contracts all the time. The most common contract is the nurse-employer contract, but other contracts exist between nurses and their patients, physicians, and schools of nursing.

Although many hospitals require the nurses they hire to sign written contracts, there are many other hospitals that have oral employment contracts. Whether written or oral, elements such as exact work hours, salary, raises, sick leave, vacation time, overtime compensation, and job expectations should be expressed clearly. In some settings, the "Employees' Handbook" serves as the written list of expectations and duties and may even have the legal force of a contract in a court of law. Whether written or oral, once agreed upon, all contracts have the same weight before the law.

Once the contract is accepted and agreed upon by both parties, it is in force until it is broken, or until one or the other party terminates it. It is generally accepted that the contract lasts as long as the pay period, and, at that time, is automatically renewed or terminated. The employee may terminate the contract by presenting the employer with a formal letter of resignation at least 2 weeks before the effective date. It is often more difficult for an employer to terminate an employee's contract for misbehavior such as unsafe or negligent care than it is for the employee to terminate the contract. However, in cases where the decision has been made to terminate an employee, employees are to be given the same 2- to 4-week termination notice as the employer is given. If there is no written contract, some states use a "fire-at-will" policy, which does not require notice or a reason.

Both written and oral contracts should be based upon the two ethical principles of justice and fidelity. Under the principle of justice, the employer owes the nurse a safe, comfortable place to work plus a just salary that is equal to the work being performed. Often included under the umbrella of the term *just salary* are benefits such as health insurance, sick leave, vacation time, and so on.

The principle of justice also demands certain requirements on the part of the nurse employee. In general, the nurse owes the employer a provision of patient care that is in line with the reasonable standards and qualities of the profession. More specifically, the nurse employee should meet or exceed the standards set by the Nurse Practice Act, continue to upgrade his or her skills through education and practice, seek the highest standards and quality of care for patients possible, and be a patient advocate seeking to follow the patient's wishes as closely as possible. Often included in these requirements for the nurse-employee is the obligation to "float" or work in areas of patient care to which the nurse is not usually assigned.

The ethical principle of **fidelity** is one of the key building blocks of accountability, and without accountability, there can be no claim to professionalism. Although the definition of fidelity seems simple, "fidelity conflicts" often arise in the work setting due to opposing demands from various forces. For example, the employer hospital or institution may experience a fidelity conflict between fidelity to its employees to provide modest raises and job security, and fidelity to a board of directors that is seeking reductions in overall institutional expenses by salary cuts and reduction in positions.

Nurses often experience fidelity conflicts in their day-to-day provision of care. It is usually agreed that fidelity to patients and their needs is the highest priority, yet nurses have fidelity obligations to the hospital, to the profession of nursing, to other nurses, to the government, and to society as a whole. For example, government regulations and certain accrediting organizations such as the Joint Commission on Accreditation of Healthcare Organizations (JCAHO) require certain types of documentation on the part of nurses. This documentation adds to the overall load of "paperwork" that the nurse is required to do. Many times nurses are placed in a situation where they must use valuable bedside care time to fill out forms and write lengthy notes. This conflict is really a fidelity conflict.

Although the balance of obligations in the hospital-employer, nurse-employee contract seems to fall to the nurse, the hospital also incurs serious obligations in the contract agreement. Awareness of the underlying ethical principles as well as the legal intricacies will aid the nurse in fulfilling his or her obligations in a professional manner as well as seeing that the hospital also meets its obligations.

OBJECTIVES

Upon completing this chapter, the reader will be able to:

1   Discuss the principles of basic contract law.
2   Define the technical language used in contracts.

3 Explain the value of using alternatives to the court system.

4 Describe when contracts should be used.

5 List contract requirements.

6 Explain the basis for enforcement of contractual rights.

INTRODUCTION

As an alternative to the traditional employer-employee relationship, nurses are increasingly striking out on their own, opening the doors of their own businesses, entering into partnerships with other health care providers, establishing corporations, and offering their expertise to the public independent of the health care facility employer. Particularly at the executive level, nurses are entering into contractual arrangements similar to those of executives in other industries. This chapter includes an overview of contract law and focuses on the contractual needs of the nurse as an independent contractor, a consultant, and an executive.

DEFINITION AND ELEMENTS

A **contract** is an agreement consisting of one or more legally enforceable promises between two or more parties—people, corporations, or partnerships. There are four elements in a contractual relationship: the offer, acceptance, consideration, and breach.

Box 12–1   ELEMENTS IN A CONTRACTUAL RELATIONSHIP
Offer
Acceptance
Consideration
Breach

The person or entity making an offer to keep a promise is called the **offeror.** The person or entity accepting the offer is the **offeree.** An example of a contractual relationship, then, would be a nurse (offeror) who contracts with a hospital (offeree) to perform certain nursing services. The offeree has the "power of acceptance." If the offeree accepts the offer, a contract is created.

Consideration can be defined as the economic cost of an agreement. Consideration is what the offeror bargains and exchanges for the promises. For example, a nurse who owns a consulting business offers to analyze medical records for a lawyer for a fee. When the lawyer accepts the nurse's offer and "promises" to pay a fee, a contract is made.

If, after the nurse analyzes the records, the lawyer refuses to pay, the nurse can file a lawsuit against the lawyer and ask the court to enforce the contract between the two parties. Refusal to pay constitutes a breach of contract.

STATUTE OF FRAUDS

The *statute of frauds* is a principle of common law which states that a contract does not have to be in writing to be enforced. However, there are exceptions, which include agreements involving suretyship, marriage, the sale of land or interests in land, the sale of goods, and those agreements that cannot be performed within 1 year.

Box 12–2   ENFORCEABLE CONTRACTS WHICH MUST BE IN WRITING
Suretyship Marriage Land Sale of goods Agreements that cannot be performed in 1 year

In lawsuits involving contractual rights, the parties may need to prove to the court the express terms of the contract. A written agreement, expressing all of the parties' intentions, is the most concrete evidence. However, subsequent communications about a written agreement can be oral, written, or behavioral and can serve as evidence of terms agreed to that are different from the original written agreement.

MERGER CLAUSE

The merger clause is a statement in a contract indicating that the document is the final agreement between the parties. The terms cannot be modified unless reduced to writing, signed by all parties, dated, and made a part of the original contract.

Box 12–3   MERGER CLAUSE
A statement of final agreement, which may be modified only if: ■ In writing ■ Signed ■ Dated

REMEDIES

Monetary Damages

The principal remedy for breach of contract is monetary damages. As a general rule, the goal of the courts is to place the damaged or injured party in the same economic position he or she would have been in if the promise had been kept. For example, the nurse cited above, who was not paid by the lawyer for analyzing records, can expect the court to grant judgment against the lawyer for an amount that is at least equal to what the lawyer promised to pay for services.

If a nurse is working under an employment contract as an executive and the employer breaches the contract by wrongfully terminating him or her before the expiration of the contract, the nurse may enforce the contract by bringing a lawsuit to recover salary and other economic benefits agreed to for the remainder of the contract.

Duty to mitigate is the right to decrease or reduce the damages or award of the injured party. The nurse may expect the court to reduce this sum by the amount the nurse earned, or will or could earn, with reasonable effort, during the period the parties had agreed the contract was to run.

Other Remedies

Only in certain circumstances does a court enforce a contract by requiring that a promise that cannot be measured financially be kept. For example, to prevent someone from either unjustly benefitting from or suffering a loss, a court may require restitution to the aggrieved party by canceling a contract.

Box 12–4   REMEDIES
Money Return damaged or injured party to the same position Duty to mitigate Enforcement of a contract

ALTERNATIVE DISPUTE RESOLUTION PROCESSES

For a nurse, the publicity of a lawsuit can mean considerable demands on his or her professional and personal life. Today, there are several alternative legal options that include mediation, binding and nonbinding arbitration, neutral fact finding, and summary jury trial.

Mediation

Mediation is an excellent technique when parties want to maintain a relationship. It involves the use of **mediators**—neutral third parties who facilitate agreements by helping both sides to identify their needs and work toward agreeable solutions. Through this option, the nurse who wants to continue reviewing records for a lawyer is much more likely to achieve that goal by mediating the dispute than by suing the lawyer. Costs for the mediator and the associated scheduling and paperwork can be shared by the parties.

Arbitration

The **arbitration** process often works best for technical cases such as medical malpractice and certain employer-employee contracts. Both sides select a neutral third-party arbitrator with technical knowledge in the area of contention who hears the case and renders a decision and award.

Depending upon what the parties agreed to before the arbitration began, the decision can be binding or nonbinding.

Fact Finding

Fact finding is most often used in complex multistate and multiparty cases. However, a neutral fact finder may be used whenever the facts of any particular case are in dispute.

Summary Jury Trial

A **summary jury trial** is an abbreviated, privately held trial. It is often used to give the parties an indication of the strengths and weaknesses of their cases and possible outcome if the case goes to trial.

Nurses' contracts should contain a statement that provides for the use of one or more *alternative dispute resolution processes*. It may be necessary to consult legal counsel for the appropriate wording for each situation.

Box 12–5   ALTERNATIVE DISPUTE RESOLUTION

Cost saving: Court costs, lawsuit expenses, and lawyers fees can be greatly reduced.

Time saving: Parties meet on their own schedules: do not have to wait for a court calendar date.

Private: The process and the result are private.

Less traumatic: Money can be saved; the process is speedier; sensitive materials are not shared with the press and general public; and parties have access to remedies that are not available in the court system.

TYPES OF CONTRACTS

The Nurse as an Independent Contractor

A nurse who is an independent contractor undertakes a specific job for either a person, a hospital, or a corporation using his or her own means and methods. The person, hospital, or corporation for whom the work is performed has no authority over the nurse. Unlike the employer or employee, neither party has the right to terminate the contract at will. The key to independent contractor status is: How much "control" does the person, hospital, or corporation have over the nurse?

When to Use an Independent Contractor's Contract

The traditional private-duty nurse is perhaps the nursing profession's oldest example of an independent contractor. Today, midwives, nurse anesthetists, and nurse practitioners are among the nurse specialists who are taking advantage of the financial and professional rewards available to the independent contractor, as are nurse brokerage firms, quality review specialists, and nurse paralegals. The Internal Revenue Service (IRS) has also issued private letter rulings permitting several nurses who work for nurse brokerage firms to be classified as independent contractors. However, this is a rapidly changing area of tax law, and nurses should seek legal counsel before deciding about their own classification.

Box 12–6   INDEPENDENT CONTRACTOR

Turns on the issue of control or "work in its entirety."
Employer has no right to give instructions or training.
Does not have to render services personally, may work for others.

Continued on the following page

Box 12–6   INDEPENDENT CONTRACTOR (Continued)

May hire assistants, use own tools.
Does not have to keep set hours.
Does not have to work on employer's premises.
May perform work in any sequence but has no right to quit—cannot be fired.
Paid by the job, on commission, by the hour, week, month, or year.
Assumes own expenses, can bill for same.

Requirements in an Independent Contractor's Contract

The first section of a contract should contain the full names and addresses of parties to the contract and their role in the contract, such as owner or corporation, or family, and nurse.

Second, a section on recitals is needed. It should address the type of business the owner or corporation is engaged in, or the needs of the family or individual requiring care. It should also state that the nurse will provide nursing services for the specified persons under the terms and conditions in the contract in consideration for the promises listed in the contract.

Third, the contract should list a reasonably complete description of all the work the nurse will provide. For example, a private-duty nurse's description of work might be "all nursing care essential to Baby Doe's health between 7:00 A.M. and 3:30 P.M., each Monday through Friday, until, in my judgment, in collaboration with the Doe family, all of Baby Doe's health care providers, and all other professionals interested in Baby Doe's welfare, Baby Doe no longer needs such nursing care."

The contract should also contain the total fee owed to the nurse and the fee schedule to be followed.

The contract should have a statement about the nurse's liability insurance coverage in an amount acceptable to the other party. In some instances, a corporation may want the nurse to have a clause inserted that would hold it harmless and indemnify it from all costs arising out of the nurse's negligence or other actions. These clauses are varied and complex and have numerous and significant effects on the nurse's business. The nurse should seek legal counsel for advice and assistance in the contract negotiation process to ensure that all areas are properly covered in the contract.

The duration of the contract should be clearly spelled out, the day it starts and the day it ends. In the case of Baby Doe, described above, a specific end date should be inserted, perhaps the day the health insurance coverage ends, plus the clause that "services, in the nurse's judgment in collaboration with those mentioned above, may terminate sooner." A clause allowing either party to terminate before the end date should be inserted, provided written notice is given by one party to the other.

Also, a provision asserting the relationship between the professional nurse as an independent contractor and the employing party should be included, emphasizing that the nurse is not an employee. This type of paragraph is especially helpful in dealing with certain governmental agencies, such as the IRS, for the validity of certain business deductions. In fact, all of the above inclusions are good evidence that the parties intend to pursue an independent contractor relationship, should any such agency inquire. If the employer breaches the contract by not paying according to schedule, the nurse has documented evidence of the employer's promise.

Finally, the contract must have a section for signatures and dates signed. Technically, a contract does not have to be signed for a court to enforce it, but the nurse's case is stronger if such formalities are performed. Although none of the promises made by the nurse and the other party to the contract have to be written for the court to enforce them, the specific terms of the contract need to be proved, and a written contract can be clear evidence of what was promised.

**Box 12–7   ELEMENTS OF INDEPENDENT
CONTRACTOR'S CONTRACT**

Identification of parties
Recitals
Description of work
Contract price and payment schedule
Liability insurance statement
Duration of contract
Independent status
Items unique to each contract
Signatures and date

WHEN TO USE A CONSULTING CONTRACT

The traditional role of the consultant has been principally that of advice giver. This role has expanded so that it often includes performing work on or off site for an employer. For example, a nurse may be hired as a consultant to advise a law firm on setting up a system to review and analyze medical records. Subsequently, the firm may want to contract with the nurse to implement that system. A nurse's consulting contract is really a variation of the independent contractor's agreement. Some of the provisions in the consulting contract, such as identifying the parties and the recitals, can be virtually identical. Other provisions are tailored for the consultants, an option that many nurses are choosing by taking consulting assignments for federal, state, and local governments; multinational corporations; insurance companies; law firms; and national health care providers, to mention just a few.

REQUIREMENTS IN THE NURSE CONSULTANT'S CONTRACT

The description of the nurse's duties and responsibilities in the body of the contract should focus on the consulting role. The contract may include a statement about making suggestions to employees and management concerning a particular aspect of the corporation's business.

The location of the nurse's workplace should be mentioned. Consultants often work out of their own offices, libraries and research facilities, or corporate offices or places where the corporation has contracts.

The amount of time needed by the consultant to do the work should be included. Usually, consultants are paid a flat fee for a job to be finished by a certain date, but the speed at which it is accomplished is the consultant's prerogative.

Some corporations may request that a nurse consultant obtain the corporation's written approval before working with competitors. A noncompete clause is a clause prohibiting a nurse from doing business that competes with the business of a client or an employer. Noncompete clauses vary as to the type of restrictions, length of time required when the nurse cannot compete, and geographical areas restricted. If a noncompete clause is requested, the nurse should consider the full implications of this restriction on practice. Similarly, a related clause restricting the nurse from providing similar consulting services to certain types of corporations may also require the services of counsel to negotiate.

The payment schedule clause should address the issue of reimbursement for all travel expenses incurred away from home or office. Seeking reimbursement and complying with IRS audit demands require scrupulous documentation of such expenses.

In the duties and responsibilities clause, the correct title, or titles, should be included. The nurse's duties and responsibilities should be negotiated carefully and inserted in this section, with as much specificity as possible, replacing what is often found in a job description.

An optional issue for inclusion is that of military service, because federal law does not protect salary and benefits for the person called to active duty.

Box 12–8   REQUIREMENTS FOR THE NURSE EXECUTIVE EMPLOYMENT CONTRACT
Compensation (including benefits and bonuses) Duties and responsibilities Disability Term of employment Alternative dispute resolution Termination

SUMMARY

How nurses are compensated for their work has changed almost as rapidly as the health care delivery system. Nurses are now no longer confined to hourly wages. They function as consultants, business owners, executives, and independent contractors. Consequently, nurses need to know when to use a contract—a document containing one or more promises, mutually agreed to, that the law will enforce.

The easiest contracts to enforce are those in which the terms are committed to writing, signed, and dated.

Enforcement proceedings in a court can be expensive, time consuming, and emotionally draining. Consequently, use of the appropriate alternative dispute resolution mechanism can eliminate these problems.

SAMPLE CONTRACT FOR THE NURSE
WHEN WORKING AS AN INDEPENDENT CONTRACTOR

This contract is made on _____, 19____,
between _____, whose address is _____,
City of _____, County of _____,
State of _____, hereinafter referred to
as Corporation, and _____ of _____,
City of _____, County of _____ [address],
State of ____, hereinafter referred to as Nurse.

Corporation owns and operates a _____ [type of busi-
ness] business at the address above, and Corporation wants to have certain nursing
services performed for Corporation's business.

Nurse agrees to perform those services for Corporation under the terms and conditions included in this contract.

In consideration of the mutual promises contained herein, it is agreed by and
between Corporation and Nurse:

Relationship of Parties

The parties to this contract agree that Nurse is a professional person, and that
the relation created by this contract is that of employer-independent contractor. Nurse
is not an employee of employer, and is not entitled to any benefits provided by
employer to its employees, including, but not limited to, pension plan, withholding of
federal and state income taxes, FICA, Workers' Compensation, Unemployment Compensation, and other insurances. Nurse may practice nursing for others during those
periods when Nurse is not performing work under this contract for Corporation. Corporation may, during the length of this contract, engage other nurses to perform the
same work that Nurse performs under this contract.

Duties and Responsibilities

The work to be performed by Nurse includes all services which are usually performed by [insert type of practice] nurses including, but not limited to, the following:
[insert type of nursing services to be rendered]

Payment Schedule

Corporation will pay Nurse the total sum of _____ Dol-
lars ($ ____) for the services to be provided under this contract, according to the
following schedule:

Professional Liability Insurance

The nursing service to be provided under this contract will be accomplished at
Nurse's risk, and Nurse assumes all responsibility for the condition of his/her own
equipment used in the performance of this contract. Nurse will carry, for the length of
this contract, liability insurance in an amount [insert limits of professional liability insurance coverage you carry].

Length of Contract

Either party may cancel this contract on _____ month(s)' written notice; otherwise, the contract remains in force for a period of _____, from date of execution of this contract by both parties.

Dispute Resolution

For all disputes arising under or in connection with this contract which cannot first be resolved through good faith negotiations, the parties shall mediate those disputes with the assistance of a third party neutral. Costs for such mediation shall be borne equally, unless otherwise agreed to during such mediation. If the parties cannot resolve any such disputes in mediation, they shall submit such disputes to binding arbitration.

[SIGNATURES]

[DATES]

SAMPLE CONTRACT FOR THE NURSE WHEN WORKING AS A CONSULTANT

This contract is made _____, _____, 19____, between a corporation organized under the laws of the State of _____ with its principal place of business at _____ [address], City of _____, County of _____, State of _____, hereinafter referred to as Corporation, and _____ of _____ [address], City of _____, County of _____, State of _____, hereinafter referred to as Nurse Consultant.

Corporation is in the business of _____ [type of business], and wants to have the following services, as a consultant, accomplished by Nurse Consultant.

Nurse Consultant agrees to accomplish these services for corporation under the terms and conditions contained in this contract.

In consideration of the mutual promises contained in this contract, it is agreed by and between Corporation and Nurse Consultant as follows:

Duties and Responsibilities

Nurse Consultant will perform consulting services on behalf of the Corporation with respect to all matters relating to: [insert description of duties and responsibilities]

Location of Work

Nurse Consultant's services will be rendered at _____ [address], City of _____, State of _____, but that Nurse Consultant will, when requested, come to the Corporation's address at _____ [address], City of _____, State of _____, or such other locations as designated by the Corporation, to confer with representatives of the Corporation.

Amount of Time Devoted to Work

In the performance of the services, the services and the hours Nurse Consultant is to work on any particular day will be completely within Nurse Consultant's control and Corporation will rely upon Nurse Consultant to work such number of hours as is necessary to fulfill the intent and goal(s) of this contract. It is estimated that this work will take approximately _____ [days of work per month]. However, there may be some months during which Nurse Consultant may not provide any services or, in the alternative, may work the full week.

Payment Schedule

Corporation will pay Nurse Consultant the total sum of _____ Dollars ($_____) each year payable in equal monthly installments on or before the _____ day of each month for services rendered in the prior month. In addition, Nurse Consultant will be reimbursed for all traveling and living expenses while away from the City of _____, State of _____.

Length of Contract

The parties to this contract agree that this contract is intended to be for five (5) years from date hereof, but the contract shall be considered as a firm commitment on the part of the parties hereto for a period of _____ one (1) year commencing _____, 19_____. At any time before _____ [month and day] of any year, either party hereto can notify the other in writing that the arrangement is not to continue beyond the _____ [month and day]. In the absence of any such written notification, this contract will run from year to year up to the maximum period of five (5) years.

Status of Consultant

This contract contains the performance of the services of the Nurse Consultant as an independent contractor and Nurse Consultant will not be considered an employee of the Corporation for any reason, including, but not limited to, payment of taxes and insurances.

Services for Others

Because Nurse Consultant will acquire or have access to information which is of a confidential and privileged nature, Nurse Consultant shall not perform any services for any other person or firm without Corporation's prior written consent.

Services After Contract Ends

Nurse Consultant agrees that, for a period of one (1) year following the termination of this contract, Nurse Consultant shall not perform any similar services for any person or firm engaged in the business of _____ [specify business] in the County of _____, State of _____.

Dispute Resolution

For all disputes arising under or in connection with this contract which cannot first be resolved through good faith negotiations the parties shall mediate those disputes with the assistance of a neutral third party. Costs for such mediation shall be borne equally, unless otherwise agreed to during such mediation. They shall submit such disputes under this contract to binding arbitration if they cannot be resolved first through good faith negotiations and mediation.

[SIGNATURES]

[DATE]

SAMPLE OF A NURSE EXECUTIVE EMPLOYMENT CONTRACT

AGREEMENT made this _____ day of _____, [month], 19____, between HEALTH CARE FACILITY, INC., a _____ [state] corporation, with its principal place of business _____ [address], _____ [state], hereinafter called "Employer," and _____, R.N., _____ [address], _____ [state], hereinafter called "Employee."

1. Length of Employment

The Employer hereby employs the Employee and Employee hereby accepts employment with the Employer for a length of _____ years beginning the first day of _____, of _____ years beginning the first day of _____, _____ [month], 19____. This Contract may be terminated earlier or renewed as hereinafter provided.

2. Duties and Responsibilities of Employee

A. **General Duties:** The Employee is hereby employed as a Vice President and Chief of Nursing Operations of Employer's Corporation. The Employee shall carefully and accurately perform all the duties and tasks of the Chief of Nursing Operations and perform all duties commonly discharged by Vice Presidents and Chief of Nursing Operations and such other duties of a similar nature as may be required from time to time by the Employer.

B. **Specific Duties and Responsibilities:** The Employee is specifically engaged by the Employer to:

C. **Other Duties and Responsibilities of the Employee:** In addition to the above-described duties and responsibilities, the Employee shall perform such other work as may be assigned to her/him subject to the control, instructions, and directions, of the Employer, provided only that such additional duties shall be during the hours and at the place of employment specified in this Contract and shall be reasonably related to the goals of Employer.

D. **Changes of Duties and Responsibilities:** The duties and responsibilities of the employment may be changed from time to time by the mutual consent of the Employer and the Employee. Despite any such change, the employment of the Employee shall continue under the Contract as modified.

E. **Place of Performance:** At the commencement of his employment, the Employee shall perform her/his duties and responsibilities at the office of the Employer located at _____ [address], _____ [state]. However, at any time deemed necessary or advisable by the Employer for business reasons, the Employee shall work at such other place or places as may be determined by the Employer; provided, however, that if the place designated by Employer is outside the [agreed-upon geographic area] for a period in excess of one (1) month, Employer shall pay Employee [agreed-upon amount] a day fee in addition to the expenses and other compensation provided in this Contract.

F. **Hours of Employment:** The Employee shall work those hours necessary to get the functions of the Corporation accomplished. The Employee is in a management position and as such shall not be required to work a minimum or maximum number of hours.

3. Disability

If the Employee at any time during the term of this Contract should be unable because of personal injury, illness, or any other cause to perform her/his duties under this Contract, the Employer may assign the Employee to other duties and the consequent compensation to be paid to the Employee shall be negotiated by the Employer and Employee. If the Employee is unwilling to accept the modification in duties, or if the Employee's inability to perform is of such extent as to make a modification of duties and responsibilities in this Contract not feasible, this Contract shall terminate within [number of days agreed upon] after that.

4. Compensation

A. **Base Compensation:** As compensation for services rendered under this Contract, the Employee shall receive from the Employer a salary of _____ Thousand Dollars ($) a year for the first year, payable in semimonthly installments on the 1st and 15th day of each month during the length of employment, prorated for any partial employment period. Employee's salary shall be increased by _____ Percent (%) a year each year of the Contract. Salary increases pursuant to renewals of the Contract shall be limited to _____ Percent (%) yearly unless otherwise agreed to in writing by the parties.

B. **Additional Compensation:** In recognition of the Employee's special value to the Employer and as a special inducement to the Employee, and in order to retain Employee's special expertise, the Employer agrees to pay to the Employee the sum of _____ Thousand Dollars ($) payable over a _____ (   ) year period, in equal increments of _____ Thousand Dollars ($) per year, payable on the first day of each year, until the total of _____ Thousand Dollars ($) is paid to the Employee. The employment inducement money shall be paid Employee regardless of whether she/he stays with _____, Inc., for a full _____ (   ) year term or whether she/he is terminated for cause or otherwise during the first _____ (   ) years of this Contract. If termination occurs for any reason, including death, before the completion of the _____ (   ) years, the balance owed Employee under this clause shall be paid in full on termination date. This shall be treated and is in fact additional salary being paid the Employee, but for purposes of the _____% salary increase annually for each year of the Contract shall not be subject to this clause. This employment inducement salary shall not be included in any renewal of this Contract. This clause does not prevent Employee from being eligible to participate in any bonus, dividend or other program for employees established by Employer.

5. Employee Benefits and Bonuses

A. **General:** The Employee shall be entitled to participate in the qualified pension plan, qualified profit sharing plan, medical and dental reimbursement plan, group life insurance plan, disability insurance, and any other employee benefit plan that Employer establishes, in accordance with the terms of any such plan.

B. **Vacation Privileges:** The Employee shall be entitled, after she/he has been employed for a period of one (1) year, to an annual vacation leave of six (6) weeks, at full pay. The Employer shall determine the vacation time of the Employee in order to assure the efficient and orderly operation of the Health Care Facility, Inc.

6. Reimbursement of Employee Expenses

The Employer, in accordance with the rules and regulations that it may issue, shall reimburse the Employee for business expenses incurred in the performance of his/her duties.

7. Noncompetition Restrictive Covenant by Employee

In consideration of the Employer's employing the Employee in a position wherein she/he has and will gain specific knowledge an expertise and will establish personal relationships with the Employer's contractors and patients, confidential files, and other employees, the Employee agrees as follows:

A **During Term of Employment:** During the length of this Contract, the Employee shall not directly or indirectly, either as an employee, employer, consultant, agent, principal, partner, stockholder, corporate officer, director, or in any other capacity, engage or participate in any health care facility that is in competition in any manner with the business of the Employer.

8. Military Service

A. **Military Training Leave** If the Employee is or becomes a member of a Military Reserve or National Guard unit she/he shall be granted a leave of absence for a period of fourteen (14) days plus travel time each year to attend training camp. During such leave, the Employee shall receive full compensation, and such leave shall be in addition to any vacation or other leave to which she/he may be entitled to under this Contract.

B. **Effect of Military Service:** In the event that the Employee is drafted or is otherwise inducted into the Armed Forces of the United States, she/he shall be entitled to receive full compensation under this Agreement during the period of such military service. At the expiration of such military service, the Employee shall be fully reinstated in his/her employment and shall be entitled to continue to render services for the balance of the time which remains under the Contract. If the Employee is not qualified to resume his/her former position by reason of a disability sustained during military service, the Employer shall employ her/him in such other position, the duties and responsibilities of which she/he is qualified to perform, as well provide him/her like seniority status, and compensation consistent with the then existing circumstances, unless it is impossible or unreasonable at that time for the Employer to do so.

9. Renewal

This contract may be renewed if the parties agree for three (3) one (1) year terms. Such agreement shall be in writing and signed at least sixty (60) days before the expiration of this Contract or any renewal period.

10. Termination

A. **By Employer for Cause:** If Employee willfully breaches or makes it a habit to neglect the duties and responsibilities that she/he is required to perform under this Contract, Employer may terminate this Contract by giving written notice to the Employee without prejudice to any other remedy to which the Employer may be entitled.

B. **By Employee:** This Contract may be terminated by the Employee by giving thirty (30) day's written notice of termination to Employer.

C. **Remedies:** Termination by either party shall not prejudice any remedy that the terminating party may have.

D. **Option to Terminate if Employee Permanently Disabled:** If the Employee becomes permanently disabled because of illness, physical or mental disability, or any other reason, so that it reasonably appears that she/he will be unable to complete her/his duties under this Contract, Employer may terminate this Contract by giving thirty (30) days written notice of termination to Employee. Such termination shall be without prejudice to any right or remedy to which the Employer or Employee may be entitled.

E. **Effect of Termination on Compensation:** In the event of the termination of this Contract before the completion of the length of employment specified in it, Employee shall be entitled to the compensation earned by her/him before the date of termination as provided for in this Contract computed pro rata up to and including that date, and said compensation shall be paid by Employer within thirty (30) days of the termination date. Employee shall be entitled to no further compensation as of the date of termination except that provided in clause 4(b).

11. General Provisions

A. **Notices:** Any notices to either party required under this Contract may be given by personal delivery in writing or by mail, registered or certified, postage prepaid with return receipt requested. Mailed notices shall be addressed to the parties at the addresses listed in this Contract, unless changed and noticed according to this clause. Notices delivered personally shall be deemed communicated as of time of actual delivery; mailed notices shall be deemed communicated as of thirty (30) days after mailing.

B. **Entire Agreement:** This Agreement supersedes any and all other agreements, either oral or in writing, between the Employer and Employee with respect to the employment of the Employee by the Employer and contains all of the representations, covenants, and agreements between the parties with respect to such employment in any manner whatsoever.

C. **Arbitration:** Any dispute arising out of or in connection with this Contract which cannot be resolved by good faith negotiations between Employer and Employee shall be submitted to binding arbitration under the rules of the American Arbitration Association.

D. **Governing Law:** This Agreement shall be governed by and construed in accordance with the laws of the State of _____, and the only venue for legal action hereunder shall be the Court of _____ in the State of _____.

E. **Payment of Moneys Due Deceased Employee:** If Employee dies before
the expiration of the term of employment, any moneys that may be due her/
him from Employer under this Contract as of the date of her/his death shall
be paid to the executor or administrator of her/his estate.

[SIGNATURES]

_____
EMPLOYER

_____
EMPLOYEE

[DATE]

Points to Remember

▶ A contract is an agreement the law will enforce.
▶ The elements in a contractual relationship are the offer, acceptance, consideration, and breach.
▶ Once the offer is accepted, the contract is created.
▶ "Consideration" is the amount paid by the offeror in exchange for a promise or agreement.
▶ To be enforced, most contracts do not have to be in writing. However, to prove what the terms of the contract are, it is helpful to have them documented.
▶ Monetary damages are the usual remedy for a breach of contract.
▶ Using alternative methods to resolve disputes is less expensive, faster, less traumatizing, and more private than pursuing a lawsuit in court. The types of methods include mediation, arbitration, fact finding, and a summary jury trial.
▶ The appropriate alternative dispute method should be included as a contract term.
▶ Independent contractors and consultants must arrange to pay their own federal and state income taxes, and social security and unemployment obligations.
▶ Breach of employment executive contracts by either party is often handled through binding arbitration.

Study Questions

1. Discuss the four elements in a contractual relationship.
2. What is the purpose of a merger clause?

3. Why should an alternative dispute resolution be included in a contract?

4. Discuss contractual remedies.

5. a. Describe three types of contracts and when they should be used.

   b. Describe the employment issues that should be covered in each type of contract.

   c. Develop a sample contract using one of the three types of contracts discussed.

6. Discuss the similarities and differences between the four methods of resolving disputes.

7. Explain the advantages of using alternatives to the court system to resolve disputes.

8. Why should a contract be in writing?

9. Why should nurses understand basic contract law?

10. Discuss instances when legal counseling is helpful in the contract process.

▶ **ETHICS IN PRACTICE**

Betty A., RN, graduated from an Associate Degree program 2 years ago and is now the 3 to 11 P.M. charge nurse on the medical unit of a small rural hospital. Most of her experience for the past 2 years has been in the medical unit, although she has occasionally floated to the maternity unit, emergency room (ER), and intensive care unit (ICU). The usual staffing for her unit on her shift is an RN, an LPN, and an aide.

One Friday evening, the nursing supervisor called Betty at the beginning of her shift and stated that she needed Betty to go to the 6-bed ICU to cover for 1 to 1½ hours because the scheduled RN for the ICU had been in a minor accident on the way to work. The supervisor felt Betty was the best qualified of the nurses that were in the hospital at that time and that the medical unit was quiet enough so that the LPN could handle it while Betty was gone.

Betty quickly went to the ICU where she received an abbreviated report on the four unit patients from the 7 A.M. to 3 P.M. nurses who were waiting to leave for the weekend. The day shift RN also mentioned that there was a patient in the ER who was experiencing some chest pain and might be admitted to the ICU.

Within minutes of receiving the report, the ER called and said they were admitting a 46-year-old male with an acute anterior myocardial infarction (MI) to the ICU. They also relayed the facts that they had begun streptokinase therapy and that the patient required very close monitoring for dysrhythmias, blood pressure changes, and bleeding.

Betty had never administered or cared for a patient receiving streptokinase and felt incompetent to care for such a patient. Although the

LPN working with her had worked with these types of patients, she was not permitted to administer any of the many IV medications this type of patient requires. Just as the patient was being brought through the ICU doors, Betty called the nursing supervisor to let her know that she would need help with this patient. The nursing supervisor said that because of call ins, there was no help available at this time, but that Betty just needed to admit the patient. The regular ICU RN should be in at any time.

Betty assessed the patient and checked his vital signs. He was cold, diaphoretic, and a pale, gray color. His blood pressure was 88/42 with a pulse of 52, and he was having frequent premature ventricular contractions (PVCs). The monitor technician also informed Betty that he was in a 2:1 AV block. Betty wanted the supervisor to come to the floor and relieve her of the responsibility for the care of this patient. Betty did not know the ICU protocols for dysrhythmias and did not feel competent to care for this seriously ill patient. It would be at least another 45 minutes before the regular RN arrived.

What are Betty's obligations under her contract with the hospital? What are the hospital's obligations in this situation? Where do the issues of justice and fidelity fit into this situation? Are there any "fidelity conflicts" in this situation? How should Betty resolve the dilemma?

Documentation

ETHICAL CONSIDERATIONS

▼ The universal dislike of paperwork in general, and charting in particular, is the one issue in health care that probably all nurses agree upon. The amount of time nurses spend completing forms, filling out checklists, and organizing progress notes has increased in proportion to the amount of government regulation and the ever-increasing complexity and specialization found in today's health care system. Although most nurses realize the importance of accurate and timely documentation of patient care, they also see it as an activity that removes them from the patient's bedside and that increases their overall work load. Seldom is documentation included as an element in the nurse's proficiency evaluation, thus reducing its importance as an activity for nurses. The one aspect of patient care that is most likely to be abbreviated during a nurse's busy day is charting.

In recent years, the medical record (that is, patient's chart) has attained tremendous stature as a key element in most lawsuits brought against health care providers, including nurses. Because of this increased interest in documentation by the legal system, the ethical and legal principles involved in documentation have been welded into one inseparable issue. Yet, the ethical principles that underlie good charting also serve to form the underpinnings of the legal value of that charting in a court of law.

First and foremost, the ethical principle of veracity serves as the bedrock issue in documentation. Although veracity (truth telling) is an important element in all aspects of health care, it loses its ambiguity when it takes on a written form. It is a generally accepted principle that health care providers should ''tell the truth'' to patients concerning their health care. Yet most nurses realize that truth telling is not an absolute principle. Telling the truth to a patient can have a number of meanings ranging from giving the patient all the information available, to providing the patient with the information he or she ''needs,'' to withholding information that is considered to be harmful to the patient's health or recovery.

About the only activity that is prohibited in relation to truth telling and patient care is outright mistruths or lies.

In documentation, there is no room at all for misinformation involving patient care. The patient usually does not have easy access to the chart, so that there is little need to protect him or her from disturbing information. The main purposes of charting are (1) to furnish other health care providers with information about the patient's condition and the care already rendered, and (2) to protect the health care provider from the legal system should something adverse or unexpected happen to that patient.

Not only is dishonest charting a violation of the ethical issue of veracity, but also a violation of the legal system. Charting activities that were not done, observations that were not made, or vital signs that were not taken constitute fraud in the eyes of the legal system. Depending on the situation and the state where it occurred, fraud may be treated as a crime punishable by either a fine and/or a jail term.

Another ethical principle that underlies charting is that of *beneficence*. To do good for the patient is a well-accepted principle in health care. A nurse must believe that accurate, truthful, complete, and timely charting aids in the cure of patients' diseases and hastens their recovery. The antithesis must also be accepted, namely that inaccurate, untruthful, incomplete, and late charting is harmful to patients' cures and recoveries.

Finally, as a practical issue in charting, it is important to consider what may possibly be done with that chart in the future. It would seem that the quality of nurses' charting, particularly the nurses' notes, would improve drastically if nurses kept it in the back of their minds that this chart may eventually turn up in a court of law. As nurses chart, they need to ask themselves: "How would this entry sound if it were read to me while I sit on the witness stand in front of a judge and a jury?" Professionalism is more than wearing a clean uniform and providing competent patient care. Professionalism is reflected in how nurses speak, how they present themselves to patients and the public, and how they record the activities of patient care in the chart.

OBJECTIVES

Upon completing this chapter, the reader will be able to:

1 Identify appropriate documentation, as required by the current health care system, including computerized documentation systems.
2 Discuss pitfalls that lead to weak documentation and potential problems.
3 Relate the process of continuing quality improvement (CQI) to documentation.
4 Identify the appropriate use of variance, incident, or occurrence reports.
5 Identify the appropriate use of employee health records, including postexposure tests to human immunodeficiency virus (HIV) and hepatitis B virus (HBV).
6 Relate the importance of confidentiality in patient care documentation.
7 Discuss reasons for documentation.

8 Identify potential areas of legal liability in charting.

9 Relate charting do's and don'ts.

10 Discuss case law involving documentation errors and problems.

INTRODUCTION

Documentation is the cornerstone of all health care decision making. The old adage, "If it was not documented, it was not done," is as true today as ever before. The nurse is responsible for the largest part of the patient care record. Documentation recorded by the nurse is a critical factor from a legal-ethical perspective, a patient outcome perspective, and a continuous quality improvement perspective.

PURPOSES OF DOCUMENTATION

In addition to serving as a confidential record that identifies the patient and health care services provided, the medical record is a business and legal record that has many uses and serves multiple purposes. The primary purposes of the record are to identify the patient's status in order to document the need for care and to plan, deliver, and evaluate that care. The following are secondary purposes for nursing documentation:

1. Evidence of the provision of quality nursing care.
2. Evidence of the nurse's legal responsibilities to the patient.
3. Information for personal health protection.
4. Evidence of standards, rules, regulations, and laws regarding nursing practice.
5. Statistical information for standards and research.
6. Cost-benefit reduction information.
7. Communicational risk management information.
8. Information for student learning experiences.
9. The protection of patient rights.
10. Documentation of professional and ethical conduct and responsibility.
11. Data to ensure appropriate reimbursement.
12. Data for planning future health care.
13. Data on nursing and medical history for future admissions.
14. Data for quality-of-care review.
15. Data for continuing education and research.
16. Data for billing and reimbursement.
17. Data to record nursing care, which forms the basis of evaluation

by the Joint Commission on Accreditation for Healthcare Organizations (JCAHO) agencies.

18. Communication between the responsible nursing professionals
    and other practitioners contributing to managing patient care.

EFFECTIVE DOCUMENTATION

Communication is one of the most important skills and activities
nurses use on a daily basis. Nurses gain most of their knowledge about
their patients through effective communication. Effective written communication skills are essential in order to precisely document nursing practices and to describe the nursing care delivered. Documentation forms the
framework for all nursing activities, and documentation standards establish specific regulatory guidelines and policies. Documentation skills are
necessary in order to provide evidence of application of these standards
through accurate, timely, and complete record entries.

Effective documentation includes the following:

1. Written communication of essential facts in order to maintain a
   continuous record of events over a period of time.
2. Preparation and maintenance of accounts of events through charts,
   records, or documents.
3. Entries into patient records to give evidence of the need for care,
   to identify patient problems, and to plan, deliver, and evaluate that
   care.
4. Professional monitoring and evaluation of the patient, nursing
   judgments and actions, the patient's progress with regard to health
   or illness, and the outcomes.
5. Entries of nursing activities performed on behalf of the patient.

DOCUMENTATION STANDARDS

Standards governing documentation come from various sources such
as federal and state laws, the American Nurses' Association (ANA),
JCAHO, institutional policies and procedures, and other health care
organizations.[1]

Standards must be "reasonable." If the standard at your facility is set
at providing the optimal level of care, nurses will be held to the higher
standard of care even though the national standard is lower. Keep this in
mind when writing your policies and procedures.

CONTINUOUS QUALITY IMPROVEMENT

Nursing has been concerned with the process of assuring quality patient care since the time of Florence Nightingale. The initial primary focus on patient care quality began with single events and single settings. Dissatisfaction by consumers with both the cost and the quality of care led to attempts to change health care through intense regulation and reliance on legal decisions to support patients' rights. Health care leaders responded by focusing on entire patient care episodes and recognizing the importance of synergy between the provider and the system in affecting quality outcomes. **Continuous quality improvement (CQI)** is a desirable method for bringing about needed changes. This approach has been embraced by the JCAHO as part of its agenda for change.

The origins of CQI lie in the work of Joseph Juran and W. Edward Deming, Americans who developed effective processes for implementing them as consultants to the Japanese manufacturing industries following World War II. Juran and Deming refer to CQI as total quality management (TQM) or quality improvement processes.

In the past, facilities have used quality assurance and risk management to manage and control the quality of care and financial losses. Quality assurance is a process used to evaluate the type and level of patient care that is given by the health care provider. Patterns and recurring incidents are evaluated to determine how to change them so that a more optimal level of patient care can be achieved.

Risk management is a quality assurance process used by facilities to prevent financial losses before they happen, by identifying, analyzing, minimizing, and preventing risks in problem areas that result in claims by injured patients, staff, or visitors.[2] Risk management tools commonly used include incident, variance, or occurrence reports; surveys; committees; training and retraining of staff; communication between patient and staff and among health care providers; patient and staff education; monitoring of risks and injuries; and accurate and comprehensive documentation.[3]

CQI is a more mature process than quality assurance (QA) or quality control (QC) and assumes that work groups are experts about their work and should be the focus for monitoring quality, identifying problems, and devising solutions. Data for improvement purposes is collected from the nurses' documentation and is used to assist in problem verification, analysis of problems, measurement of improvement over time, and conformance to standards of care.

The staff nurse responsible for implementing patient care services actively participates in the actual patient care processes and is in the perfect position to analyze those processes with a view toward system improvement and to document those processes appropriately. Merely to monitor the status quo is inadequate.

TYPES OF DOCUMENTATION

The best type of documentation is concise, factual, accurate, and timely. This type of documentation allows for a more efficient and effective method of patient care and communication among health care providers.

Although it may be difficult to do with 10 seriously ill patients and no aide or licensed practical nurse (LPN), timely documentation can be critical for patient care. For example, if a dose of insulin is given but not documented and a supervisor or a medication nurse tries "to help out" and does not talk to the nurse who actually gave the insulin, the patient could be overdosed and suffer severe consequences.

It is also important to chart accurately. Mistakes have been made with medications in failing to chart the dosages accurately. For example, if an order is given for Demerol 25 mg and is written on the medication record as Demerol 125 mg, this could be detrimental to the patient depending on his or her condition.

Charting should also not be used to state personal feelings about patients. For example, "Mrs Stacey is bullheaded and obnoxious and won't take her medicines." Although the statement may be true, if insulting or derogatory remarks are made by the staff and the patient is unhappy with the care rendered, a lawsuit is more likely to result.

Documentation should also be factual. Documentation that is falsified can lead to serious problems if a patient sues for medical negligence and it is discovered that records are altered or falsified or if there are accusations of Medicare and Medicaid fraud and abuse.

INCIDENT, VARIANCE, OR OCCURRENCE REPORTS

Many times when the standard of care is breached or an unusual occurrence takes place with regard to patient care or a visitor, an *incident, variance, or occurrence report* is completed. These reports are used for quality improvement and should not be used for disciplinary action against staff members. No mention of the report should be made in the patient's record. Also, it should not be charted that an incident report has been written because it is a red flag to a plaintiff's attorney. Also the incident report must not be made a part of the employee's personnel file because the file may be subpoenaed by the plaintiff's attorney. If the entire file is subpoenaed and the incident report is a part of the file, the otherwise confidential report may be discoverable.

When reporting an incident or occurrence, one should state only the facts. No assumptions; hypothetical, derogatory, or inflammatory remarks;

opinions; judgments; or recommendations on how to avoid or prevent such an incident in the future should be made on the report.[4]

The ideal type of incident report is one that is primarily a checkoff list, where there is a limited area for an actual narrative report. There should be an area for a brief factual description of the incident. There should not be an area for physician comments. Again this is a nursing incident report, not a physician report. Many times physicians make statements that are very damaging to the nurse and hospital in order to cover their potential exposure.

Only the facts should be stated in the actual nursing notes and in the actual incident report. For example, if the wrong medication is given to a patient, the following type of documentation should be noted in the record:

1. Medication given versus medication that should have been given.
2. Vital signs of patient.
3. Adverse effects, if any.
4. Name, date, and time when physician was notified and orders given, if any.
5. Treatment or procedures done per physician's orders.
6. Patient's response.

EXAMPLE

1. Aminophylline 200 mg is given instead of Amoxil. Aminophylline 200 mg given PO at 8 A.M.
2. Dr. Stamp called.
3. Orders noted. VS—T98.6, P80, R20, B/P 120/80. Skin warm and dry. In no distress.
4. Amoxil 250 mg given at 8 P.M.

Documenting Incidents in Your Diary

Any personal notes that are used to prepare for a deposition or trial can be obtained by the plaintiff's attorney. When there is the possibility of a lawsuit, it is advisable to be cautious in writing facts or assumptions about an incident in personal notes. Always show any such material to your attorney prior to your trial or deposition.

TELEPHONE ORDERS AND VERBAL ORDERS

With regard to telephone orders, it is crucial that the orders be written and cosigned according to the hospital policy and procedure. It is also very dangerous to obtain telephone orders for a **Do Not Resuscitate**

(DNR) order on a patient. If there is any type of controversy regarding the death of a patient on a DNR order, the nurse may be exposed if the physician states that he or she did not give the order and refuses to cosign. If there is a certain circumstance where a DNR order must be obtained over the telephone, it is imperative that the nurse and another witness on the telephone sign and verify the fact that they have heard the DNR order given by the physician.

DO NOT RESUSCITATE ORDERS

Do Not Resuscitate orders must be written in order to protect the health care provider in situations where there is a potential for a medical malpractice suit. There should be policies regarding DNR orders, and a time limit should be placed on the orders so that they are renewed periodically. A patient's status may change, and the need for DNR orders may no longer be required. Also, any discussions regarding DNR orders with the patient or family should be documented. Institutions may also want to develop a form for DNR cases that explains what happens if the patient is not resuscitated and the implications of that. This form should be signed and dated by the patient and family member who consents to such an order. A copy should be given to the patient and a copy can remain on file.

EMPLOYEE HEALTH RECORDS

Employee health records are essential to care for the staff of any facility. Those records may be reviewed by outside agencies and generally should be carefully constructed to provide adequate information without divulging privileged or confidential information. Of particular concern, following implementation of the Occupational Safety and Health Administration's (OSHA) Standard for Prevention of Transmission of Bloodborne Pathogens in the Workplace, is test results following occupational exposure to hepatitis B virus (HBV) or human immunodeficiency virus (HIV). It is suggested that those records be segregated from the balance of the employee's health record and maintained in a separate medical file so that the results are not provided to attorneys who subpoena a nurse's personnel or health file.

FAXES

With materials that are faxed, there is the potential for breaches of confidentiality if the fax machine is in an area that is not limited to the individual's access. Policies and procedures must be developed regarding the kind and types of information that can be faxed and the information that is too confidential, such as HIV and HBV test or status reports. Policies and procedures must also be developed when information that may be considered confidential is transmitted to the wrong person or received by the wrong person or facility.

DISCHARGE PLANNING AND DISCONTINUATION OF HOME HEALTH SERVICES

When planning for a discharge, it is of the utmost importance that there be documentation that the patient or the patient's family is aware of the fact that treatment and care will be discontinued on a specific date and the consequences; alternative resources; and specific plans that must be put into action after the effective date. It is wise to develop a specific form that can be signed and dated where there is documentation of the information that is discussed with the patient. Both the patient and the family member should sign and date the form. They should be provided with a copy and a copy should remain on the patient's medical records. This may decrease the possibility for exposure if there is a claim of medical malpractice and abandonment. (Unilateral termination of care and treatment by the health care provider without the patient's consent.)

DOCUMENTATION WEAKNESSES

In documentation, every word counts. Legally speaking, your documentation is just as important as the care you provide. It must indicate assessments noted and the interventions performed in response to those assessments. Furthermore, a summary of actions that are taken but lacking a record of follow-up on those actions presents a legally damaging document. An attorney, a risk manager, or another health care provider should be able to review the patient record and reconstruct the care the patient received, even if months or years have passed. If key facts or notes on follow-up are not documented, it is difficult to defend.

To be certain that your documentation is complete, address these three vital aspects of care: *assessment, intervention,* and *patient response.* Be particularly alert in the following instances, where documentation weaknesses commonly occur:

When Vital Signs Are Abnormal. Any significant deviation from normal—whether it is elevated or decreased temperature, elevated or decreased blood pressure, or accelerated or slowed respiratory rate—demands a notation showing what is being done about it. When notifying a physician or other provider, record the time, the provider's response, and whether you acted on those instructions. Note also when you are unable to reach the primary provider as well as when you re-attempted to contact the provider or contacted someone else.

If your response to abnormal findings is to monitor the patient more closely (and frequently), specify that in your documentation, and note whether the patient's condition improves or deteriorates, and your response to that change in condition.

When a Patient Codes.   An unexpected bad outcome often results in legal action. Documenting what happened during a code or other emergency is especially crucial, since it is often argued that monitoring was inadequate and intervention occurred too late.

Emergency situations are precisely when documentation is apt to fall short. To avoid documentation gaps, many facilities keep code sheets on crash carts, and documentation is assigned to one member of the team who does only the documentation.

Once a crisis is over, check the documentation to be sure it is complete and review the chart to see that nothing crucial was omitted.

When a Patient Is Transferred.   Any patient moved—from the emergency department to intensive care unit, or other department, even from one medical-surgical unit to another—calls for a patient assessment. Document the condition of the patient soon after he or she arrives on your unit, and again right before he or she leaves. It should go without saying that the chart should contain a record of the patient's condition on admission to your institution, and that assessments are updated at the beginning and end of each shift or change of staffing.

FAILURE TO DOCUMENT VITAL INFORMATION

Failure to document vital information that would be used by other health care providers in rendering treatment can result in a malpractice action. In a Louisiana case, the hospital was held liable because a hospital employee was told by the family and patient that a knife used in the stabbing of the patient had a broken blade. Because this information was not charted on the patient's history and not communicated to the emergency room physician, no X-rays were taken. Two months later, X-rays were done because of continued pain and swelling in the shoulder, and knife blade fragments were found[5] [*Brown V.E.A. Conway Memorial Hospital,* 588 So.2d 295 (La. 1991)].

MEDICATIONS

When administering a medication, you must document the name of the medication, route, site, time, your name or initials, and the patient's response. It is extremely important to document the site, because if there is a lawsuit, for example, claiming sciatic nerve damage of the right leg, the attorney will focus on which nurses administered injections in the right gluteus maximus during the crucial time period.

It is also important to thoroughly read any affidavits given regarding your nursing care. In a sciatic nerve injury case that was settled out of court, a statement was prepared by an attorney to aid in proving that the hospital's nurses were not negligent in their method of administration. However, neither the attorney nor the nurse who signed the affidavit read it. Unfortunately, it stated that the nurse always gave her injections in the right *lower inner* quadrant of the gluteus maximus—a damaging statement resulting in immediate settlement of the case.

AMA DOCUMENTATION

When a patient leaves **against medical advice (AMA),** proper documentation must be made to decrease the potential liability exposure for the health care providers.

The physician should inform the patient of the risks of leaving without proper treatment. For example, if a patient is having chest pains radiating down the left arm, the patient should be warned that he or she could suffer damage to the heart and death if not treated. A form devised by your hospital attorney should be given to the patient to sign which states that he or she has been advised of the risks and dangers of leaving the hospital AMA. If the patient refuses to sign, document what was told to the patient and that he or she refused to sign the form.

If the physician is not available to discuss the dangers of leaving AMA, the nurse should discuss them with the patient. Documentation of the conversation should be made in the nurses' notes.

Also document the mental status of the patient and the patient's reason for leaving in his or her own words. Document that other family members or friends are present and have been informed of the dangers of leaving and given instructions about what to do. Instructions on follow-up care and drugs or prescriptions given to the patient must also be documented. If relatives who are not with the patient are notified, document the name, time notified, and what information was relayed. Finally, document the destination of the patient, how he or she is being transported, who is accompanying him or her, the time that he or she left the facility, and his or her mental and physical condition.

ADMISSIONS IN CHARTING

Avoid any admission of liability involving patient care when charting. In a New Hampshire case, a hospital was held liable when a nurse documented in her chart that the patient was found on the floor and had apparently crawled out of bed while trying to get to the bathroom. She wrote that the patient had called for help, but "there was not a quick enough response."

Only facts should be charted in patient's records. Speculations and admissions like those above will greatly aid the plaintiff's attorney in proving liability against the nurse and hospital.[6]

CHARTING DO's AND DON'Ts

The following are charting recommendations that should be utilized when doing any type of patient charting:

1. Have the patient's name on each sheet of the medical record. Many times charting may take place on the wrong chart because the nurse has not checked the actual patient's name on the chart. A word of caution: If you are aware of a lawsuit or anticipate a lawsuit regarding a particular patient, do not completely rewrite your nurse's notes. Attorneys and experts review charts and can detect when the actual records have been rewritten. An important point for a nurse to remember is that the top of a chart has the patient information that is routinely put on by the addressograph. If the chart is later rewritten, it will not be stamped. Secondly, handwriting analysis can be done on each chart to determine the date and type of ink as to when the actual recordings were made.
2. Read the nurses' notes prior to caring for a patient before charting your care. It is important that you know the status of your patient prior to charting to determine whether or not there has actually been any deterioration of the patient's status.
3. Make entries in order of consecutive shifts and dates. Remember, it is acceptable to document late entries if you have forgotten to put something in your records. The farther away from the actual time period that you actually document, the more suspicious it becomes to a judge or jury that you are trying to add information to cover yourself from potential exposure.
4. Write the complete date and time of each entry. This is important because if there is a medical negligence case involving a patient, a chronology of events will be developed in order to pinpoint the exact times when events occurred and whether or not timely intervention

would have changed the outcome. Military time is more effective because you do not have to determine if treatment was done in the "A.M." or "P.M."

5. Use concise, factual, concrete, and specific terminology. Describe reported symptoms accurately. "The reddened area on the left lower calf is 2 cm long."

6. Use the patient's words in describing symptoms whenever these words are helpful. Examples:
   a. "My back feels great today."
   b. "I am not having any pain in my stomach."

7. Use acceptable hospital abbreviations. Be sure that you know what the abbreviations in your hospital mean. For example, do not use "h/a" for "headache" *and* "heart attack."

8. Avoid using such words as "apparently" and "appears to be." For example, on the 11 to 7 shift the nurse documents that the patient "appears to be sleeping." There are no objective facts documented as to the patient's status. The 7 to 3 shift arrives, make rounds, and finds that the patient has been dead for several hours. The only documentation is that the patient "appears to be sleeping."

9. Avoid the use of phrases such as "in no acute distress."

10. Sign each entry with your name and title.

11. Do not leave any space between your last entry and your signature. This is very dangerous because you are allowing others the opportunity to document information that may be detrimental to the care and treatment that you rendered to the patient and may expose you to legal liability.

12. Do not chart in advance. Medical records have been discovered that have had, for example, "patient tolerated procedure well" documented when in fact the patient died during the procedure. Although this may not seem to be that terrible a charting error, it does lessen the credibility of the health care provider regarding what else might not have been properly done.

13. Do not chart until you have checked the patient's name to make sure that you are charting on the proper record.

14. Do not backdate, tamper with, or add to notes previously written. Use the appropriate charting procedure for late entries.

15. Do not skip lines between entries.

16. Do not write relative statements such as "wound is healing." Describe the wound.

17. Do not use slang.

18. Do not use medical terms unless you know their meaning.

19. Do not chart for anyone else, especially nursing actions performed by another nurse. Remember, it may be crucial to you if a lawsuit ensues and several years later the only documentation that could protect you

from exposure is the charting by another nurse. You may not remember that patient and what exactly happened, which could be detrimental to you.

20. If you have made an error in your charting, draw a line and follow the procedure noted in your hospital's policy and procedure manual. Many hospitals today direct staff to draw a line through the entry, write "void" or "error," and then initial it. Many hospitals are eliminating the use of "error"—it implies that something was done wrong and again it becomes a credibility issue that an attorney can use to attack a nurse during a trial.
21. Do not erase.
22. Do not use liquid correction fluid.
23. Chart only in ink.
24. Do not allow long periods of time to elapse between entries, because it may appear that the patient is abandoned.
25. Do not spell words incorrectly because this can cast doubt on your credibility. For example, if a nurse spells "aspirin" incorrectly, although it has nothing to do with the quality of the care and treatment rendered by her, the plaintiff's attorney will blow up the chart that has the word spelled incorrectly on it to insinuate and imply that the nurse cannot properly take care of a patient if she cannot even spell such a simple word.
26. Remember that the record will be used in a court of law in any type of medical negligence claim, personal injury case, or worker's compensation claim.
27. Describe only what you actually observe or assess.
28. The nurse must stay current in terminology and pathophysiology, new diseases, and new assessment tools in terms of ongoing illnesses.
29. The record contains confidential information and must not be placed where unauthorized persons, facility personnel, family members, or strangers can access it.
30. Do not blame others in your charting for acts or omissions that occur in patient care and treatment.

Case Example—Inadequate Documentation

Was the nurse's documentation inadequate to protect the hospital and nurses from legal exposure in a patient fall case? A 62-year-old stroke patient was admitted to the hospital. The doctor ordered that she wear a restraining jacket and that the bed rails be raised at all times. One month after the patient's admission, a nursing assistant found her on the floor where she apparently had fallen from the bed and fractured her right hip. The family of the patient sued the hospital for malpractice and the jury returned a verdict in favor of the hospital. The plaintiffs moved for a new trial. The trial judge granted the motion and awarded $225,000 for general damages and $60,897.37 for medical expenses.

The hospital appealed the award. What did the nursing notes document? The nurses' notes documented that the patient had "escaped from her retraining jacket and left the bed on several occasions." On the morning that she fractured her hip, it was documented that at 6:30 A.M. she was resting quietly in bed and the restraint was on and the side rails were up. At 7:15 A.M. a nursing assistant found the patient on the floor still wearing the restraints and the side rails were up. However, the nurse's notes actually contradicted the nurse's contingent that she actually saw the patient at 6:30 A.M. In fact, she actually did not check on the patient until 9:30 A.M.

The head nurse spoke to the husband about the problem and voiced her concern that he was unfastening her jacket and forgetting to retie it, which he denied, and asked that his wife be checked on almost constantly. This was documented in the notes. The head nurse informed him that she would require private duty nurses. The problem with the documentation was that there was no notation about the conversation showing that the husband was informed of the problem of his wife getting out of bed. The documentation on the chart showed that the hospital took no special steps to protect the patient. The court ruled that the conversations of the head nurse with the patient's husband did not relieve the hospital of the duty to take extra precautions and that the damage award was not excessive.[7] [*Keyworth v. Southern Baptist Hospital*, 524 So.2d 56 (La. App. 4th Cir. 1988).]

REVIEW OF MEDICAL RECORDS: AN ANALYSIS BY THE PLAINTIFF'S ATTORNEY OR EXPERT

When a plaintiff feels that there has been medical negligence involved in his or her care and treatment, he or she seeks an attorney who specializes in the area of medical malpractice. This attorney reviews the records or obtains an expert to review the records. The following are just some of documents reviewed to determine whether or not there has been a breach of the standard of care that has caused damage to the plaintiff:

History and physical, admit face sheet, physician orders, physician progress notes, nurses' notes, flow sheets, narrative notes, medication records, nursing care plan, vital signs sheets, surgery documents (including the record of the operation, anesthesia record, operating room nurse's notes and post anesthesia records), emergency room record, consultations, ambulance run sheets, consents for treatment or surgery, discharge teaching, X-ray reports, discharge summary, autopsy reports, records of treatments and care given by physical therapist, occupational therapist, respiratory therapist, dietitian, and social services, hospital/clinic/physician records and medical bills (itemized statements).

Medical records can be obtained by the patient from the medical records department of the facility. Medical records can also be obtained after a lawsuit has been filed by a *subpoena duces tecum* (SDT), which means "to appear and to bring with you." After a lawsuit has been filed, the plaintiff may also obtain medical records through a request for production of the documents.

COMPUTER CHARTING

The trend for the future is computer charting. Many hospitals and facilities are converting to this type of system.

Computer charting has many advantages, such as: (1) more accurate and timely charting; (2) easy access to patient information; (3) more efficient method of communicating; (4) help with providing patient confiden tiality; and (5) more legible patient information. Many times, nurses or physicians are included in a lawsuit because the care rendered cannot be determined because of illegible handwriting.

Along with this type of system are various potential legal problems regarding confidentiality issues. Both storage of medical records and access to such records is of primary concern to facilities. Policies and pro cedures must be developed limiting the time period that information is left on a screen if the nurse has to leave the station for some reason. Also the access codes for the nurse-employees or health care providers should not be alphabetical and in numerical order, which could be deciphered by someone. Access codes should be a random choice of numbers and letters. Computer terminals also should be placed in an area where there is limited access by other individuals. A mechanism must also be built in to determine which individuals are requesting sensitive information such as HIV results so that leaks of confidential information can be traced.

ETHICAL ISSUES

The ethical issues surrounding computer charting include privacy, accuracy of the information, accessibility by patient and health care providers, and property rights or who owns the records.[8]

Privacy of information obtained from the patient and family members must be protected from those who may "abuse" such information. Policies and procedures must be developed so that health care providers have guidelines for making sure that the information obtained is entered into computerized records accurately and in a timely manner. Orientation and training programs must be developed so that employees' computer skills can be checked and policies and procedures can be instituted for charting.

Policies and procedures must be developed to designate the process of who has accessibility; how they can obtain accessibility; why (for what reasons) they wish to access information; what information can be accessed; and what information is confidential and has limited access.

Patients also have a right to a copy of the medical records. However, with computerized charting, policies and procedures must be developed as to when a patient or a patient's attorney can actively obtain a copy of the computerized chart. Since the computerized chart can be printed out immediately, decisions such as whether a partial chart can be released or whether the patient must be discharged before he or she can obtain a copy of the chart must be made.

Points to Remember

▶ The primary purposes of documentation are to identify the patient's status in order to document the need for care and to plan, deliver, and evaluate that care.

▶ Continuous quality improvement (CQI) is a process which assumes that work groups are experts about their work and should be the locus for monitoring quality, identifying problems, and devising solutions.

▶ Four types of documentation are contemporaneous, accurate, fraudulent, and inappropriate.

▶ Incident, variance, or occurrence reports should only state facts surrounding an incident.

▶ Policies and procedures must be developed for telephone orders, DNR orders, verbal orders, and faxed materials to protect the health care provider and patient confidentiality.

▶ Several problem areas in documentation are when vital signs are abnormal; when the patient codes; when the patient is transferred; and medication administration.

▶ The plaintiff's attorney or an expert may review the entire medical chart, autopsy protocol, ambulance run sheet, and so on, to determine if there are breaches of the standard of care based on the documentation noted in the records.

▶ Computer charting policies and procedures must be especially sensitive to the potential risk of liability based on breach of a patient's privacy and confidentiality.

Study Questions

1. List five reasons for documentation.
2. What is ''effective'' documentation?
3. Discuss the continuous quality improvement (CQI) method.

4. Discuss three important aspects of the incident, variance, or occurrence report.

5. Outline and discuss 10 charting do's and don'ts.

6. Discuss current documentation and the nurse.

7. Outline important points that should be remembered when dealing with a DNR order.

8. Relate ethical and legal issues involved with computer charting.

9. Discuss what must be documented with an AMA patient

10. Relate three areas in nursing of potential danger and legal exposure when documenting.

REFERENCES

1. Iyer, P, and Camp, N: Nursing Documentation—A Nursing Process Approach. CV Mosby, St. Louis, 1991.
2. Fishbach, F: Documenting Care—Communication, the Nursing Process, and Documentation Standards. FA Davis, Philadelphia, 1991.
3. Northrop, C, and Kelly, M: Legal Issues in Nursing. CV Mosby, St. Louis, 1987.
4. Springhouse Corporation: Better Documentation. Springhouse Corp, Springhouse, Pa, 1992.
5. Tammelleo, AD: The Regan Report on Nursing Law, vol. 32, no. 9, February 1992.
6. *Brookover v. Mary Hitchcock Memorial Hospital,* 893 F.2d 411 NH (1990).
7. Nursing 90 Court Case: A question of inadequate documentation. Nursing 90: November 1990.
8. Faaoso, N: Automated patient care systems: The ethical impact. Nursing Management, vol. 23, no. 7, July 1992.

BIBLIOGRAPHY

Arikian, VL: Total quality management: Application to nursing service. Journal of Nursing Administration 21(6):46, 1991.
Deming, WE: Out of Crisis. Massachusetts Institute of Technology, Cambridge, Mass 1982.
JCAHO Transition: From QA to CQI—Using CQI Approaches to Monitor, Evaluate, and Improve Quality. Oakbrook Terrace, Ill, 1991.
Juran, J: Juran on Leadership for Quality. Free Press, New York, 1989.

▶ ETHICS IN PRACTICE

It was an extremely busy 3 to 11 P.M. shift on the surgical unit of a large city hospital. Because it was a Wednesday evening, the unit was not only receiving fresh postoperative patients from surgery but was also in the process of discharging patients and admitting new patients for the next day's surgery schedule.

Melinda L., RN, charge nurse for the 3 to 11 shift, had worked on the surgical unit for 2 years. She had a reputation as being a well-organized, competent, and hard-working nurse who seemed to be able to bring order out of chaos. On this particular shift, even her considerable skills in organization were failing to settle the unit to a point where she felt in control.

Mrs. Star J., a 66-year-old diabetic, was being admitted at 4:00 P.M. to the surgical unit because of poor circulation in her legs and possible infection of her right foot. One of her admission orders was to culture the drainage from the sore on her great right toe. In checking the orders after the unit secretary had noted them, Melinda decided to do the culture herself because the staff was already tied up in other activities. Melinda explained the procedure to Mrs. J. and then proceeded to culture a draining sore on her *left* toe. The culture was taken to the lab with the appropriate slips by the unit secretary.

During supper, a patient aspirated and coded. Later that evening, a patient fell while attempting to climb out of bed with the bed rails up. It was almost 11:45 P.M. when Melinda finally got to sit down and do her charting. After all that had happened that evening, she was having some trouble remembering what she had done earlier in the shift.

When she came to Mrs. J.'s chart, she remembered that she had gotten a culture and checked back on the orders to make sure it was actually ordered. The order said "C&S right great toe," so Melinda charted, "1630—Culture of right great toe obtained and sent to lab. Procedure explained to patient." And signed it.

On her way home that night, Melinda was thinking about how busy the shift was and all that had happened. She wondered if she had done everything that was supposed to be done, and charted everything that needed to be charted. She also began thinking about Mrs. J. and the culture. By the time she reached home, she felt pretty sure that she had cultured the wrong toe. She would correct the chart in 2 days when she worked again.

When Melinda returned after her 2 days off, she discovered that Mrs. J. had had a below-the-knee amputation of her right leg. The physician had decided to do the amputation because the culture that was sent to the lab had grown *Clostridium perfringens* (gas gangrene). Melinda feels that she is responsible for this mistake. What should she do? If she "tells" or tries to correct the chart, could she be open to a lawsuit?

LOBBYING: HOW TO IMPLEMENT CHANGE

Today nurses must be active in the legislative process in order to be heard on issues affecting nursing practice. There are many ways that nurses can become involved, such as gathering information on issues, visiting or writing to senators and representatives, and **lobbying** for specific **bills.** Legislative bills must go through a lengthy process before actually becoming law. (See "Path of a Bill from Conceptualization to Law".)

HOW TO LOBBY

1. Develop your plan of action. Consider, rework, revamp, and define your plan in advance of your trip to the legislator's office.
2. Practice, practice, and practice until your presentation is smooth. While legislators do not expect health care professionals to be polished lobbyists, a good presentation is much more impressive than an unprepared, bumbling attempt.
3. *Never lie!* If the answer is not available, promise to get it and then communicate that answer to the legislator or aide as soon as possible.
4. Be patient. Whether elected or appointed, officials have many people competing for their attention. Practice your presentation while you wait.
5. Courtesy is imperative. Officials and their aides are above all human. The old adage "common courtesy never cost a dime" applies here in capital letters. These individuals may respect you

PATH OF A BILL FROM CONCEPTUALIZATION TO LAW

Idea for legislated change ─────────→ Group takes idea and develops a proposal

Board of directors ←─────── Proposal presented to ←─────── Proposal discussed
approves plan　　　　　　　organization's board　　　　　with members of
　　　　　　　　　　　　　　of directors (i.e., ANA,　　　　professional orga-
　　　　　　　　　　　　　　AANA, etc.)　　　　　　　　　nization (Govern-
　　　　　　　　　　　　　　　　　　　　　　　　　　　ment Relations
　　　　　　　　　　　　　　　　　　　　　　　　　　　Committee, Legis-
　　　　　　　　　　　　　　　　　　　　　　　　　　　lative Action Com-
　　　　　　　　　　　　　　　　　　　　　　　　　　　mittee, etc.)

Public Relations ─────────→ Government Relations ─────────→ Sponsor brings
Committee launches　　　　Committee seeks leg-　　　　　　bill to House
public information　　　　islative sponsors for　　　　　or Senate
phase—Health　　　　　　bill
fairs, news releases,
articles in print, talk
shows (radio & TV),
town meetings, etc.

Health Committee ←─────── Health Committee holds ←─────── Senate President
recommends bill　　　　　public hearings and　　　　　　or House Speaker
to House or　　　　　　　nurses testify　　　　　　　　refers bill to Health
Senate　　　　　　　　　　　　　　　　　　　　　　Committee for
　　　　　　　　　　　　　　　　　　　　　　　　　review

Bill passes House or ─────────→ Bill referred to that ─────────→ That chamber's Health
Senate; it is then　　　　chamber's Health　　　　　　Committee holds pub-
sent to the House if　　　Committee　　　　　　　　lic hearings or nurses
the bill started in　　　　　　　　　　　　　　　testify
the Senate or sent
to the Senate if it is
started in the
House

Bill passes with changes to ←─────── Chamber's Health Commit-
original form or Bill rejected by　　　tee recommends bill
other chamber with the
changes made in the previous
chamber

Conference Committee of both ─────────→ Bill accepted by both House
chambers irons out difficulties　　　and Senate with Confer-
　　　　　　　　　　　　　　　　ence Committee
　　　　　　　　　　　　　　　　recommendations

President or governor signs bill ←─────── Bill sent to governor or president
into law　　　　　　　　　　　　for signature

and respond in a more helpful manner if you treat them with courtesy.

6. Be brief. Officials are often on busy schedules. Get in and out in an expedient amount of time while getting your point across.
7. Be direct. Get to the point but personalize the issue if possible. Use your own experience, or how the issue will affect your practice directly.
8. Keep it simple. Do not use jargon or get too detailed or too complex. Get to the point but make sure the official understands your point.
9. Do not travel in a pack. Keep your group small so as not to detract from your issues with the sheer numbers (not to mention the time lost in all those introductions).
10. Close effectively. Ask for the official's support or vote for your issue.
11. Follow up with a thank-you letter. Include a summary of your position and ask for the cooperation of the legislator in working on their hard-to-convince colleagues.

Handling Opposition

The committee hears testimony from interested parties and then decides to recommend the bill as is or amend the bill. Should the committee oppose the bill, they will simply let it "die" in committee. If a number of bills regarding the same issue are pending, the committee may report out a *clean bill,* which brings the features of the other similar bills in and provides totally new provisions. **Amendments** or clean bills can range from perfecting or helping a bill to gutting the original proposal and changing the meaning of the bill. Amendments must be carefully scrutinized.

A bill reported out of committee is put on a **calendar** for a vote by the full House or Senate. If your bill is placed on the *consent calendar,* on the date specified it will be called and passed without debate if no one objects. If your bill is placed on the regular calendar, as are all major bills and nonroutine minor bills, it will be called for debate and voted on the date indicated on the calendar. Of course, calendars are always subject to change.

As soon as your bill is out of committee, begin contacting each member of the full House or Senate. *Do not wait for the date of the vote!* Each member should be contacted formally by the group.

On the day of the vote, there must be enough volunteers in the galleries and in the lobbies of the capitol so that their numbers are noticed.

Wear badges identifying yourselves. Pay close attention to your bill when it is debated on the floor of the chamber because it may be amended. Amendments can improve or destroy a bill. The sponsor must be advised as to whether or not acceptance of an amendment is appropriate or opposition imperative.

To become law, a bill must be passed by both houses in identical form (except in Nebraska, which is unicameral). When one version of a bill is passed in the Senate and a different version in the House, a **conference committee** composed of members of both houses irons out the differences. Unless one version is totally objectionable, there is little to be done at this time. If your group simply cannot "live" with one version of the bill, your group must contact the members of the conference committee and try to gain support for the appropriate version of the bill.

Once the bill clears the conference committee, it goes to the president or governor. He or she may sign it into law, let it become law without his or her signature, **veto** it and send it back to the Congress or legislature, or *pocket veto* it (that is, leave it unsigned after the legislature adjourns). Unless there is evidence that the governor or president is in opposition to your bill, do nothing, or if it is major legislation, arrange to participate in the bill signing. If you think you are in trouble, get to the governor. If the bill is vetoed, your chance for mounting a campaign to override the veto is small unless the original vote was by a sizable margin and the governor does not command party loyalty. If the pocket veto is used, you can do nothing except start your planning for the next year.

Do not be discouraged if your program is defeated. Major social reform is a series of defeats often stretching over a generation followed by victory. Try again.

GETTING YOUR SENATOR OR REPRESENTATIVE TO VISIT YOU

When the legislator is in the home district, invite him or her to your office, hospital, operating room, or business to meet the people who work with you or invite the legislator to speak to your professional group. Scheduling for senators and representatives is handled by an appointment person in the local office in the major cities in the senator's home state or the representative's district. Following a visit, write a thank-you letter to your elected senator or representative or the aide and restate your position.

You may also invite the members of your state's congressional delegation to lunch or breakfast. This has been done in Washington for several

years with success. Remember, legislators need direct contact and expo
sure to their constituents and their views.

WRITING TO YOUR LEGISLATORS

Do not hesitate to write your congressional representative if you have
something to say. Legislators are sensitive to grass-roots opinions. Letters
from constituents are the best way for legislators to feel the pulse of their
district or state. The simple Do's and Don'ts list below will help you and
your professional organization in developing and implementing a sound
communication channel with your representation in the government.

Do's

1. Spell all names correctly and address the letters correctly.
2. Write legibly or type. Handwritten letters are perfectly acceptable
   so long as they can be read.
3. Use personal stationery. Indicate that you are a registered nurse.
   Sign your full name and address. If you are writing for an organization, use that organization's stationary and include information
   about the number of members in your organization, the services
   you perform, and the employment settings you are found in. For
   example, "I am a Certified Registered Nurse Anesthetist, and
   President of the Louisiana Association of Nurse Anesthetists. We
   are a 700-member group of advanced practice nurses who provide
   safe, cost-effective anesthesia services for the citizens of Louisiana. In this country C.R.N.A.s perform between 60 and 80% of the
   anesthetics in the rural sector and approximately 60% of the anesthetics for Medicare recipients."
4. If you are a constituent, state this. If you campaigned for or voted
   for the official, say so.
5. Identify the issue by number and name if possible or refer to it by
   the common name ("Clean Air Act").
6. State your position clearly and state what you would like your legislator to do. "I would like you to support the reauthorization of
   the funding for the Center for Nursing Research."
7. Make the letter your own words—your own thoughts.
8. Refer to your personal experience of how a bill will directly affect
   you, your family, clients, members of your organization, or your
   profession. Thoughtful, sincere letters on issues that directly
   affect the writer receive the most attention and are those that are
   often quoted in hearings or debates.
9. Be timely. Write in time for your legislator to act on an issue—

after the vote is too late. If your senator or representative is a member of the committee that is hearing the issue, contact him or her before the committee hearings begin. If he or she is not on the committee, write just before the bill is due to come to the floor for debate and vote.

10. Write the governor promptly for a state issue, after the bill passes both houses, if you want to influence his or her decision to sign the bill into law or veto it.

11. *Be appreciative!* Especially of past favorable votes. Many letters legislators receive are from constituents who are unhappy or displeased about actions taken on an issue. Letters of thanks are greatly appreciated.

12. Be brief in your writing. Most letters should be one page long. Make your point quickly and discuss only one issue per letter.

13. Remember, you are the expert in your professional area. Most legislators know little about the practice of nursing and respect your command of knowledge. Offer your expertise to your elected representative as an advisor or resource person to his or her staff when issues arise.

14. Ask for what you want your legislator to do on an issue. "We would like you to support H.R. 2143." Ask him or her to state his or her position in the reply to you.

Don'ts

1. Don't begin a letter with "as a citizen and a taxpayer." Legislators assume that you are a citizen, and all of us pay taxes.

2. Don't threaten or use hostility. "I'll never vote for you again if you . . ." will get no positive response. Most "hate" mail is ignored and rarely gets a response.

3. Don't send carbon copies of your letter to other legislators. Write each legislator individually. Don't send letters to legislators from other states—they will refer your letter to your congressional representative.

4. Don't write House members while a bill is in the Senate and vice versa. A bill may be amended many times before it gets from one house to the other.

5. Don't write postcards; they are tossed.

6. Try to avoid form letters. In large numbers these get attention only in the form that they are tallied. These letters tend to elicit a "form letter response" from the legislator.

7. Don't apologize for writing and taking their time. If your letter is short and presents your opinion on an issue, they are glad to have it.

How to Address a Letter to a Legislator

House of Representatives

Dear Congressman or Congresswoman (Full Name):

The Honorable (Full Name)
United States House of Representatives
Washington, DC 20515-(+ four-digit zip code)

Senate

Dear Senator (Full Name):

The Honorable (Full Name)
United States Senate
Washington, DC 20510-(+ four-digit zip code)

PREPARING YOUR MEMBERSHIP FOR AN EFFECTIVE LETTER-WRITING CAMPAIGN

The following suggestions for implementing a grass-roots effort should help you and your nursing organization in planning strategies:

1. Assess the knowledge level of your members concerning the legislative process and the issues that impact your organization. Use this information to plan educational sessions with the goal of improving the political sophistication of your members.
2. Give your members information about the bill in question and how this bill would directly affect your practice. State to them clearly what action the legislative body needs to take to meet your goal and include the specific bill number and name.
3. Develop a plan. What are the goals of this grass-roots letter-writing campaign, and how do you plan to get there?
4. Set up an effective telephone network that can contact key members quickly. Often legislative issues are scheduled and moved up quickly on that schedule, requiring an immediate change of plan. Fax networks or computer modem setups can facilitate the need for instant communications.
5. Identify and set up contacts with the key legislators involved in your issue.
6. Set numerical goals for how many letters will be generated in your efforts.
7. Get the timing right. The time to mount your campaign is just before the committee hearings begin or just prior to the vote on the floor. Too early is ineffective—too late is wasted effort; therefore, it is of importance to follow the progress of your issue closely

so as to mobilize your members at the right time. Have members refer to the list of Do's and Don'ts of letter writing.

STATE MONITORING OF LEGISLATION AND REGULATIONS

Legislation

1. Contact with the legislature:
   a. Identify key committees and subcommittees in the house and senate.
   b. Identify and develop communications with the members of those committees.
   c. Identify and develop communications with staffers who work with committee members.
   d. Contact committee chairs and ask for notification of any hearings on pertinent bills.
2. Volunteer for campaign work and develop contacts with legislators.
3. Identify the Documents Room in both the house and senate for the purpose of getting copies of bills.
4. Get the general telephone number for the state government and the mailing addresses for correspondence.
5. Develop liaisons with other health professionals and utilize them as information sources and allies in lobbying for health care issues.
6. Register a member of your group as a lobbyist—the fee is generally inexpensive.
7. If possible, hire a lobbyist.

Regulations

1. Subscribe to the State Register (which contains all state regulations under consideration).
2. Identify and develop contacts with state agencies which exert control on or impact your practice and ask to be added to their mailing lists. A limited list includes:
   a. Nurse practice **act:** rules and regulations.
   b. Medical practice act: rules and regulations.
   c. Pharmacy act: rules and regulations.
   d. Dental practice act: rules and regulations.
   e. Hospital licensing act: rules and regulations.
   f. Ambulatory surgical center licensing act: rules and regulations.
   g. Insurance statute: rules and regulations.
   h. Trauma center statute: rules and regulations.

    i. Department of health.

    j. Podiatric act; rules and regulations.

SOURCES OF INFORMATION

The federal information centers located in the major cities of the country are a good place to start your search. Information specialists in these centers are there to help you locate the correct office for your needs. Find the number in the White Pages of the telephone book under "U.S. Government." Once you know what agency you need to contact, you can then call the information officer at that agency who can direct you to the proper department.

For information about Congress there are many sources:

1. **Staff members of senators and representatives.** Look in the *Congressional Staff Directory* and call directly.
2. *Congressional Staff Directory* (most libraries have a copy). An annual publication listing names, room numbers, and extensions of staff members of legislators, committee members, and subcommittee members. This also lists key personnel of the executive departments.
3. *Congressional Record.* A record of the verbatim proceedings on the floor of the houses of Congress. This is issued daily when Congress is in session.
4. **Government Printing Office.** Orders all of the printing for Congress and the departments of the federal government. It has bookstores in 20 major cities around the country and branches in Washington. It carries 25,000 titles and deals in mail orders. For information on publications, contact Superintendent of Documents, Government Printing Office, Washington, DC 20402 or call (202) 793-3238. Request a copy of *Consumers' Guide to Federal Publications.*
5. *United States Government Manual.* Official handbook of the federal government; gives information on the agencies of the legislative, judicial, and executive branches plus on international organizations in which the United States participates, boards, committees, and commissions.
6. **Library of Congress.** Primarily responsible for services to Congress. Admission to most research facilities is open to anyone over high school age. No special credentials required. Contact the Information Office, Library of Congress, 10 First Street, S.E., Washington, DC 20540 or call (202) 287-5108.
7. *Congressional Directory.* Complete directory to all government

offices, congressional committees, executive and judicial branch offices, maps of congressional districts, embassy locations.

8. ***Federal Register.*** Used to make information about the federal regulations available to the public. Includes proposed changes. Conducts workshops on how to use the *Federal Register.* Contact Office of the Federal Register, National Archives and Records Service, Washington, DC 20408 or call (202) 523-5235.

9. Other sources of information:

To determine status of legislation:

House Bill Status Office
3669 House Office building
Annex #2
Washington, DC 20515
(202) 225-1772

Senate Bill Status Office
Senate Library
The Capitol, S332
Washington, DC 20510
(202) 224-2971

10. To obtain copies of House or Senate bills and documents:

House Documents Room   Senate Documents Room
The Capitol, H226   The Capitol, S325
Washington, DC 20515   Washington, DC 20510
(202) 225-3456   (202) 223-4321

11. To obtain information about the government:

Federal Information Center
General Services Administration
7th and D Streets, S.W.
Washington, DC 20407
(202) 755-8660

12. ***Congressional Quarterly.*** Weekly magazine that gives the highlights of major congressional events and the events of the agencies and judicial and executive branches. Publishes a book on congressional procedures and issues before Congress. Congressional Quarterly, 1414 22nd St., N.W., Washington, DC 20037; (202) 296-6800.

13. ***Washington Monitor.*** Publishes the *Congressional Monitor,* a daily newsletter when Congress is in session; the *Congressional Record Scanner,* a synopsis of the *Congressional Record,* published

daily when Congress is in session; the *Regulatory Monitor,* covering all real and rumored regulatory activity in terms of proposed and finalized rule making processes—weekly. The *Washington Monitor* also conducts seminars. Washington Monitor, 499 National Press Building, Washington, DC 20045; (202) 347-7757.

14. ***National Journal.*** Monthly magazine with article on topical governmental subjects—legislative, media, and regulatory updates. National Journal, 1730 M. Street, N.W., Washington, DC 20036; (202) 857-1491.

15. **Bureau of National Affairs (BNA).** Collects and disseminates information of the activities of governmental agencies and regulatory bodies with daily, weekly, and monthly reports on labor, law, economics, environment, safety, management, taxation, and finance. Workshops and seminars on management development, employee communications, and sales training available; produces and distributes films, video, and audiocassettes. Bureau of National Affairs, Inc., 1231 25th Street, N.W., Washington, DC 20037; (202) 452-4200.

16. **Your nursing associations.** Most professional associations are actively monitoring the issues that impact their members. Many have active government relations departments and can give information about current legislation. Get involved with your professional organization's legislative action committee.

SAMPLE CONTACT SHEET

Date of Contact _____

Representative/Senator _____

Staff Aide in on Discussion _____

Reaction of Legislator or Staff _____

(Use other side for additional comments.)

This Representative or Senator will help us in what specific ways:

☐ Sponsor   ☐ Oppose
☐ Cosponsor   ☐ Remain neutral
☐ Support   ☐ Not sure

Comments _____

_____

_____

Your Name _____

Home Address _____

Home Telephone _____

Business Telephone _____

DRAFT LETTER NO. 1
REQUESTING SUPPORT OR OPPOSITION

Date

Honorable (Full Name)
United States Senate/United States House of Representatives
Washington, DC (zip code four digits)

Dear Senator/Congressman or Congresswoman Doe:

Brief explanation of *what* you would like to gain support for or opposition to and refer to the bill name and number if possible.

Give reasons why you feel this issue warrants the support or opposition of this legislator.

Request this support or opposition.

"Thank you for your support for this issue in advance."

If you are going to be in the state capitol or Washington, ask for an appointment with the legislator or staff member to discuss the request for support for or opposition to the issue.

Sincerely yours,

Mary E. Jones, RN
123 Any Street
Any Town, Any State 12345-6789

DRAFT LETTER NO. 2
REQUESTING A CHANCE TO SPEAK WITH A REPRESENTATIVE OR STAFF MEMBER

Date

Honorable (Full Name)
United States Senate/House of Representatives
Washington, DC (zip code + four digits)

Dear Senator/Congressman(woman) Doe:

Briefly state what you are attempting to gain support for or opposition to.

Give your position.

Request an appointment with the elected official or staff member (''I shall be in Washington on June 6 and would like an opportunity to discuss this issue with the senator or his aide . . .'').

Thank you very much for the opportunity to meet with you.

Sincerely yours,

Mary E. Jones, RN
123 Any Street
Any Town, Any State 12345-6789

DRAFT LETTER NO. 3
SHOWING APPRECIATION FOR SUPPORT OR OPPOSITION

Date

Honorable (Full Name)
United States Senate/House of Representatives
Washington, DC (zip code four digits)

Dear Senator/Congressman or Congresswoman Doe:

''I would like to take this opportunity to thank you for your support of (or your opposition to) H.R. 1843.''

What the legislator supported or opposed (briefly).

Why he or she was correct in this action.

Thank you again for your. . . .

Sincerely yours,

Mary E. Jones, RN
123 Any Street
Any Town, Any State 12345-6789

BIBLIOGRAPHY

American Society of Association Executives: Plugging in to Washington; How to Communicate
        with Congress. American Society of Association Executives, 1575 Eye Street, N.W., Wash-
        ington, DC 20005, 1980.
Berglund, JF: Develop a Position Paper. Minnesota Licensed Beverage Association.
Bodenhorn, KA, Hardy-Havens, D, and Sharp, NJ: Writing to Your Member of Congress. Spe-
        cialty Nursing Forum, Spring, 1989.
Brandt, SF: Legislative Action at the State Level. Action Guideline. National Mental Health
        Association, 1800 North Kent Street, Arlington, Virginia, 22209.
Charton, S: Thou Shalt Lobby. Association Management, August 1989, p 234.
Gynn, KH: "All the Right Stuff" for Successful Lobbying. American Society of Association
        Executives, July/August 1990, pp 4–6.
Hardy-Havens, D: From the Capitol, How to Write Your Member of Congress. Capitol Asso-
        ciates, Washington, DC.
Legislative Directory of the Eighty-Sixth General Assembly of Illinois 1989–90, prepared for
        the Chicago Society of Association Executives.
Lobby? You? Of Course You Can . . . And You Should! Independent Sector. 1828 L. Street,
        N.W., Washington, DC 20036.

THE AMERICANS WITH DISABILITIES ACT

Historically, disabled individuals have been discriminated against and isolated. They face disadvantages and unequal opportunities in such vital areas as employment, health services, telecommunications, public accommodations, entertainment, and housing. Unlike other groups, the disabled have not had legal recourse to address these issues. Congress passed the Americans with Disabilities Act in 1990 to ensure equality of opportunity, full participation in the activities of daily living, and economic self-sufficiency.

The goal of the Americans with Disabilities Act is to eliminate discrimination against Americans who have physical or mental disabilities so that they can participate more fully in the workplace and social life. This act not only prohibits discrimination but also delineates clear, enforceable standards. The federal government's role is the enforcement of standards and of the Fourteenth Amendment. The Fourteenth Amendment provides due process of the law (access to the legal system) for denial of life, liberty, and equal protection under the law. Congress will regulate commerce in an effort to address daily discrimination to disabled individuals by imposing restrictions regarding employment practices and regulations.

Box B–1 FOUR PURPOSES OF THE AMERICANS WITH DISABILITIES ACT

1. Eliminate discrimination against the disabled
2. State clear standards
3. Make the federal government the enforcer of standards
4. Enforce the Fourteenth Amendment and regulation of commerce

---

The term *disability* is defined as any physical or mental impairment that limits any major life activity. This broad-based definition covers all individuals with obvious physical disabilities but also includes individuals with such disabilities as diabetes, cancer, or HIV or AIDS as well as recovering alcoholics and individuals who have completed a drug rehabilitation program and who are not involved in the illegal use of drugs. The act does not cover any individual who is illegally using drugs. The "illegal use of drugs" means possession, distribution, or use of drugs that violates the Controlled Substance Act. Also covered are individuals who have a work, social, or family relationship with disabled individuals. Because of the broad definition of impairments, there is an ongoing process of identifying additional covered disabilities. Specifically *excluded* from this act are homosexuals, bisexuals, transvestites, transsexuals, pedophiliacs, exhibitionists, voyeurs, those with gender identity disorders, gamblers, pyromaniacs or kleptomaniacs unless they have identified disabilities.

Box B–2   WHO IS COVERED BY THE ADA?

1. All individuals with one or more physical or mental disabilities that limit any major life activity
2. A record of such a disability
3. Being regarded as having a disability
4. Individuals who have a work, social, or family relationship with a disabled person

---

All aspects of public accommodation were in effect as of January 1992, and effective July 26, 1992, employers with 25 or more employees must have complied with the employment provisions of this act. Very small employers with fewer than 15 employees have until July 26, 1994, before they must comply.

TITLE I EMPLOYMENT

All employers, employment agencies, labor organizations, or joint labor management committees are covered by the Americans with Disabilities Act. No discrimination is allowed against any qualified applicant with a disability or *discrimination* against disabled individuals regarding any terms and conditions of work. This includes promotions, salary, discharge, transfer, and all other conditions of work.

The impact of the ADA in the workplace will be felt as employers eliminate most preemployment medical inquiries. Medical questionnaires will also change since employers can no longer ask about prior injuries, employee compensation claims, and diseases. The ADA prohibits any question seeking to identify the nature or severity of any individual's disabilities.

Educational institutions and other employers are now restricted to asking only about a candidate's ability to do the job safely. If a physical examination is required, it must be job specific. Employers also have the responsibility of educating all employees about the law.

The essential functions of the job have to be clearly identified by the employer, who must determine whether an applicant is qualified. In this area many disputes and litigation are anticipated. The employer does not have to hire a disabled applicant if there are other equally qualified applicants.

A *qualified individual* with a disability is someone who can safely perform all aspects of a job with or without reasonable accommodations. The employer has the right to require that the individual does not pose any threat to the health and safety of himself or others.

Reasonable accommodation refers to the employer's responsibility to provide the necessary restructuring, reassignment, equipment modification or devices, training materials, interpreters, and other accommodations for any disabled individual. This is applicable to all job applicants and employees. Disabled individuals should be prepared to seek appropriate modifications by asking the employer specifically to meet their needs. For example, a disabled person who requires an interpreter should make this need known to the employer. If the person is hearing-impaired, appropriate telephone devices may be requested.

DEFENSES TO ADA CLAIMS

There are several circumstances that can precipitate a defense to an employment claim.

Undue Hardship Defense

The undue hardship defense is an exception to reasonable accommodation by employers. If an accommodation is too expensive or difficult to implement, it may be considered an undue hardship; however, the employer must thoroughly investigate and offer data to prove this defense. A determination of undue hardship is made based on cost, the resources of the employer, the size of the employer, numbers of employees, and type of operation or function of the employer.

Qualification Standard and Health and Safety Defense

Another defense to an employment claim is that the health and safety of the individual or others is compromised. All qualification standards require that applicants safely perform their jobs. Employers can ask questions about any applicant's ability to do the job and perform safely all necessary job-related functions.

Standards of employment entrance exams must also be carefully administered without any disadvantages being imposed on a disabled person. It should be understood, however, that drug testing to determine the illegal use of drugs is not considered a medical exam.

Religious Entities Defense

Employers are not prohibited from giving preference to individuals of a particular religion.

Public Safety Defense

Public safety is a priority, and it can be a defense to an employment claim if a reasonable accommodation cannot eliminate the risk of transmittal of infectious or communicable diseases to others. For example, if a nurse's aide is hired for a job, and through a physical exam it is discovered that he or she has active tuberculosis, the job offer can be rescinded based on the public safety defense.

Box B–3   DEFENSES TO EMPLOYMENT CLAIM

1. Undue hardship
2. Qualification standard and health and safety defense
3. Religious preference
4. Public safety

ENFORCEMENT OF THE ADA

Enforcement of this act requires coordination of agencies with the authority to avoid duplication of effort and prevention of conflicting standards. Remedies for violation of the ADA are based upon the Civil Rights Act of 1991, and include compensatory and punitive damages. The *Equal*

Employment Opportunity Commission (EEOC) handles complaints under the ADA. Trials by jury are also allowed.

Rules and regulations protected by the Department of Justice will oversee all *public accommodations* (Title III). This includes public and many types of private entities serving food and providing lodging, shopping, entertainment, and transportation, as well as all places of education and health care providers are affected by the ADA.

Public accommodations must be accessible to disabled people without any screening that eliminates or disqualifies them from full participation, unless there is a demonstrated safety risk. Institutions or employers cannot refuse to comply because of insurance limitations. In addition, public accommodations are required to provide auxiliary aids and services to the disabled to facilitate their full participation. This includes items like amplifiers for telephones for the hearing-impaired, or braille for the visually impaired. All architectural barriers must be modified or eliminated using ramps, curb cuts, and repositioning of equipment such as doors, telephones, and workstations to accommodate easy access by the disabled.

Similarly, educational institutions, libraries, auditoriums, conference rooms, and examination rooms must be completely accessible. There is no requirement, however, for an institution to provide *personal devices,* such as wheelchairs or crutches although assistance such as cutting food may be required. All current and potential students are protected by this law.

Generally, the purpose of the bill is ensure that no one, abled or disabled, is given a greater advantage. In addition, no individual may be excluded from any school or program because of a personal or social relationship with a disabled individual. Any violation of these practices may precipitate a discriminatory practice charge.

Box B–4   DISCRIMINATORY PRACTICE

1. Denial of participation to a disabled person
2. Unequal benefit
3. Failure to provide settings suitable for use by the disabled
4. Denial to someone affiliated with a disabled person
5. Exclusion because of lack of insurance coverage

The Americans with Disabilities Act requires an end to discrimination of the disabled, with clear legal alternatives when there are violations of these standards. The ADA will be tested and continue to evolve.

THE HIRING PROCESS AND THE ADA

An individual who cannot, with or without a reasonable accommodation, perform an essential job function will not be considered a "qualified" individual with a disability under the ADA. An unqualified individual is not protected by the ADA. It is important for employers to determine whether job applicants are, in fact, qualified. This requires an affirmative answer to two questions:

First, does the individual satisfy the prerequisites for the position? You will need to review whether the applicant has the appropriate educational background, employment experience, skills, licenses, or other job-related requirements for the position. The facility does not have to provide an accommodation to an individual with an impairment who has not met the selection criteria. That individual is not entitled to a reasonable accommodation until the applicant satisfies the first prerequisite.

Second, can the individual perform the job's "essential functions" with or without a reasonable accommodation? *Essential functions* refers to fundamental job duties intrinsic to the position she holds or desires. For example, if an applicant cannot hear, but has graduated from an accredited nursing school and passed the board examination, the facility might be required to provide an accommodation in order for her to perform the job's essential functions.

An accommodation is required if it imposes an undue hardship on the facility. An undue hardship often means a significant increase in operating expenses or disruption to the business.

Essential and nonessential job functions should be identified and descriptions prepared which serve as evidence of their nondiscriminatory intent. Preparing a written job description before advertising for a position or interviewing candidates assists in identifying a qualified individual. Inaccurate, vague, or overly general job descriptions can do more harm than good and should be discarded.

Employment applications should be reviewed to make sure they comply with federal and state laws. Questions about the facility's prerequisites should be included. Questions regarding an individual's disability status, health, past medical problems, and worker's compensation claims should be deleted. Specific job-related questions to help determine whether applicants can perform the essential functions of the job should be provided where practicable.

An employment test may not be used that would screen out individuals with disabilities unless the test is shown to be job-related for the position in question and consistent with business necessity. An employment test must be selected and administered in a manner which ensures that the test results accurately reflect the skills, aptitudes, or other factors the test is designed to measure. A test designed to measure sensory, manual, or speaking skills when those skills are job-related may be used. A facility should administer written tests orally to applicants who are blind or visually impaired or who have a learning disability.

If the facility gives drug tests to applicants which may detect prescription drugs taken for a disability, such tests should not be administered until a conditional offer of employment has been made and the test is shown to be job-related and consistent with business necessity. The only preoffer drug test that should be required is one which solely detects the use of illegal drugs. No tests may be given that attempt to detect a disability prior to extending a conditional offer of employment.

If a medical examination is a required part of the hiring process, such examination should be administered to all entering employees receiving conditional job offers in the same category. The exam results must be kept confidential. Only those people with a need to have that type of information should be informed. These individuals are health care providers or security, if the disability might require emergency treatment; government officials investigating compliance with the ADA; and supervisors who need to be informed of the necessary restrictions and accommodations associated with the employee work and job description.

The major requirement of the ADA is that during the preemployment interview, applicants may not be asked if they have a disability nor may they be asked about the nature or severity of a disability. It is permissible to ask about an applicant's ability to perform job-related functions. The personnel policy manuals must be updated to reflect the ADA policy. At a minimum, the following policies should be reviewed:

1. **Attendance and lateness.** Neutral policies concerning attendance and lateness distributed to all employees should be drafted and enforced consistently. If an employee violates a neutral policy, he or she may be terminated even if the reason for the violation is excessive absenteeism to care for his or her disabled spouse. An employee with a disability may be disciplined if the violation exceeds the facility's attempts at reasonable accommodation.

2. **Leave of absence.** A facility should review its leave-of-absence policy, particularly with respect to leaves with pay. The ADA does not entitle individuals with disabilities to have more paid leave time than nondisabled employees.

3. **Work schedules.** Part-time or modified work schedules to help accommodate all employees, not only those with disabilities, should be considered by the facility.

4. **Interview, discipline, and performance forms.** Interview, discipline, and performance forms should be prepared objectively. They must indicate why an individual was hired, disciplined, demoted, and so on. They should provide a nondiscriminatory record should an individual bring a claim alleging discrimination

based on disability, or on some other protected basis such as age, race, sex, national origin, marital status, or veteran status.

The facility should develop a disability policy in compliance with procedure. A written policy that explains the facility's commitment to adhere to and enforce its obligations under the ADA and other relevant nondiscrimination laws should be distributed. It should contain a procedure for job applicants and employees to file complaints if they feel they have been discriminated against on the basis of the disability. This may prevent an employee from filing complaints with a government agency or in court and will provide a sound employee relations practice.

A facility is not liable for failing to provide an accommodation that was not requested. If no request is received, it is inappropriate to provide an accommodation. A facility must have knowledge of the limitations of an applicant or employee before a duty to accommodate arises. However, if an employee or applicant with a known disability is having problems performing his or her job, it would be reasonable of the facility to discuss the possibility of an accommodation with the employee. The employee with the disability is not required to accept the accommodation.

Once you are aware that an individual has a disability:

1. Consider discussing possible accommodations with the individual.
2. Identify the barriers to job performance resulting from the particular disability.
3. Assess the reasonableness of each accommodation in regard to its effectiveness, equal opportunity, and hardship.
4. Implement the accommodation that is most appropriate and imposes the least hardship on the facility.

An effective accommodation does not have to be the most expensive or the most difficult to implement. As long as it provides a meaningful employment opportunity, it may be the least expensive or easiest to implement. Reallocation of essential functions is not required in order to provide a reasonable accommodation. Essential functions are those that the individual who holds the job must perform, with or without reasonable accommodation, to be considered qualified for the position.

SEXUAL HARASSMENT AND DISCRIMINATION

In 1972, Title IX of the Education Amendments extended prohibition regarding sex discrimination to educational institutions receiving federal funding. In 1980, the EEOC issued sexual harassment guidelines for the workplace that applied to supervisors, employees, and nonemployees. In 1987, Title IX was clarified, making the entire institution subject to the requirements of nondiscrimination law, not just the section receiving federal funding.

The issues of sexual harassment and discrimination concern the misuse of power and control over others in "lower" positions of the power structure in both academic and clinical settings. Sexual harassment can be heterosexual or homosexual. Sexual harassment is unlawful if submission to it:

1. Is a condition of employment
2. Interferes with performance
3. Is the basis for employment decision
4. Creates a hostile and intimidating work environment.

There are two types of sexual harassment—*quid pro quo* and *hostile environment.*

QUID PRO QUO

In quid pro quo harassment the following types of behavior may be displayed:

1. Requests for sexual favors that are implicit

2. Requests that are used for a condition of employment decisions, for example, promotions, demotions, new jobs, and so on.

The following elements must be proved in a quid pro quo case:

1. Sexual advances are unwelcome.
2. Harassment is sexually motivated.
3. Plaintiff is a member of a protected group (i.e., employees of a hospital that are in a lower position in the power structure).
4. Plaintiff's reactions to the superior's advances affect an aspect of his or her employment or advancement, for example, promotion, salary increase, and so on.

For example, an institution's administrator tells a nursing faculty member that he loves good looks and brains in a woman. The educator ignores the administrator's sexist remarks and walks away from him in disgust after the comment. The administrator then suddenly finds fault with her work with no basis and fires her. [See *Chamberlain v. 101 Realty, Inc.*, 915 F. 2nd 777 (1st Cir. 1990), which illustrates the elements of quid pro quo sexual harassment.]

HOSTILE WORK ENVIRONMENT

In a hostile environment, offensive behavior creates a hostile or intimidating work environment, which interferes with the work performance of the plaintiff.

In *Meritor Savings Bank v. Vinson*, 477 U.S. 57 (1986), the victim alleged that the supervisor made repeated demands for sexual favors, fondled her in front of other employees, forcibly raped her on numerous occasions, and exposed himself to her. The court found that the allegations were sufficient for a case of sexual harassment.

In order to establish that a hostile work environment exists, it is not necessary to show that the offensive conduct was directed specifically at the plaintiff; it is enough that the behavior was observed or known by the plaintiff and affected his or her psychological and emotional status and well being. In *Broderick v. Ruter,* 685 F. Supp 1269 (Do D.C. 1988), the plaintiff had only two incidents directed at her regarding sexual relationships with the supervisor; however, she was aware that those who had sex with the supervisor received more benefits. The court ruled that this was a hostile work environment.

WHAT VICTIMS SHOULD DO

The first line of redress for victims is to consult their employer's or educational institution's sexual harassment policy. These policies are a requirement for receiving federal funding. The policy must include the EEOC (Equal Employment Opportunity Commission) language on sexual harassment. The following items must be described in the policy:

1. A grievance procedure
2. The type of forms that need to be completed
3. To whom the incident is reported
4. The hearing procedure and an alternative in case that person is the offender
5. The resolution process

The policy must protect the legal rights of all parties involved by ensuring confidentiality and due process. The policy is applicable to on- and off-campus placements, including clinical areas.

A sexual harassment complaint by a faculty member or nursing student against an employee or professional at the clinical site implicates the clinical facility and the educational institution. For example, if the complaint is against a physician, he or she is held accountable to the clinical facility's policy manual even when the physician is not an employee of the hospital. The facility itself may be liable for the actions of those who work for it. The facility is also responsible for complying with the grievance procedure stated in its sexual harassment policy. Since the educational institution has a contract with the facility, the school has an obligation to make the clinical facility aware of a sexual harassment complaint by a nursing student. If the school fails to monitor the clinical facility for any further signs or incidents of sexual harassment it may be liable to the student if further problems occur.

If the internal policies and procedures of the academic institution or the clinical facility fail to address the sexual harassment complaint, victims have the right to sue in federal court to resolve their problems.

Glossary

Abandonment: A unilateral premature termination of the professional treatment relationship by the health care provider with neither adequate notice given the patient nor the patient's consent.

Absolute privilege: The law recognizes that publications made in certain legislative, judicial, and administrative proceedings are absolutely privileged and do not give rise to an action for defamation.

Accreditation Manual for Hospitals (AMH): The purpose of the manual is twofold: (1) it serves as a basis for the Joint Commission's evaluations, and (2) it is used internally to develop policies and procedures and to assess whether health care providers and services in the institution or facility are measuring up to the AMH standards.

Act: Term for legislation that has been passed by both houses of Congress or the legislature and has been signed into law by the president or governor or passes over his or her veto, thus becoming law.

Act utilitarianism: Type of utilitarianism in which an individual's particular situation determines the rightness or wrongness of the act.

ADEA: Age Discrimination and Employment Act, 29 U.S.C. § 621 (1967), also enforced by the EEOC, prohibits discrimination by the employer against anyone forty (40) years old or older in decisions regarding hiring and promotions.

Administrative laws: Created by administrative agencies under the direction of the executive branch of the government.

Admissions of fact: Written requests to admit or deny facts regarding issues of the lawsuit. This technique attempts to limit the number of facts that actually are disputed and argued at trial.

Advance directive: Document by which a competent person (1) makes a declaration regarding future health care he or she will accept or refuse (a Living Will) and/or (2) designates another person to make health care decisions if he or she becomes incompetent in the future (a Durable Power of Attorney for Health Care or "proxy" decision maker).

AMA: Against medical advice.

Amendment: Proposal of a legislator to change the language or content of a bill or act. Usually amendments are handled as bills.

Americans with Disabilities Act: An act passed by Congress in 1990 to ensure equality of opportunity, full participation in daily living activities, and economic self-sufficiency.

Arbitration: Both sides select a neutral third party arbitrator with technical knowledge in the area of contention who hears the case and renders a decision and reward. The decision can be binding or nonbinding.

Arraignment: When a person is brought before a judge, pleads guilty or not guilty, and has bail set.

Assault: An intentional act by one person that causes another person to fear that he or she will be touched in an offensive or injurious manner—even if no touching actually takes place.

Autonomy: The right of self-determination, independence, and freedom.

Battery: An intentional act resulting in actual physical contact or touching in an offensive or injurious manner.

Beneficence: A very old requirement for health care providers that views the primary goal of health care as doing good for patients under their care.

BFOQ: Bona fide occupational qualification.

Bill: Legislative proposal originating in the House or Senate, labeled H.R. (for House of Representatives) or S. (for Senate), and then numbered. The numbers are assigned in order of introduction from the beginning of the term.

Bioethics: The ethics of life, or of death in some cases.

Bylaws: Rules that are adopted to regulate practice and privileges.

Calendar: The agenda or list of pending business before either chamber or a committee.

Capacity: Ability to understand the nature and effects of one's acts.

Categorical imperative: Absolute fundamental principle of ethics in which moral rightness or wrongness of a human action is considered separately from the consequences of that action.

Challenge for cause: An attorney can ask that a juror be dismissed from the jury because he or she is biased or prejudiced.

Civil code: Comprehensive written organization of general rules and regulations authorized by the legislature, based on Roman, Spanish, and French civil law. Louisiana is the only state in the United States with a civil code based on the Napoleonic Code.

Chamber: Meeting place for the total membership of the House or Senate (as opposed to committee rooms).

Claims-made policy: Covers injuries only if the injury occurs in the policy period *and* the claim is reported to the insurance company during the policy period or during the "tail."

COBRA: Consolidated-Omnibus Reconciliation Act.

Code of Ethics: Written list of a profession's values and standards of conduct.

Common law: Evolves from the judiciary branch of the government through court decisions and is the most frequent source of law for malpractice issues.

Competency: Level of care used to determine whether grounds exist for disciplinary action by a state licensing board; also used to assess civil liability against a nurse in a malpractice case.

Complaint or petition: Plea or document that states the parties of the lawsuit, allegations of negligence, and damages suffered by the plaintiff.

Conference committee: Committee composed of House and Senate members appointed to reconcile differences between the two groups over provisions of a bill.

Congressional Record: Daily printed account of the proceedings of both houses with debate, statements and so on, reported verbatim

Consideration: What the offeror bargains and exchanges for the promises.

Constitution: Government document that guarantees individuals certain fundamental freedoms.

Continuous quality improvement (CQI): Method developed to effect change in the health care system, it assumes work groups are experts in their work and should be the focus for monitoring quality, identifying problems, and devising solutions.

Contract: Agreement consisting of one or more legally enforceable promises between two or more parties—people, corporations, or partnerships. There are four elements in a contractual relationship: offer, acceptance, consideration, and breach.

Contract law: Area of the law concerned with agreements between two parties that involve an obligation or duty (e.g., employer/employee agreements in nursing).

Corporate negligence: Doctrine of law whereby the hospital is held liable. Two hospital responsibilities included under this doctrine are (1) monitoring and supervising all medical and nursing personnel within the facility and (2) investigating physicians' credentials before granting staff privileges.

Credentialing: Voluntary form of self-regulation seen in many health care disciplines.

Crime: Offense against the public that is prosecuted by the state.

Criminal law: Area of the law concerned with violations of criminal statutes or laws.

Damages: Money for which the defendant is sued.

Defamation: Oral or written communication to someone other than the person defamed that tends to *injure his or her reputation* (i.e., diminish the esteem, respect, good will, or confidence in which the person is held) or cause adverse, derogatory, or unpleasant feelings or opinions against him or her.

Defendant: Person or entity being sued.

Deontology: System of ethical decision making that is based on moral rules and unchanging principles, also referred to as the formalistic system, the principal system of ethics, or duty-based ethics.

Deponent: Person being interviewed or deposed.

Deposition: Structured interview in which the person being interviewed (the deponent) is placed under oath and asked questions about issues of the lawsuit.

Disability: Any physical or mental impairment that limits any major life activity.

Discovery: The stage in a lawsuit in which all information, facts, and circumstances surrounding the alleged malpractice incident are "discovered" by the plaintiff and defendant; techniques include interrogatories, requests for production of documents and things, admissions of facts, physical and mental examinations, and depositions.

Distributive justice: Obligation to be fair to all people; concept that individuals have a right to be treated equally regardless of race, sex, marital status, medical diagnosis, social standing, economic level, or religious belief.

DNR orders: Do Not Resuscitate orders.

Durable Power of Attorney for Health Care (DPAHC): Document that designated another person to make health care decisions for a person if he or she becomes incompetent to make such decisions.

EEOC: Equal Employment Opportunity Commission; enforces Title VII, which has guidelines that provide protection from sexual harassment.

Ethical dilemma: A situation that requires an individual to make a choice between two equally unfavorable alternatives.

Ethical rights (also called moral rights): Rights that are based on moral or ethical principles.

Ethics: Declarations of what is right or wrong, and of what ought to be.

Exclusions: Items not covered by an insurance policy.

Expert witness: Person used to assist the judge and jury in understanding breaches of the standard of care and damages sustained by the plaintiff.

Fact (or material) witness: Person having knowledge about circumstances surrounding the events of the alleged malpractice.

False imprisonment: Unlawful intentional confinement of another within fixed boundaries so that the confined person is conscious of the confinement or harmed by it.

Felony: A more serious crime with punishments greater than the misdemeanor level; can be grounds for nursing license denial, revocation, or suspension.

Fidelity: The individual's obligation to be faithful or loyal to commitments, agreements, and responsibilities made or accepted by self or others.

Filibuster: Device used only in the Senate to delay or prevent a vote by time-consuming talk; often used by a minority in an effort to prevent a vote on a bill that would probably pass if brought to vote; can be stopped only by a two-thirds vote of the senators present and voting.

General damages: Award given for the plaintiff's pain and suffering caused by the defendant's acts.

Gross negligence: The intentional failure to perform a manifest duty in reckless disregard of the consequences, as affecting the life or property of another.

Guideline: Recommended course of action to describe a process of client-patient care management.

Handicap: Physical or mental impairment that substantially limits one or more major life activities; may be long-term or short-term disability.

Hard damages: Damages that include medical bills, physician fees, pharmacy bills, and other items claimable as specific amounts.

Hearsay evidence: Statements made out of court that are being used in court to prove the matters asserted in those statements.

Indictment or complaint: First step in criminal procedure; written document issued to defendant, describing wrongdoing.

Informed consent: Consent obtained after the physician or other health care provider has given the patient enough information regarding the material risks, benefits of the proposed treatment, its alternatives, and consequences of no treatment, so that the patient can make an intelligent or "informed" decision.

Insurance policy: Agreement by the insurance company that states that, in exchange for a premium, the company will pay money when certain injuries are caused by the person insured by the policy.

Insuring agreement: Insurance company's promise to pay in exchange for premiums.

Intent: Acting either for the purpose of causing an injury (or an invasion of a right), or knowing or being reasonably certain that an injury or invasion will result from the act; does not imply an act is done intentionally.

Intentional infliction of emotional distress: Intentional invasion of a person's peace of mind. The conduct must be outrageous and beyond all bounds of decency; ordinary rude or insulting behavior is not enough.

Intentional tort: An intentional act that violates another person's right or property.

Interrogatories: Written questions sent by one party to the other requesting information about issues and witnesses surrounding the incident of alleged malpractice.

Intrusion upon the seclusion or private concerns of another: Consisting of intentional interference with another's interest in solitude or seclusion, ragarding his or her person or private affairs.

Invasion of privacy: Injures the feelings without regard to any effect on the property, business interest, or standing of the individual in the community. The right to privacy concerns one's peace of mind and the right to be left alone without being subjected to unwarranted or undesired publicity. The right to privacy is personal to the individual and does not extend to family members or businesses.

Joint Commission on Accreditation for Healthcare Organizations (JCAHO): Group that annually publishes the Accreditation Manual for Hospitals.

Joint Committee: Committee composed of a specific number of members of both the House and the Senate; usually investigative in nature.

Jurisdiction: The authority by which courts and judges accept and decide cases.

Justice: The obligation to be fair to all people.

Law(s): (1)Act of Congress or state legislature that has been signed by the president or governor or passed over a veto. (2) Rule of social conduct made by the people to protect society; based on concerns for fairness and justice. (3) The body of rules and regulations that governs behavior and relationships with others in society and with the state.

Legal obligations: Obligations that have become formal statements of law and are enforceable under the law.

Liability: Legal responsibility; a nurse is legally responsible for actions that fail to meet the standard of care or for failing to act, thereby causing harm.

Liability policy: Written agreement between the health care provider and the insurance company.

Libel: Defamation in written form.

Licensure: Process by which an agency of a state government grants permission to an individual to engage in a given occupation.

Limit of Liability: Amount that the insurance company agrees to pay on behalf of the insured, in exchange for premiums.

Living Will: Legal document stating what health care a patient will accept or refuse after the patient is no longer competent or able to make the decision.

Lobby: To influence the passage or defeat of legislation or attempt to create a favorable climate toward legislation.

Malpractice: A specific type of negligence that takes into account a standard of care that can be reasonably expected from such professionals a lawyers, accountants, nurses, physicians (i.e., professional negligence).

Mandatory licensure: Regulates the practice of a profession such as nursing and requires compliance with the licensing statute if an individual engages in activities defined within the scope of that profession.

Material Risk: A significant risk that a reasonable patient would want to consider when making a decision about undergoing medical treatment.

Mediators: Neutral third parties who facilitate agreements by helping both sides to identify their needs and work toward agreeable solutions.

Medical community standard: The physician's duty to inform the patient depends on the circumstances of the case and the general practice of the medical profession in such cases.

Merger clause: A statement in a contract indicating that the document is the final agreement between the parties.

Misdemeanor: A lesser crime usually punishable by fines or imprisonment of less than one (1) year.

Moral obligations: Obligations based on moral or ethical principles that are *not* enforceable under the law.

Morals: Fundamental standards of right and wrong that an individual learns and internalized, usually in the early stages of childhood development.

National Practitioner Data Bank: Addresses three types of data:
1. Information relating to medical malpractice payments made on behalf of health care practitioners.
2. Information relating to adverse actions taken against clinical privileges or physicians, osteopaths, or dentists.
3. Information concerning actions by professional societies that adversely affect membership.

Negligence: To establish malpractice or professional negligence against a nurse, the plaintiff must prove the four elements of negligence: (1) duty, (2) breach of duty, (3) proximate cause or causal connection, and (4) damages.

Nonmaleficence: The requirement that health care providers do no harm to their patients, either intentionally or unintentionally.

Normative decisions: Ethical decisions that deal with questions and dilemmas requiring a choice of actions where there is conflict of rights or obligations between nurse and patient, nurse and patient's family, nurse and physician, and so forth.

Nursing negligence: Conduct that is unreasonable under the circumstances and fails to meet the appropriate standard of care.

Obligations: Demands made on individuals, professions, society, or government to fulfill and honor the rights of others.

Occurrence-basis policy: Insurance policy that covers injuries that occur during the period covered by the policy.

Offeree: Person or entity accepting the offer.

Offeror: Person or entity making an offer to keep a promise.

Option rights: Rights that are based on a fundamental belief in the dignity and freedom of human beings.

Ordinary negligence: The omission of the care that an individual of common prudence usually takes of his or her own concerns.

Ostensible authority: A doctrine of law whereby a hospital is liable for the negligence of an independent contractor if the patient has a rational basis to believe that the independent contractor is a hospital employee.

Parties: Plaintiffs and defendants in a lawsuit.

Paternalism: Type of unilateral decision by health care providers that implies they know what is best, regardless of the patient's wishes.

Peremptory challenge: Challenge by an attorney of a juror that does not require a cause to be shown for removal of that juror from jury selection.

Permissive licensing legislation: Regulates the use of a title and requires compliance with the licensing statute only if an individual intends to use the title granted by the licensing authority.

Plaintiff: The person or entity alleging harm and bringing the lawsuit.

Policy: Overall plan or series of steps to accomplish or coordinate the general goals and acceptable procedures in a facility.

Political Action Committee (PAC): Organization formed by a corporation or association, which solicits contributions for candidates for public office.

Prescriptive authority: The limited authority to prescribe certain medications according to established protocols. Certain medications or devices incidental to routine health or family planning can also be dispensed.

Prima facie case: Case that is found in the employee's favor if no conflicting evidence is offered by the employer.

Procedural law: Area of the law that determines the form or process that regulates the legal right that is violated.

Procedure: Tools used to implement the policies. (A policy, by definition, is broader than a procedure.)

Prudent patient standard: Standard that focuses on the risks a reasonable person would consider when making a decision of whether or not to undergo treatment.

Punitive damages: Damages awarded in an amount intended to punish the defendant (or person committing the tort) for the egregious nature of the tort. The defendant's actions must be willful and wanton, and the damages are not based on the plaintiff's actual monetary loss.

Qualified individual with disability: Someone who can safely perform all aspects of a job with or without reasonable accommodations.

Qualified privilege: An exemption from liability for defamatory statements that are made in *good faith* and without malice, concerning subjects in which the person has an interest or a duty to communicate to another with a corresponding interest or responsibility.

Quality assurance: Evaluation of the role of the health care provider with the purpose of reaching as high a standard of care as possible.

Quorum: Number of members needed to conduct business. This would be a majority of the members (in Washington: 51 in the Senate and 218 in the House if there are no vacancies). Any member may object to conducting business without a quorum and force a roll-call vote to bring in absentees. Roll calls are frequently used as a delaying tactic. Much legislation is passed without a quorum present because it is noncontroversial.

Reasonable accommodation: The employer's responsibility to provide necessary restructuring, reassignment, equipment modification or devices, training materials, interpreters, and other accommodations that are reasonable for any disabled individual.

Regulations: Rules and orders issued by various regulatory agencies such as state boards of nursing.

Relevance: The degree to which evidence tends to either prove or disprove a contested matter.

Requests for production of documents and things: Requests by plaintiff or defendant for documents or things from the other party that may lead to discoverable information and pertain to the issues of the lawsuit.

Respondeat superior: A Latin term for "Let the master answer" that has been handed down from English common law; when the employer is held responsible for the employee's negligence in causing injury to a patient while in the "course and scope of employment."

Rider: A provision usually not related but tacked onto a bill which its sponsor hopes to get through more easily by including it in other legislation.

Rights: Generally defined as just claims or title or something that is owed to an individual according to just claims, legal guarantees, or moral and ethical principles.

Rule utilitarianism: Type of utilitarianism in which individual draws on past experiences to formulate rules that are the most useful in determining the greatest good.

Self-defense: Principle to avoid liability; person must reasonably believe that a danger exists to self or others and that he or she must therefore use only the force that is reasonably necessary.

Slander: Oral defamation.

Soft damages: Money awards to plaintiffs for loss of love and affection, pain and suffering, emotional distress, disfigurement, loss of parental nurturing, or loss of consortium.

Special damages: Damages based on the actual monetary loss for the past, present, and future that were caused by the defendant's acts.

Standard: An authoritative statement.

Standard of best interest: Type of decision made about an individual's health care when he or she is unable to make the informed decision for his or her own care.

Standard of care: A measuring scale based on negligence that means the average degree of skill, care, and diligence exercised by members of the same profession under the same or similar circumstances.

Standards of professional performance: Standards based on the professional activities that should be undertaken by nurses, such as continuous quality improvement, education, research, ethics, and peer review. (Standards of care and standards of performance are both described in terms of competency, rather than in terms of reasonable care or optimal level of performance.)

Statute of limitations: A procedural law that specifies the time during which a plaintiff may bring a lawsuit.

Statutes: Laws passed by the state legislature pursuant to recommendations and lobbying by such groups as the state nurses' association, special interest groups, or specialty nursing organizations.

Statutory laws: Formal written laws enacted by federal, state, and local legislative branches of the government.

Subpoena: Court order that requires a person to come to court or appear at a specific place to give testimony (e.g., attorney's office for a deposition). Failure to appear can result in punishment by the court.

Substantive law: Law that determines the specific wrong, harm, duty, or obligation that causes an action to be brought to trial.

Summary jury trial: An abbreviated, privately held trial.

Tail: An uninterrupted extension of the insurance policy period, also known as the extended reporting endorsement. See also **Claims-made policy.**

Tort: A wrongful act or private injury committed by one person against another person or property, which may be pursued in civil court by the injured party. The purpose of tort law is to make the injured party whole again, primarily through monetary compensation or damages.

Trespass to land: Unlawful interference with another's possession of land. The tort may be committed by an intentional or a negligent act; it may occur when a person intrudes onto property or fails to leave, or throws or places something on the land, or causes another person to enter the property.

Unintentional tort: An unintended wrongful act against another person that produces injury or harm.

Utilitarianism (also called teleology, consequentialism, or situation ethics): The ethical system of utility, based on two underlying principles: (1) "The greatest good for the greatest number," and (2) "The end justifies the means."

Values: Ideals or concepts that give meaning to the individual's life.

Veracity: The principle of "truthfulness," which requires that the health care provider tell the truth and not intentionally deceive or mislead the patient.

Veto: Action taken by a president or governor rejecting a bill presented to him or her by Congress or the legislature for signature. When Congress is in session, the president has ten (10) days, excluding Sundays, to veto a bill; otherwise the bill automatically becomes law.

Vicarious liability: When the law, in certain limited instances, imposes liability for the acts of another.

Voice vote: The presiding officer of either chamber calls for "yeas" or "nays" (or "ayes" or "nos") and decides the results based on this oral vote.

Voir dire: Judicial process that means "to speak the truth."

Warrant: Permission for law enforcement officers to take the person (the defendant) into custody.

Welfare rights (also called legal rights): Rights based on a legal entitlement to some good or benefit.

Writ of certiorari: Written petition by the losing party requesting that the Supreme court hear the case.

INDEX

A "t" following a page number indicates a table.

Intentional tort(s), 9, 17, 136–155
  defamation, 139–143
  emotional distress, 153–154
  ethics, 136–137
  false imprisonment, 151–152
  implications, 154
  nature of, 137–139
  trespass to land, 153
  see also Assault and battery; Invasion of
    privacy
Internal Revenue Service (IRS), 218, 220,
  221
International Council of Nurses Code of
  Ethics, 23
Interrogatories, 10, 83, 94
Interview questions, 197, 208, 273–274
Intrusion, 144–145
Invasion of privacy, 107–108
  intrusion, 144–145
  news media, 146–147, 155
  publicity, 145–146
IRS. See Internal Revenue Service

JCAHO. See Joint Commission on
  Accreditation of Healthcare
  Organizations
Johnson v. Misericordia Community
  Hospital, 196
Joint Commission on Accreditation of
  Healthcare Organizations (JCAHO),
  40, 59, 65, 71–72, 98, 180
Judicial power, 5
Juran, Joseph, 238
Jurisdiction, 9
Justice, 23

Kevorkian case, 14

Labor disputes, 153
Lateness, 273
Law, 1–19
  administrative, 5
  civil, 7, 17
  common, 5, 7
  constitutional, 4
  contract, 7–8
  court system, 5–6, 10–11
  definition of, 3, 22
  duty to disclose, 143
  ethics, 1
  government role, 4t
  jurisdiction, 9
  legal status of nursing, 2–3
  procedural, 6, 17

Roman, 7
  sources of, 3–6
  statutory, 4–5
  substantive, 6, 17
  tort, 7–9, 17
  types of, 6–9
  see also Criminal law; Lawsuit
Lawsuit, 76–94
  actions to take, 79–80
  depositions, 85–90
  discovery, 82–85
  ethics, 76
  informed consent, 104
  malpractice defenses, 80–82
  prelitigation panels, 79, 94
  trial preparation, 90–93
  types of damages, 77–79
Lawyer. See Attorney
Leach v. Akron General Medical Center, 107
Leave of absence, 273
Legal defense costs, 163
Legal implications of standards, 65–70
Legal obligations, 25
Legal rights. See Welfare rights
Legislative process. See Legislators
Legislators, 253–260
Liability, 119
  burns, 125–126
  communication, 130–132, 133
  direct, 178
  equipment injuries, 126–127, 133
  falls, 121–122
  hospital, 189–209
    corporate negligence, 191, 195–196,
      208
    employment issues, 196–209
    ethics, 189–190
    ostensible authority, 191, 193–194,
      208
    respondeat superior, 191–193, 208
  inappropriate action, 129–130, 132
  insurance, 53, 158–170, 219, 223
    company's financial strength, 164–165
    costs and benefits, 166–169, 170
    ethics, 158–159
    exclusions, 162–163
    exposure, 166–168
    individual policy, 165–170
    insuring agreement, 161–162
    limits and deductibles, 164
    parties covered, 163–164
    types of injuries covered, 162
    types of policies, 159–162
  monitoring, 128–129
  negligence and, 118–119
  recurring causes of, 120–133
  restraints, 122–124